Diary Poetics

Routledge Studies in Twentieth-Century Literature

1. Testimony from the Nazi Camps
French Women's Voices
Margaret-Anne Hutton

2. Modern Confessional Writing
New Critical Essays
Edited by Jo Gill

3. Cold War Literature
Writing the Global Conflict
Andrew Hammond

4. Modernism and the Crisis of Sovereignty
Andrew John Miller

5. Cartographic Strategies of Postmodernity
The Figure of the Map in Contemporary Theory and Fiction
Peta Mitchell

6. Food, Poetry, and the Aesthetics of Consumption
Eating the Avant-Garde
Michel Delville

7. Latin American Writers and the Rise of Hollywood Cinema
Jason Borge

8. Gay Male Fiction Since Stonewall
Ideology, Conflict, and Aesthetics
Les Brookes

9. Anglophone Jewish Literature
Axel Stähler

10. Before Auschwitz
Irène Némirovsky and the Cultural Landscape of Inter-war France
Angela Kershaw

11. Travel and Drugs in Twentieth-Century Literature
Lindsey Michael Banco

12. Diary Poetics
Form and Style in Writers' Diaries, 1915–1962
Anna Jackson

Diary Poetics

Form and Style in Writers' Diaries, 1915–1962

Anna Jackson

New York London

First published 2010
by Routledge
711 Third Avenue, New York, NY 10017

Simultaneously published in the UK
by Routledge
2 Park Square, Milton Park, Abingdon, Oxfordshire OX14 4RN

First issued in paperback 2014

Routledge is an imprint of the Taylor and Francis Group, an informa business

Typeset in Sabon by IBT Global.

Library of Congress Cataloging-in-Publication Data

Jackson, Anna, 1967–
Diary poetics : form and style in writers' diaries, 1915–1962 / by Anna Jackson.
p. cm. — (Routledge studies in twentieth-century literature ; 12)
Includes bibliographical references and index.
1. English diaries—History and criticism. 2. Authors, English—20th century—Diaries—History and criticism. 3. American diaries—History and criticism. 4. Authors, American—20th century—Diaries—History and criticism. I. Title.
PR908.J33 2010
828'.03—dc22
2009052938

ISBN 978-0-415-99831-4 (hbk)
ISBN 978-1-138-88361-1 (pbk)

"She knows all the problems that arise from treating books like people and people like books."

Hermione Lee, *Virginia Woolf*

To Diana Harris and to Saskia Voorendt

Contents

Acknowledgments

This is a project I have come back to many times since I first began writing about diaries as a graduate student, and I could not have maintained my enthusiasm for the project without the interest and support of so many people along the way. The book draws on research I first undertook as a DPhil student at Oxford, and I would like to thank Lyndall Gordon, who supervised the project in its early stages, Andrew McNeillie, who advised me as I brought the material together "towards" an argument, and Jon Stallworthy for his meticulous attention to detail as I prepared the thesis for submission. I am grateful to the examiners of the thesis, Hermione Lee and Tim Kendall, whose insightful responses have shaped the work I have done since.

I returned to this work on diaries with the support of my colleagues at Victoria University of Wellington and I am very grateful for the interest shown by my colleagues. In particular, I would like to thank Mark Williams for his generosity in reading and commenting on draft material, Harry Ricketts for his sympathetic advice, and Peter Whiteford for his support and encouragement. I thank the Faculty of Humanities and Social Sciences for a grant providing assistance in preparing this manuscript for publication.

I thank the librarians at the Turnbull Library in Wellington for their assistance as I researched the unpublished papers of Katherine Mansfield, and the librarians of the Mortimer Rare Book Room at Smith College, Northampton, for their assistance with my study of the Sylvia Plath manuscripts.

I am extremely grateful to Robert Gottlieb for his generosity in speaking to me over the telephone about his work editing the John Cheever journal manuscripts for publication, and to Ben Cheever for an extremely helpful e-mail exchange providing me not only with the information I requested but also encouragement and insights.

For permission to quote from copyright material, and assistance in arranging this, I am grateful to the Cheever family, Susan Chitty, Faber and Faber, Edward Orloff at the Wylie agency and Sarah Lewis at Curtis Brown. I thank Karl Stead for permission to use lines from his poem "Yes,

T.S.," and Ronald Koertge for the permission to quote his poem "Diary Cows."

I look forward to handing a copy of this book to my husband, Simon Edmonds, who has been sceptical about my claims to have finished it, as I have made the same claim so often over the years. I would never have finished it so often if it were not for the extraordinary kindness of my mother, Nicole Jackson, who has come to my rescue as various deadlines approached and got stuck in alongside me sorting out all the details of presentation and referencing that can seem insurmountable. Most of all I thank her for her unfailing enthusiasm and extremely helpful criticism as this book's most constant reader. I am very grateful too for the support of my father, Mac Jackson, who is always ready with advice or assistance over matters big and small.

Two friends in particular have been so intimately involved in this project that it feels like their book as much as mine. Diana Harris was finishing her own PhD at the same time I was finishing mine, and I think we both found ourselves more interested in each other's work than we were in our own. Eight years later, Saskia Voorendt helped me prepare this book for submission to Routledge, knowing it through all its incarnations as Dora and as Doris. It is easy to find the words for what these friendships have meant to me, because I only need to look to the bookmark Saskia gave me with the quotation on it from Emily Dickinson: "My friends are my estate."

Introduction
Form and the Diary

Oh Form!
honourable suitcase
battered
covered with labels
have you anything to
declare?

C.K. Stead, from "Yes, T.S."

In 1945, the schoolgirl diarist Sylvia Plath asked her mother not to give her the dated diaries she had been given other Christmases, because "When the big moments come, one page is not enough."[1] Plath would go on to experiment with the formal possibilities for diary writing all her life. She filled a hard-cover journal with entries that she numbered, rather than dated; she used loose-leaf pages to make diary entries outside the journal format; she kept brief, setting-specific travel journals that combined written and drawn sketches; she wrote unposted letters to lovers and to herself; she built up portfolios of typed-up notes on neighbours, adding diary entries periodically to the files. Plath's diaries have been read mostly, as Tim Kendall has observed, by readers "hoping for scandalous new revelations,"[2] but my interest is in that negotiation between experience and form that Plath began experimenting with in 1945.

The diary tends to be thought of as a genre that is virtually formless. It is this sense of the diary that is represented by Virginia Woolf's often-repeated metaphor for the diary as "some deep old desk, or capacious hold-all, in which one flings a mass of odds & ends without looking them through." Harriet Blodgett borrows this metaphor for the title of her collection *Capacious Hold-All: An Anthology of Englishwomen's Diary Writings* (1991), one of several anthologies of diary extracts published in the 1980s and 1990s, almost all arranged thematically and almost all restricted to writing by women.[3]

Sarah Gristwood introduces her selection of diary entries *Recording Angels: The Secret World of Women's Diaries* with the question, "How better to fill in some of the gaps, flesh out the skeletal picture of women's lives over the last centuries, than through their diaries?"[4] The diary form contains the "mass of odds & ends" that historians can look through at last, as a way of adding "content" to representations of past lives. The thematic arrangement of these anthologies reflects the interest in the lives that the diaries relate, rather than the formal aspects of the narratives that relate them.

While the interest is in the lives represented by the diaries, the autobiographical aspects of them, it is only relatively recently that the diary has been included in the field of autobiography studies. In the 1950s and 1960s, autobiography scholars such as Wayne Shumaker, Barrett John Mandel, Georges Gusdorf, and Roy Pascal were concerned with establishing autobiography as a legitimate literary genre, and this involved distinguishing autobiography from letters, journals, and memoirs. Robert Fothergill's 1974 study of the diary, *Private Chronicles*, was the first substantial work on the diary as a genre published in England. This deliberately evaluative study of the diary, which distinguishes the "literary diary" as a form of autobiography from "the great mass of diary-writing . . . interesting only to the antiquarian or social historian"[5] and focuses on qualities such as presence, style, tone, self-projection, and the importance of the unconscious, perhaps looks less out of date now than it came to look in the 1980s. His argument that the diary should be considered as "serial autobiography," however, made little impact on the studies of autobiography written after it. Studies such as William C. Spengemann's *The Forms of Autobiography* (1980) and Paul Jay's *Being in the Text: Self-Representation from Wordsworth to Roland Barthes* (1984) push the limits of inclusion in terms of genre, including fiction and poetry as forms of autobiography. James Olney's 1972 *Metaphors of Self* was ground-breaking in this respect, proclaiming the concern of autobiographical studies to be "what is man?" and noting therefore, "I do not [. . .] intend to speak very strictly when it is a question of literary genre."[6] Yet none of these studies of the autobiographical self include any consideration of the diary.

The situation is completely different today. The diary has received an enormous amount of attention over the past two decades, in part perhaps because of the increased interest in autobiography initiated by scholars such as James Olney. More important, however, has been the work done by feminist autobiography scholars, who have recognised that to extend the question "what is man?" to include women involves rethinking the whole tradition of autobiography studies and the genre boundaries that have been established. Domna Stanton's 1984 collection of essays *The Female Autograph* is one of the early works of feminist autobiography scholarship to present "a collage of pieces" from different disciplines, breaking down distinctions between genres. Her determination to avoid a "facile presumption of referentiality," however, which accounts for the elision of the "bio" from what she prefers to call "autography," has not been shared by later theorists.[7] Bella Brodzki and Celeste Schenck's 1988 collection of essays, *Life/Lines: Theorizing Women's Autobiography,* deliberately sets out "to restore the *bio,*" through a similarly eclectic range of essays that include pieces on poetry, letters, and even painting and film as autobiography.[8]

Writing on diaries as autobiography is included in the 1989 collection of essays edited by the Personal Narratives Group, *Interpreting Women's Lives: Feminist Theory and Personal Narratives.*[9] This collection presents a less literary sense of autobiography, reflected in the substitution of the term "personal narratives" for "autobiography." It is one of the first collections to include work on oral narratives and working-class autobiographies. Liz Stanley is another to protest against the excision of the *bio*, including a chapter "The Presumptive Feminist: Reinscribing the 'Bio' in Autography" in her book *The Auto/biographical I: The Theory and Practice of Feminist Auto/biography.*[10] Like the Personal Narratives Group, Stanley focuses on content rather than form to analyse the ideology of auto/biography, and shifts attention away from more literary works to a wider range of autobiographical writing. She alternates the use of the terms "auto/biography" and "life writing" to reflect the breaking of the boundary between autobiography and biography. Marlene Kadar includes the term "life writing" in the title of the 1992 collection *Essays on Life Writing: From Genre to Critical Practice,* a collection which includes essays on diaries as well as on oral narratives, fiction, and biography.[11] Again the defining principle of the collection is content rather than form, with the term "gynocritics" used to refer to a practice of writing on "literature which has been identified according to its subject matter"—that is, women's lives (5).

The diary, then, receives increasing attention in the 1980s and 1990s as a form of "life writing." At the same time, the attention is directed away from the diary *as diary*, as generic differences are elided in order to focus on content rather than form, on women's lives rather than texts, on *bio* rather than *graphy.* The first collection of academic essays on the diary, edited by Suzanne Bunkers and Cynthia Huff, is called *Inscribing the Daily,* suggesting the attention to the process of writing and the periodic form of the diary that some of the contributions offer.[12] But even more significant than the inclusion in the title of the word "Inscribing" is the relegation to the subtitle of the book's focus as a collection of "Critical Essays on Women's Diaries." The focus on women's diaries and indeed on "gender as an analytical category" (2) is indicative of the collection's roots in the growing interest in women's autobiography and other forms of "life writing."

The work of feminist scholars has been tremendously important in opening up new ways of thinking about autobiography and allowing for new interpretations even of canonical texts. At the same time, new patterns in theorising autobiography and what can be seen as a new process of canon formation has introduced new problems in autobiographical criticism. In particular, the trend towards considering the diary as one form of life-writing among others, and, in particular, as a form of *female* life-writing, fails to take into account the particular demands of the diary as a genre. Whereas the dominance of the canon of autobiography by male writers led to a false universalising of a masculine tradition, which has since been revised to accommodate writing by women, the dominance of an emerging canon of diary writing by women has had the opposite effect. Stylistic features of diary writing have been theorised as expressions of femininity or as responses to women's social conditions, when in fact they are common to diary writing by men and by women and should rather be recognised as responses to the formal demands of the genre itself. The diaries of Joe Orton and John Cheever have their own gaps and silences and are just as "fragmentary, interrupted" as diaries by women writers.

Diary writing can be under-theorised as well as over-theorised. Interpretations of individual diaries or diary extracts are often used to support a larger project of interpretation of the work or the life of the writer, and these interpretations often similarly fail to account for the ways in which diary writing is shaped by the demands (and possibilities) of the genre. Diaries are read as even more authentic source material than other primary sources, such as letters. When Plath's journals seemed to tell a different story than the story told in her letters to her mother, the assumption has been that the journals reveal the truth that the letters conceal. But both letters and diary extracts are used as evidence for psychological states of mind and opinions about people and events, as well as providing primary source material for biographical facts. As Tracy Brain has pointed out in an article on the dangers of reading any of Plath's writing confessionally, even the facts recorded in the diaries and other personal writings are not as unmediated as biographers' use of them suggests. She takes the example of the visit Plath and Hughes made to Yellowstone Park, where their encounter with bears provided the basis for Plath's later short story, "The Fifty-Ninth Bear," and compares the different accounts of the occasion given in the biographies by Anne Stevenson and Paul Alexander. Both accounts clearly draw on Plath's journals and letters, while altering factual details in line with the different interpretations being presented of Plath's character. The minor alterations each biographer has made of the details given in Plath's own written accounts are fascinating, and very revealing of the different stories each biographer is telling of the same life. But while the alterations immediate draw attention to the work the biographers do in constructing a narrative based on the facts, the status of the facts recorded by Plath herself is much less obviously an issue. As Brain remarks, no biographer or critic writing about the source for this story has ever taken the basic step of checking out Plath's account of the man-eating bear, yet the historical records show that the only fatalities ever caused by bears in Yellowstone Park occurred years away from the time Plath and Hughes camped there.[13]

Autobiographical theory has led to a greater recognition of the problems involved in interpreting and constructing the representation of a writer's "self" through his or her autobiographical writing. Even so, whenever there are different editions of a diary published, the more complete version is assumed to be a more accurate representation of the author—an "intimate portrait," as the blurb to *The Unabridged Journals of Sylvia Plath* declares, of "a more rounded, grounded figure."[14] Like most scholars, I like to see the full edition of a diarist's journals being published (and like other Plath scholars, I cannot help hoping that the famous locked trunk in the Hughes archives at Emory University might, when it is opened at the end of the embargo period in 2023, turn out to be holding Plath's missing journal "lost" by Hughes in 1962). But the publication of a more complete version of a journal text is not simply equivalent to a more complete representation of the writer's self.

For instance, the complete edition of the diaries of Katherine Mansfield, edited by Margaret Scott and published in 1997, presents a radically different portrait of Mansfield from the pure, rather fey, aesthete of the *Journal of Katherine Mansfield* as it was edited by John Middleton Murry in 1927.[15] The assumption has been, however, that all the artifice was in Murry's editing and that with the new, restored edition, readers at last had access to a "true" portrait of Mansfield. But Mansfield's diaries are unusual in that she rarely kept what she considered a diary, and most of the diaries she did keep she destroyed. Scott's edition of *The Katherine Mansfield Notebooks* is a collection of diary-type entries and other manuscript material, such as recipes, gardening notes, plans for writing, drafts of letters, and so on. This version of a Katherine Mansfield who moves from the poetic to the mundane almost in one breath, who wills herself to write but cannot finish a story without getting up to bake and eat another stodgy pudding, is as much an editorial construction as the version Murry came up with when he selected only the more aesthetically significant material from the notebooks. What the different editions of Mansfield's diaries, with their radically different portrayals of Mansfield, really make apparent is the power of the diary form itself to give significance to the kinds of juxtaposition that arise between different bits of text, how the diary form knits up fragments of writing into a text which constructs a portrait it is difficult not to identify with the writer's self.

This study of the diary focuses on the formal qualities of the diary: how the structure of periodic entries creates particular literary effects and allows for a range of literary effects controlled by the individual writers. There has been only one significant book-length study of the diary as literature published recently, Elizabeth Podnieks' extensively researched study of four twentieth-century women diarists, *Daily Modernism*.[16] Podnieks looks at the diaries of Virginia Woolf, Antonia White, Elizabeth Smart, and Anaïs Nin as modernist texts, which, like many other modernist works by women, extend and disrupt a modernist canon and a theory of modernism based on T.S. Eliot's insistence on impersonality. Like many feminist scholars, Podnieks considers the diary a "subversive" genre for women, but her interest is in how the diary form is used by women to disrupt a conservative and misogynist modernist movement. She presents a strong case for considering the diary as a literary genre and for considering the diaries of these women writers as important "modernist achievements."

In shifting the emphasis away from the diary as life-writing—or, rather, in approaching life-writing itself as a modernist strategy—Podnieks avoids the problems that I have identified with life-writing approaches to the diary. It also falls outside the scope of her study to really address these problems. Like Podnieks, I am interested in the literary and formal possibilities of the diary as a genre. I have found that the comparison of different editions of particular diaries, and the comparison of writing by the diarists in other genres with their writing in the diary form, allows me to return to issues around the representation of self, the relation between the diary form and women's writing, the role of the editor, and the concept of "voice," with an approach grounded in an understanding of the diary form and its literary effects. My interest is above all in the sequential nature of the diary, and how individual entries made over time come to piece together a text with a larger, more coherent significance. I suggest that the autonomy of the entry, on the one hand, and the unifying effects of the sequence, on the other, can be seen as opposing forces.

My first three chapters focus in particular on the autonomy of the entry, and the autonomy of the detail within the entry, in the diaries of Antonia White, John Cheever, and Joe Orton. I examine the ways in which the effects of the autonomous entry, and the detail within the entry, disrupt the unity of the sequence, opening up gaps between entry and sequence and between the positions of the reader and the writer of the diary. Looking at Antonia White's diaries in comparison with her fictional writing makes it particularly obvious how the "continuous present" of the diary narrative creates a structure of irresolution. The lack of an ending, except for the continually shifting, provisional, ending of the diary as it is written, means there is no definitive perspective from which to interpret textual detail. This is strikingly different from how White's fiction works, with the ending of a short story or novel typically offering a revelatory perspective, which throws a new light back onto the rest of the story. Whereas the fictional narratives, to borrow a metaphor from White's diary, "digest" details by placing the detail in the text in such a way as to point to a new interpretation of the story, detail in the diary remains "undigested," only making sense across the grain, when the reader aligns details into new patterns against the grain of the text. It is almost impossible reading White's diaries not to wish to intervene in her life, or offer interpretations she seems almost wilfully to resist making. Reviewing the diary, novelist Jenny Diski expressed dissatisfaction as much with the form of the diary as the particular contents, unsure what to make of the "miasma" of unstructured detail. Yet if the irresolute structure is read not just in terms of White's personal failure to gain perspective on her life, but at least in part as a formal quality of the diary allowing for particular effects and requiring particular reading strategies, it is possible to enjoy the present tense of the diary and the interpretative possibilities it opens up.

The chapter on John Cheever looks further at the role of the detail in holding open interpretation, even in a text which relates interpretation to narrated detail in a much less conditional and indeterminate way. Unlike White, Cheever typically concludes his diary entries with an interpretation of the events and details he has just been recounting. It is interesting, then, to see how the structural effect of the form of the diary works to undo the closure Cheever tries to provide. Individual entries often have the "past perfect" perspective of a piece of fiction, with the descriptive details of the narrative accounted for by an interpretation of their significance in abstract, often moral, terms. A confused and fragmentary account of an irritating afternoon visit concludes with the vow to love his enemy and love his brother; an afternoon spent in an as yet undefined relationship with "A." ends with their parting as "the student and the teacher"; an entry written sick with a fever, moving from current complaints and anxieties to memories of old pastimes and family occasions, concludes with "nothing to say, really, but a thanksgiving." Even when the entries end with a detail—the cat wandering from room to room meowing, the different shows on television upstairs and in the kitchen—the details seem deliberately placed to act as Eliot-like objective correlatives of some coherent mood or theme now revealed as the overall subject of the passage. And yet, when the diary is read as a whole, the sequence of entries provokes further analysis and reinterpretation of Cheever's resonant details in relation to more continuous, shifting, and conditional patterns of effect. Cheever's own interpretations seem less convincing, as other narratives and other themes develop across the entries. At the same time, the curious resonance of the detail in Cheever's diaries is not just a structural effect of the diary. In this chapter, I explore the curious tension I find between detail and interpretation in Cheever's fiction as well as in his diaries, and suggest that some of this uneasiness with the detail can be explained by Cheever's dissatisfaction with his writing—and his masculinity—evaluated in terms of the masculine aesthetic Cheever shared with such writers as Mailer, Hemingway, and Updike, an aesthetic which devalues the detail as feminine.

Chapter 3 looks at the diaries of Joe Orton, a writer who shows no uneasiness with the detail. Whereas reading White's diaries provokes analysis of the juxtaposition of details that goes against the grain of White's own analysis, Orton uses the juxtaposition of detail to deliberate effect. Interpretative, even judgemental, comments are sometimes slipped into a descriptive account of events and people, but it is the details themselves, and the comic juxtapositions between them, that are the point of the passages. It is interesting, then, that the two dramatic adaptations of the diaries, by John Lahr and Alan Bennett, both dramatically change the focus of the diaries in order to subordinate the detail to a narrative interpretation. Alan Bennett's screenplay for the film *Prick Up Your Ears,* directed by Stephen Frears, is particularly striking in its insistence on closure, using the flashback frame as a device to ensure all the details of the film are interpreted in the light of an ending set up to be as "revelatory" as the ending of an Antonia White story.[17] Once again, an uneasiness is shown with the lack of an ending, and consequent lack of perspective, of the diary.

The next three chapters turn the focus away from the autonomy of the individual entry, and the role of the detail within the entry, to examine more closely the effects of sequence. I look at different editions of the diaries of Katherine Mansfield, Virginia Woolf, and Sylvia Plath, in order to compare the effects of different sequential arrangements of entries and extracts from the diaries. The autonomy of the individual entry that I have discussed, and the role of the reader in interpreting details within diary entries often against the grain of the diarist's own perspective, might seem to suggest an editor would have a free hand to select extracts at will from their suspension in a diary. Indeed, in looking at the questions of authorship and authority raised by the very different editions of Mansfield's diaries, I argue that much of the authority comes from the location of each diary entry in a "moment of writing" belonging at once to the diarist and the diary entry. It is this aspect of the diary that enables an editor to select, extract, and collate entries from a diary, or even a number of different notebooks, and still publish it under the authorship of the diarist.

But the sequencing of the periodic entry is as important as its autonomy. Since Mansfield never actually kept a diary as such, each of the editions that have been published are very much editorial constructions, which piece together different combinations of diary-like writing from various notebooks and other texts. What the various editions of Mansfield's papers reveal is how powerful the effects of the diary form are, even on pieces of writing which the writer herself never placed in the sequences in which they have subsequently appeared. Both the *Journal,* edited by John Middleton Murry, and the *Notebooks,* edited by Margaret Scott, have their own integrity as texts; and both present very different, yet curiously compelling, "portraits" of a Mansfield "self". The sequential form, it turns out, has very powerful effects of its own, whether determined by the diarist or the editor.

Unlike Mansfield, Woolf did *keep* a diary, maintaining over the many volumes a remarkable continuity of form and style. She wrote her diary entries in beautifully designed books, with the intention of keeping one volume every year, although many, if not most, of the diary volumes begin with apologies for not starting with the "proper flourishes," usually because she is still writing in the old book so as not to waste the blank pages left over. A proper division of time and narrative into volumes and into discrete entries is constantly disrupted by Woolf's sense of the "andness" of life. Entries frequently begin with "and," "but," or "so," continuing a story or complaint from the entry before, even, occasionally, at the beginning of a new year or a new volume. Woolf assumed that neither the careful structuring of the diary into year-shaped volumes, nor the impulse towards a continuity that ran stories and responses across structural divisions, could be preserved in a published edition of the diaries, which she supposed Leonard Woolf would "make up" into a "little book" after her death. Leonard Woolf's edition of the diaries, published as *A Writer's Diary* by the Hogarth Press in 1953, fulfils both Virginia Woolf's expectations for his treatment of the "body" of the diaries and his own stated editorial policy to extract "practically everything which referred to her own writing."[18] But the full text of *The Diary of Virginia Woolf* as it is edited by Anne Olivier Bell, with the five volumes appearing between 1977 and 1985, is a much fuller expression of "a writer's life" and of writing as a *part* of life.[19] This sense of a writer's life is expressed as much in the rhythms of the shifts of content as in the content itself. Her sense of the diary as a complete work allowed Woolf to control from day to day the rhythms of the text, counterpoising the leaps and shifts in content against the "ands" and "buts" of her fluid, water-surface prose style.

Plath's various experiments with the diary form are as interesting as the remarkable continuity of Woolf's diary. As in the case of the Mansfield papers, the different published editions of the Plath papers all tend to produce an effect of coherence and a sense of narrative that cuts across the divisions according to genre, format, and purpose that are so evident in the original manuscripts. Looking at the original volumes and loose-leaf notes that she kept, held in the Smith College archives, makes it especially apparent how much Plath experimented with the diary form and how conscious she was of putting together different kinds of diary texts. All of these individual diaries go beyond the "moment of writing" in the ways they construct narrative, represent the self, and develop imagery and themes. Most interesting of all are the "Notes on Neighbours" that she compiled in Devon. Here, a loose-leaf approach allows for the development of a new kind of diary form, with a new form of continuity.[20] The piecemeal approach to the publishing of the Plath materials—with the publication of the *Letters Home* in 1978, Ted Hughes' heavily cut edition *The Journals of Sylvia Plath* in 1982, and finally the complete edition *The Journals of Sylvia Plath, 1950–1962* in 2000—has tended to focus criticism on what is withheld from each textual representation of Plath's life and marriage. The 1982 edition of the *Journals* was hailed by some critics as revealing the "true" self which the letters withheld and was reviled by others for being "maddeningly incomplete,"[21] with the ellipses, indicating omissions, described by one reviewer as "stud[ding] the text like angry scars."[22] By the time the 2000 edition was published, scholarly work analysing the papers in the archives, including the original journal manuscripts, was well under way, and archival work continues to be a source of fresh approaches and further insights, as is testified by the recent collection of essays *The Unraveling Archive: Essays on Sylvia Plath* edited by Anita Helle.[23] But if the 2000 edition has seemed to hold no real surprises, this is less because of the work of scholars already working with the manuscript texts and more because of the effect of the Plath myth in determining a reading of the new edition as just another "thousand pages of Plath's self-incriminating testimony."[24] This chapter shifts the focus from the Plath myth, and from the journals as the revelation of Plath's self, or "voice," to look at the different ways Plath uses the diary form and how her experiments with different formats affect the autobiographical project.

The last three chapters narrow the focus to a closer study of prose stylistics, looking at diary writing at the level of the sentence and the paragraph. Each of these three chapters examines in detail one particular stylistic feature associated with the diary: the dash, the sentence fragment, and the use of the personal pronouns "I" and "you." In an article reviewing the Elizabeth Bishop *Selected Letters,* "Writing to the Moment," Tom Paulin calls for "a poetics of the familiar letter."[25] In fact, this article itself goes a long way towards establishing such a poetics, with detailed analyses of particular passages from Bishop's letters supporting general points about letter poetics. Many of Paulin's key points about letter writing are equally applicable to diary writing, so that in this one article he has gone a long way, too, towards contributing to a poetics of the diary. The "idea of expressive motion, a paradoxical form of always-unfinished processive completeness or constantly deferred closure" (221), the role of the detail, the "spirit of newness and nowness" (224), the "chancy or chanced-upon quality" (226) of randomness, and the deployment of speech patterns, a "prose that speaks itself actively all inside what's happening in the moment" (231)—these are key features of the diary as well as the letter. The letter is primarily distinguished from the diary by its specificity, and historicity, of address; its role within "the dynamics of [. . .] relationship" and the "dialogic energy" (216) it possesses as a result. Yet even the diary shares more of that "dialogic energy" than might be expected of a form without an addressee, as I suggest in the chapter on the use in the diary of the pronouns "I" and "you."

This section, then, builds on Paulin's contribution towards a "poetics of the letter" and is intended as a contribution towards the "wider poetics of prose" that Paulin calls for. At the same time, the analysis of particular stylistic effects in these chapters continues to build on the poetics of form established in the previous chapters. The paradoxical and contradictory effects that emerge from the diarists' distinctive ways of employing these features can be seen to reflect the paradoxes of the diary form itself. To an extent, of course, variability in the effects of prose features is to be found in the prose writing of different writers in any genre.[26] Yet the variant effects of the features characteristic of diary stylistics in the diaries I look at in the final three chapters are so strikingly contradictory as to suggest such contradictions are produced as a result of the diary form.

The diary's periodic form can be understood as a paradoxical form, with its structure as a series of entries combining the contradictory principles of autonomy and sequence. The contradictory effects of the stylistic features analysed in these chapters all reflect the contradictions of the diary form. The dash, for instance, used at the end of a sentence reflects the deferral of closure that characterises the open form of the diary; within a sentence, the indefinite relationship between syntactic units that the dash allows reflects the indefinite relationship between diary entries, at once sequenced and autonomous. Yet in Mansfield's diary prose the dash becomes, frequently, a marker of precision, directing the sentence towards a singular effect of a *mot juste*, as singular as the single entries from which her diary is in part made up. Similar contradictory effects can be found with the sentence fragment, which typically contributes to a narrowing of focus to the local, often being used with a kind of postcard-like economy to note details such as weather conditions, yet can also be used to evoke a sense of wider significance, the details or objects referred to in the fragment expanding in a meaning that is unrestricted by narrative grammar. Perhaps most intriguing of all is the curious tendency of the pronouns "I" and "you" to swap effects in the diary, so that it is often the "you" who is most closely identified with the diarist, while the "I" is referred to almost as a second, or third, person.

A discussion of the use of personal pronouns more obviously relates to the discussion of self and addressee, the subject that has been the focus of most diary criticism, in place of my own focus on form. Diary criticism from before the 1980s, when autobiography theorists were working to define autobiography in formal terms, represented formlessness as a quality of the diary inextricably linked to the diary's lack of an addressee, the private nature of the text. Some diary scholars saw the private nature of the diary as limiting its potential as a literary text, while other, more partisan, scholars of the diary looked for evidence of uncrafted writing—a lack of unity in the plot, a strict periodicity of tense, indeterminacy, and gaps in the information provided—as proof of an authenticity and sense of writing for the self alone that can be valued as the distinguishing qualities of the diary genre.[27] The feminist interest in the diary as a woman's genre has also emphasised the importance of privacy, often making a connection between privacy and resistance.

This association between the formlessness (or particular use of form) of the diary with the privacy of the diarist has required radical rethinking with the emergence of the internet diary in the late 1990s, which by now is probably the most widely-used format for diary writing, far more popular than the traditional manuscript diary. On-line diarists not only publish their diaries as they write them but invite, sometimes even require, readers to respond by signing "guest-books" or posting comments. In an article which begins with a "confession" (her own distaste for much of the ungrammatical writing in the genre), Laurie McNeill explores in detail the new confessionalism of the on-line diary and how traditional associations of the genre with truth-telling and authenticity are invoked and reworked in the new relationships created between on-line diarists and their readers.[28] Madeleine Sorapure's study of the shaping of "autobiographical selves and stories" by on-line diarists also emphasises the public nature of these texts and how they "challenge our current conception of diary writing as a private act."[29]

Yet both these articles focus at least as much on the form of the on-line diary and emphasise the ways in which the relationship between reader and writer is mediated by the formal constraints and potential of the on-line format. McNeill investigates aspects of literary style, the use of hypertext, and the levels of privacy and protection that are possible within a single text, as part of her discussion of the community-creation that she argues is an essential function of on-line diary-keeping. Sorapure notes that the *Diarist.net* Awards, which give a good indication of the on-line diary-keeping community's values, include several categories of awards that are essentially about design aspects of the diary and the diarist's use of the Web as a publishing medium (for example Best Design and Best Use of Multimedia). At the same time, she sees the aspects of diary form carried over from the traditional print diary, its paratactic and fragmentary nature, as continuing to define the kinds of writing, and self-presentation, the on-line diary allows. Indeed she further argues that not only does the form lend itself to fragmentary and disconnected narratives which "shape [the diarist's] self-representation," but that this mode of narrative might shape even the diarist's own sense of self. Surprisingly, it is Woolf's metaphor of the diary as a "capacious hold-all" which is taken up again and again by on-line diarists, providing a title, epigram, or explanation of purpose for blogger after blogger. It is the capacious form of the diary, and the way it can hold together a "mass of odds and ends," which on-line diarists have taken up as they construct this newly public performance of the self that on-line publication involves.

While I, too, am fascinated by the on-line diary and the ways in which it develops the poetics of the diary form, I continue to be even more fascinated by the book-based diaries that this study is concerned with. Woolf worried that her diaries were not "book-length" enough to be published, even while she kept each bound volume as a book, often with a title page. Plath designed the length of diary entries according to the different formats of the volumes she wrote in. Writing between 1915 and 1962, before the internet was invented, before Jonathan Franzen's "Age of Television," before the "death of the novel," the six writers in this study wrote manuscript or typescript journals kept in bound volumes or as piles of paper indistinguishable from their poetry or fiction typescripts.

They were literary writers, who wrote both for a market and for posterity. Mansfield wrote reviews and short stories for literary periodicals *The New Age*, *Rhythm*, and *The Athenaeum*, and with Murry was involved in the editing and production of *Rhythm* and, as it later became, *The Blue Review*; Woolf wrote essays and reviews for publications as various as *Vogue* and the *Times Literary Supplement*, and through the Hogarth Press she ran with Leonard Woolf published the work of James Joyce, T.S. Eliot, and Katherine Mansfield, amongst others; White made money writing advertising copy and freelance fashion writing, worked for a time as an editorial assistant for *Life and Letters*, published stories and reviews for publications including *Punch* and *The New Statesman,* and, even after Carmen Callil of Virago Press began republishing White's works in the 1960s as Modern Classics, continued to make most of her income as a translator of French novelists such as Maupassant and Colette. Cheever's first story was published in *The New Republic* when he was just seventeen; later his most notable association was with *The New Yorker,* with whom he published over 120 stories, while early in his career he supplemented his income writing book synopses for MGM and television scripts which included the "Life With Father" series. The first step in Plath's career as a writer was the internship with *Mademoiselle* she later famously fictionalised in *The Bell Jar*; she remained as focused on achieving publication in *The Saturday Evening Post* and *Ladies Home Journal* as in *The New Yorker*, taking her commercial fiction as seriously as the poetry that would make her name. When Orton's success with *Loot* saw him rising "up, up, up," as he wrote to a friend in 1965, it was the commercial success and attendant celebrity to which he was referring. It was as the author of *Loot* that Orton negotiated (unsuccessfully) with the Beatles to write the screenplay for the feature film in which they would star, and it was also as a successful dramatist that Orton wrote his diaries, written on the advice of his literary agent Peggy Ramsay, always with publication in mind.

Each of these writers wrote professionally in a period when opportunities for commercial publishing were expanding, while a growing range of periodicals published serious literary criticism and the growth of English departments in universities provided criticism with an institutional base.[30] While Orton may have been the most commercially driven of the six diarists discussed in this book, he nevertheless anticipated the impression he would make would be lasting; he compared himself with Aristophanes, Oscar Wilde, and Congreve, and, as his friend Kenneth Cranham observed, "He'd talk to you about his diary" thinking "he was a very important writer." [31] Plath famously measured herself against "Sappho, Elizabeth Barrett Browning, Christina Rosetti, Amy Lowell, Emily Dickinson, Edna St Vincent Millay." Her most immediate living rival was Anne Sexton, against whose output and success she compulsively measured her own, but she measured herself even more in terms of the standards of the magazines she sent work to, expressing her satisfaction with her short story "This Earth Our Hospital" with the judgement, "It would be a Best American Short Story."[32] Cheever similarly measured his success in terms of publications on the one hand, and in terms of his own comparisons of his work with the work of the writers he saw as his rivals, Norman Mailer, John Updike, and Saul Bellow. But he too also saw his work having a lasting significance, describing himself as "endeavouring to be a serious writer,"[33] and comparing himself with Hemingway, Whitman, and, perhaps more surprisingly, though even more aptly, George Eliot. White worried that "the 'literary world'" had expectations of her she wasn't meeting, giving her the "uncomfortable feeling that it is not *me* they mean at all,"[34] and yet her constant anxiety about her writing and consequent writer's block was the result of her own high expectations for herself as a literary writer—she had no writer's block when it came to producing commercial fiction, non-fiction and translations. She was generous in her appraisal of the new novels by Barbara Pym, Doris Lessing, and Elizabeth Jane Howard, yet when writing about such canonical writers as Lawrence, Mansfield, Woolf, George Eliot, and Kafka, it is to compare her talents with theirs, analyse their shortcomings, and identify aspects of their writing she might develop in her own: about Mansfield, she writes, "I feel a curious kinship with, dislike of, yet pity for Katherine Mansfield . . . I see all my weaknesses in her, admire her for her frantic attempts to be honest and deal with them. I can now read her, feeling her equal . . . "[35] Woolf, too, of course, measured herself against Mansfield, a rivalry and a relationship explored in detail in Angela Smith's study *Katherine Mansfield and Virginia Woolf: A Public of Two.*[36] Throughout her life Woolf made critical judgements of authors, contemporary and canonical, and worried in turn about how her own work would be judged, by her contemporaries and by posterity. Mansfield's greatest fear was that she would not have time to complete her work for posterity: "How unbearable it would be to die, leave 'scraps', 'bits', nothing real finished."[37] She had good cause for the sense of urgency with which she approached her writing, or her "work" as she called it, but she expresses a view very much of her time when she writes in her journal that this work "takes the place of religion—it *is* my religion . . . it *is* Life."[38]

The diary was not quite "work" for these writers in the same way. Although Woolf in particular fretted about her failure to meet her self-imposed obligations towards her diaries, the diary represented a space for experiment, free of the critical judgement that could make writing for publication so difficult. Such a comparison holds for each of these writers, most strikingly for White, who suffered terribly from the writer's block that she described so fluently and frequently in her voluminous diaries. Yet while Orton is the only one of these writers who set out writing a diary with publication in mind, Woolf supposed that after her death Leonard Woolf would publish an edition of her diaries, White typed up edited versions of some of her diaries and left instructions for her daughter Susan Chitty to decide what to do with the manuscript material, and Cheever handed his journals over to his son, Ben Cheever, who understood that "When he discovered he had written the story of his life, he wanted that published, too. I think the prospects of publication somehow lessened the fear of death. Suddenly death was an opportunity."[39] Elizabeth Podnieks has commented on the importance to Woolf, White, Nin, and Smart of published diaries they were reading by Pepys, Evelyn, Burney, Barbellion, Boswell, Dorothy Wordsworth, Gide, and Mansfield; Peggy Ramsay suggested that Orton model his diary "à la Gide". The nineteenth century saw the publication of the diaries now regarded as canonical: John Evelyn's journal, kept from 1620 to 1706, was published in 1818; Pepys's diary, kept from 1660 to 1669, was published in 1825; and Fanny Burney's diaries, kept from 1768 to 1840, were published between 1842 and 1889. By the early twentieth century, with the publication in English translation of Marie Bashkirtseff's enormously popular journal in 1891 and the success of W.N.P. Barbellion's diary, published in 1919, the diary was established as a literary genre, with diaries being published, widely read, reviewed, and imitated by other writers.

Of course, the vast majority of diaries kept have not been published, and even fewer have received the kind of attention of these canonical examples. Jennifer Sinor's edition of the diary of nineteenth-century Dakota homesteader, Annie Ray, acknowledges in its title "The Extraordinary Work of Ordinary Writing." She points out the extent to which theorising of the diary as a genre is skewed by the selection of particular sorts of diaries for critical attention: the "diary literature" that exhibits "plot, action, suspense, length, allusion, metaphor, linearity, sparkle, self-reflection, extraordinary events, deep introspection, and/or some kind of authorial presence."[40] She finds none of these qualities in the writing of Annie Ray, yet values her diary nevertheless. Conversely, many of these qualities can be found in diaries which have not been published, and in diaries by diarists who are not otherwise writers. Amateur diarists were also influenced by diaries such as Pepys's, Burney's, Bashkirtseff's, and Mansfield's, and they were influenced too by other forms of literary narrative, as Steven Kagle and Lorenza Gramegna have discussed in "Rewriting Her Life: Fictionalization and the Use of Fictional Models in Early American Women's Diaries."[41] Before I settled on my selection of diarists for this study, I read a wide range of diaries, only some of which were by professional writers. Some of the diaries by writers whose published work I find endlessly intriguing simply failed to interest me as diaries. On the other hand, Hermine Demoriane's *The Tightrope Walker* balances descriptions of her growing competence as a tightrope walker with historical information as nimbly as she herself came to balance on the rope she strung up between trees in her backyard, while *Life Star,* the diary of her pregnancy, was just about the only diary I wanted to read, and re-read, for nearly nine months of the time I was working on this research. One of the most remarkable experiments in the diary is the visual diary, with written captions, kept by Charlotte Salomon, which I read in the 1963 edition *Charlotte: A Diary in Pictures*; it has recently been republished as *Charlotte Salomon: Life? Or Theatre?*, using the title she herself gave her diary.

However, rather than write on some diaries by professional writers and others by diarists who were not otherwise writers, I decided to make a more narrow selection, looking only at diaries by literary writers. By literary, I mean not only professional, writing for money, but committed, as Mansfield puts it, to writing as a life's *work*. Each of these writers had a keen sense of genre and an interest in the formal constraints and possibilities of the forms in which they worked, whether they aimed to fulfil the requirements, as Plath did, of what she defined as a "*New Yorker* poem" or the "*Sat Eve Post* style," or whether they aimed to go beyond the conventions of genre altogether, inventing, as Woolf aimed to do, an "essay-novel" (*The Years*), a "play-poem" (*The Waves*), a "series of contrasts . . . to end with a play" (*Between the Acts*), something "new . . . to supplant 'novel' . . . But what? Elegy?" (*To the Lighthouse*).[42] I see this same interest in form and in the possibilities of genre as informing the writing in all six of the diaries I have selected. Even when they were writing only for themselves, whether to record daily life for later reminiscence, to analyse relationships for a deeper understanding, or even just to make a "bridge" as Woolf called it between one form of writing and another (allowing her to move between journalism and fiction, for instance, by writing in the more neutral mode of the diary in between), they didn't stop being writers, or being conscious of the literary effects of their writing and the form in which they were writing it. The diaries I have selected to write about are all diaries I find particularly interesting in their structuring of daily entries, in the relation between entry and sequence, and in the construction of narrative, style, and tone across entries and in different formats. I *like* these diaries, and I like the diarists, at least most of the time.

Choosing diaries by published authors allows me to make comparisons across the genres in which each diarist has written. In the introduction to his edition of Plath's journals, Ted Hughes emphasised the continuity he saw between Plath's writing in the journals and the poetry particularly of her last collection, *Ariel*:

> *Ariel* and the associated later poems give us the voice of that self. They are the proof that it arrived. All her other writings, except these journals, are the waste product of its gestation [. . .]
>
> A real self, as we know, is a rare thing. The direct speech of a real self is rarer still [. . .]When a real self finds language, and manages to speak, it is surely a dazzling event—as *Ariel* was.[43]

Without claiming the same connection between a "real self" and a writer's "voice" that Hughes sees as linking Plath's poetry and diaries, I am interested in the way a writer's particular concerns and characteristic ways of working with language can be compared across different genres and literary forms. When writers pick out the same kinds of details to characterise the people they observe and the characters they create, or build prose passages or stanzas of poetry around similar patterns of repetition, the importance of genre and formal structure in determining the significance and the literary effects of these kinds of features is thrown into relief. Conversely, the differences in each diarist's writing in their diaries, compared to their writing in other literary forms, can be understood, at least arguably, as their response to the particular demands of the diary form.

I have also deliberately chosen diaries which have already been written about and used as source materials for a variety of interpretations and representations of the writers' lives. Extracts from these diaries have been used to support critical interpretations of their other literary works and as evidence for narrative accounts of the writers' lives. I see this as all the more reason to consider the formal demands and generic expectations the diarists were working with, and to think through, as Hermione Lee puts it, "the problems that arise from treating books like people and people like books," problems that have always accompanied the reading of diaries.[44]

These are all diaries that have been published in at least one edition, and which are readily available for reading and rereading. In the chapters that examine the process of editing, while I do draw on archival research, I have chosen to look at diaries available in two different editions, one abridged and one intended to be "complete." Readers can compare my account of the differences between the different editions with their own sense of the effects such differences produce. All of the diaries in this study are, moreover, diaries that are read not only by academic readers but by Virginia Woolf's "common reader." I read Joe Orton's diary when I was a schoolgirl, not sure if I should be allowed to, and based my bedroom decoration on the collaged walls of the flat he shared with Kenneth Halliwell. I carried Katherine Mansfield's journal around with me for months after a relationship break-up left me, at the age of twenty-two, looking for consolation in the pared-down, aesthetics-focused vision of the world John Middleton Murry's edition presents. On-line diarists continue to draw on the print volumes of Woolf's diaries to define a tradition of diary-keeping that the new web-based format develops in new directions.

The diarists, of course, did not write in "print volumes" but in exercise books, notebooks, hard-bound volumes, sometimes loose-leaf sheets of paper. Reading the originals produces a vivid sense of how the writing process was shaped by the actual form of the volume the diarist was writing in, as well as the periodic form of the diary genre. The pen, too, had its effect on the writing, as Woolf was always observing. Reading the Katherine Mansfield papers in the Turnbull Library in Wellington, New Zealand, I was particularly affected by the preserved kowhai flower I came across between two pages in a notebook. After all this time, there it still was, still yellow, still between the same two pages Mansfield had placed it between all those years ago. A piece of the world she wrote about was right there as a piece of world, still, not a piece of writing. This is the diary as the capacious hold-all in a surprisingly literal sense. But the capacity of the diary that fascinates me above all is its capacity to contain the contradictory effects of the autonomy of the entry and the sequencing of the structure: to contain the paradox of its form.

1 Antonia White

The *Diaries* of Antonia White, in the volumes edited by Susan Chitty, opens with notes made in Paris, in 1926, listing "Canaries, wireless, heavy vans, incessant bells, piano with a sharp always recurring in wrong place."[1] These vivid details, apparently listed at random, powerfully evoke a sense of Paris and of the diarist observing, even though in this first extract White writes little about herself. The diary proper begins in 1933, with White recording an intention to write up a comparison between Carlyle and Lawrence. It is unlikely she ever did fulfil this intention and not only because of the way she describes herself "veer[ing] about so" (18) in her feelings towards Lawrence. White is always recording intentions for the future in these diaries and almost as often regretting her failure to carry her own resolutions out.

By insisting on the importance of form to a poetics of the diary, I am arguing against the general assumption, already discussed in the introduction, that the diary is a formless genre. It is this sense of the diary as formless which has kept the diary, until recently, from being included in studies of autobiography as a literary genre. As Donald Stauffer explains this position, "the diary has scant claim to consideration, for it makes no pretense to artistic structure."[2] Yet all diarists must work with the sequential form that the diary, by definition, has to take. A diarist cannot compose even a single entry without shaping it, and as soon as the diary consists of a sequence of entries the diarist begins to work with the effects of juxtaposition on the one hand, and, on the other, continuities of narrative and theme. Nevertheless, it is true that such necessary attention to form does not provide an artistic structure in the sense that a novelist might structure his or her work of fiction, or a poet a poem, editing and re-editing the material as they work to define its design. Arguably, this can be seen as the work of a diary's editor, perhaps most successfully though controversially in the case of John Middleton Murry's editing of the Mansfield papers. But an artistic structure might not necessarily only be understood in terms of editing. Woolf, for instance, was clearly alert to the ways in which a structure of accretion could have its own aesthetic, working across entries not only to provide continuity but to highlight continuity as a literary device (as I will explore further in Chapter 5).

No such "pretense to artistic structure" is shown in the diary of Antonia White, nor in its editing. Her diary is the most obviously "formless" of all the diaries I look at in this book, incorporating lists, accounts of dreams, plans, analysis notes, notes for future writing, and various approaches to recording autobiographical facts, but offering little in the way of a sustained narrative. Any sense of plot, or narrative momentum, is difficult to hang on to, as questions are raised, characters introduced, events interpreted and reinterpreted, without any follow-up or conclusion. In the chapter Elizabeth Podnieks includes on White's diary in *Daily Modernism,* which represents the only considered study of White's diary that has ever been published, she makes a case for the diary as more formally composed than it first appears.[3] She gives an excellent account of how the diary was structured in relation to the particular material volumes White used, the hard or soft cover, spiral or ring-bound notebooks. She notes how often White records herself re-reading the diaries and argues that White clearly intended the diaries to be published, at least in some form, at some point. Podnieks' reading of the diaries takes a thematic approach, teasing out from the heterogeneous content four main themes: White's sexual relationships, her Catholicism, her relationship with her father, and her sense of herself as a woman, mother, and artist. In contrast, I want to return to the "formless" impression given by White's diary and look more specifically at how the diary structure might differ from the "artistic structure" Donald Stauffer requires of a literary work. White's diary can be seen as providing a particularly good example of the open-endedness that characterises the diary, and which I suggest can be analysed as a formal characteristic in itself.

It is the open form of the diary, as a succession of autonomous entries, that necessitates the use of a tense distinctive to the diary, described by Margo Culley as the "continuous present."[4] This "continuous present" refers not so much to the grammatical tense of each sentence but to an overall "narrative" tense; that is, it is a structural quality of the text. Each entry of a model diary gives an account of the period from the time the last entry was written, up to and including the time of writing the current entry. If reminiscences dating back beyond the last entry are included, they are still anchored in the present tense of the writer reminiscing as he or she writes. The grammatical tenses used tend to be the present and the perfect, with the future tense used on occasion. The "continuous present," however, describes the narrative structure created by the succession of entries written in the present tense or the recent past of the moment of writing, with a periodically shifting position in time. The diary is, in its structure, typically endless, every entry the latest in a series that has no predetermined limit. While every diary does of course have an end, in the process of keeping it, the end is a continually shifting one. It is this endlessness that is often considered a lack of form.

White's published fiction suggests an unusual talent for form and for endings. *Frost in May*, her first and most successful novel and Virago's first "Modern Classic," is most memorable for the devastating impact of the ending.[5] Although it was to be the first of a series of novels, White was always troubled by the difficulty of starting again, with the need to recapitulate the past. She changed the name of her heroine from Nanda to Clara, and the first novel is usually read alone.

Her skill with endings is apparent in her collection of short stories, *Strangers*.[6] Most of the stories lead up to a revelatory ending, which throws light back onto the rest of the story. "The Moment of Truth" becomes the title of one story. "Strangers", the story which gives its title to the collection, could have equally well been called "The Moment of Truth": in this story, the wife discovers at the end that it is not her husband's body she has been weeping over but the body of a stranger. But White wrote far more beginnings than endings. "I have a superb collection of beginnings," she remarked once on her ability to start a novel and inability to finish it.[7] And she wrote more easily in her diary than anywhere else, in that form without an ending.

Her preference for beginnings can be detected in a list of likes and dislikes she makes in 1934 (32–33). Her likes include "being out of debt," which for White means being free to start spending again, "clean clothes" that are ready to start wearing again, "sound of crockery when someone is getting tea for me" rather than the tea itself, "starting a relationship" and "decorating rooms" which means getting rooms ready. Her dislikes are many and various but include dirt in her clothes, her mother's "sweetish corruption", and "feeling fat" which she blames on overindulgence, or having *already* eaten. Her dislike of "being pregnant" might look like a dislike of a beginning, but given her indifference to her daughters as babies and her much greater attachment to the men she was involved with, I suspect "being pregnant" seemed more a consequence than a beginning to White. (She later blamed Sue's birth for ending her marriage with Eric Earnshaw Smith.) The lists she makes frequently throughout her diary are another form of writing without ending, since a list can go on as long as there are things to add to it and an interest in adding them. She lists discouragements, interesting thoughts, characteristics of herself and other people, expenses, friends, and, most often, resolutions.

So many resolutions are striking in writing so irresolute. Her resolutions are often concerned about waste: in a list from 1933, she resolves "not to waste time, thought and money" on clothes, to read without waste "not frittering away my reading," to tidy "so as not to have these orgies of getting straight," and generally to "get as much time as possible out of each day" (23). She castigates a friend as "the most ruthless waster of other people's time I know" (26). She seems always to hold herself to account for her time, providing frequent summaries like balance sheets. One of her more thorough reviews in 1951 attempts to cover the last five years of her life (229).

The metaphor of having things on account, which is in fact how she literally acquired most of her possessions, is one she uses frequently. She associates writing with money, making a curious slip in one passage:

> I spend money recklessly in a fantasy of unlimited wealth. Perhaps it is the same with writing. I want the certain consciousness of unlimited talent without the necessity of having to give any evidence of money at all. Now that was quite unconscious. I meant to write talent. (75)

It is as if she wants to have talent "on account" with writing being the payment she must make for it. Even her relationship with her daughter she analyses in terms of a debt owed: "I have got to 'earn' Sue. I've had her 'on account' as you might say. Now the bill has come in" (198).

Resolutions can be seen as a way of ordering future behaviour on account, but in White's case, the behaviour rarely follows. The diary is full of broken resolutions: "It is breaking a resolution though perhaps not an important one to write in this book in pencil" (77), and "I rang him on an impulse though I had resolved not to" (85). She recognises that it "is no good my making resolutions," yet it does not stop her making them, any more than does her resolution to make "*no* new year resolutions, however tempting" (27).

White in fact refers to the future more often than any of the other five diarists of this study, with Cheever coming closest with about a third as many references. She also refers to the past more often than average, though to a far less striking degree. Perhaps this quantity of writing in the future tense accounts in part for a certain lack of substance to the writing. The novelist Jenny Diski criticised Antonia White's diaries in a review article in *The London Review of Books* (in which they are grouped, curiously enough, with Andrew Morton's biography of Princess Diana and Lyndall Gordon's auto/biography *Shared Lives*), complaining of their "shapelessness." [8] In this review, Diski contrasts the "sharp eye" of the writer as a novelist with "the miasma of self-deception and silliness" she finds in the diaries. She concludes the article, "What we own of Antonia White is her published fiction, stories and novels, and that is all we can ever own." Ownership is an interesting idea to bring in, a further extension of the term "mastery" to mean understanding. Diski mentions a desire to "get a grip" on the writing and on the writer. There is a real difficulty in getting a grip on so formless a genre, so piecemeal a representation of "self."

Yet it would be more fair to write of a "miasma of self-awareness" than a "miasma of self-deception," or at least of a "miasma of self-examination." White is *always* examining herself, with at least the intention of honesty. She undergoes clinical analysis a number of times and uses the techniques of analysis throughout her diary. She tries to see herself from all angles: recording what other people say about her, summing up her sense of herself, interpreting her unconscious. She picks up on slips of the pen, such as the substitution of "money" for "talent", as a way of getting in an extra glimpse of self-awareness on the sly. Yet Diski argues, "It is in the fiction that we see most clearly what White increasingly doubts the existence of through this period of the diary: the 'core' of herself." The difference seems to me less one of honesty than of perspective and tense.

Hermione Lee, in her introduction to White's collected stories, contrasts "the controlling writer, digging up her past" with "the unredeemed, 'untreated' self in the fiction, unable to make coherent shape of, or distance herself from her state of mind."[9] The past as shaped by the fiction is at a remove from its analysis. A section of time is set apart and written of in a narrative which moves in a steady chronology, looking neither backwards nor forwards. The heroine is defined by her thoughts, feelings, and behaviour, in the present tense of the story.

Secondary characters in White's fiction, like the heroines, are not analysed but simply presented. Nanda, the heroine of *Frost in May*, resists analysis, "always reverent towards the people she liked." Her best friend Leonie is described as peculiarly static in appearance: "her deeply cut mouth and beautiful sallow brows seemed like the stamp of a medal rather than the changing growth of a face." [10] This strange yet vivid description reveals how the absence of a relationship to past and future is linked with clarity and definition.

The passage of time is deftly handled in *Frost in May*. The reader is never allowed ahead of the heroine. Time passing is barely referred to: the reader is always in the present tense of the narrative, which, when necessary, simply skips over a week (as it does between the first and second chapters) or two years (as it does after the death of Theresa Leighton). The reader's attention is focused, as is Nanda's, on immediate material details, such as the hair on Clare's arms and on Nanda's struggle to learn and to resist the intricacies of the convent rules and ideology. Nanda's response is, like the response called for in the reader, emotional rather than analytical. The narrative, written in the past tense, looks back with immediate feeling, belonging always to the present tense of the story itself.

The short stories are even more focused than the novel. Each has a single viewpoint and chronological narrative. Even the shifts in self-perception recorded in the story based on White's memory of her psychosis, "The House of Clouds," are described simply, with no analysis, each development given its place in a lucid chronology. While the heroine of this story may be "unable to make coherent shape of, or distance herself from her state of mind," the reader has only to follow the narrative of it to have possession of the whole story.

In the diary, White is writing from inside experience. There is relatively little narrative, compared to the amount of analysis. While she frequently reviews a past year, she can gain no perspective on the present, which will depend on future developments for its context. Her state is always conditional: at most she can state, "At the moment, thank goodness, I am not in that miserable and familiar state of being between two men," making no claims beyond the "moment".[11] Even this conditional state she hopes might be temporary, writing in 1936, "I have a feeling that in a year's time a great many things may be clear to me which I now only apprehend in the dimmest, most erratic way. If I can hold on, I really do believe . . . that I shall have learnt a new language and that at last I may have a base on which to build" (73).

In the meantime, and throughout her diary, she asks questions: "What things have made me happy lately?" (33); "Shall I go all out for freelancing?" (122); "What can one say to the dying who do not know and who do not believe?" (291). Some of these questions are rhetorical, but usually White attempts to answer her questions, often surprising herself with what she comes up with. It is as if she needs to distance herself from her thoughts by writing them out, to find out what she thinks.

She finds out too what she feels. By concentrating on her feelings, she anchors her analysis in the present tense: whatever the meaning or future development of an event, she has complex feelings about it *now*. She notes her feelings in careful detail: "I am feeling aggressive, bitter and impotent" (111). Yet the feelings she records perhaps the most often are relief and disappointment: feelings in relation to the past and to past anticipation of the future. Her feelings themselves are subject to resolutions. She resolves to be grateful, to enjoy writing, to be calm, to "try as he [Spinoza] says to convert passive emotions into active ones" (171).

Her frequent use of the phrase "of course" is an attempt to regulate her emotions. She uses it most often about something that is painful to her, something she minds about, often something that would not normally be thought of as a matter of course at all but a matter of tragedy. Thus she can write a sentence like, "Tom, of course, is like someone partly hypnotised" (240). She often writes of her disappointments in her daughters as if they are a matter of course. Her pleasure in Sue's financial independence from her is tempered by the realisation that "Sue is of course relying not on her pay but on the 21st birthday money and that of course came from the family so is indirect support from parents" (231). Of her daughters' relations with the Church, a subject she cares very strongly about, she writes, "I do think even now she takes a sort of interest in it. Lyn of course takes none" (234). Sue's estrangement from her becomes a continual source of pain which she notes in postscripts: "I have been quite extraordinarily blest and fortunate for the past six months. Except, of course, for Sue" (270). At the same time, she uses the same technique to regulate her emotions over much smaller tragedies: "lack of boxroom is a nuisance, of course" (234). She uses the word "obviously" (or sometimes "certainly") in a similarly prescriptive, rather than descriptive, fashion. What she declares "obvious" is never literal fact, but rather the much less obvious interpretation she gives fact. Usually, it is her self, and her unconscious, she is interpreting. She states, for instance, "I am obviously still terrified of being disapproved of" (225).

In many of White's stories, interpretations of fact seem "obvious". Often, interpretation is guided by religion. In *Frost in May*, the children are taught to read everything for signs of their religion, to see the robin's red feathers as a sign of the Precious Blood, to hear a cock crow "*Christus natus est*" and the sheep bleat "be-e-thlehem."[12] What seems obvious, however, is often shown to be misleading. In "The Saint" the children's prejudice leads them to mistakenly attribute the signs of sanctity they recognise to their favoured nun. It is only with the story's denouement that all becomes clear.[13]

In *Frost in May*, Nanda is finally expelled because the nuns and Nanda's father interpret her novel before she has written the conclusion, which was to justify all the colourful scandal of the main part of the novel by the dramatic conversion of the villains. The injustice of their interpretation, not just of the novel but of Nanda's character, is keenly felt. Yet there is no doubt that Nanda relished writing the scandalous beginning to her novel. Like White herself, Nanda shows a preference for the misleading beginnings, over the revelatory endings.

The diary does not lend itself to revelatory endings, and White's diary ends with her longing for painkillers and visitors. No new revelation confirms or denies her earlier interpretations. And the reader shares the diarist's perspective, restricted to the continuous present where analysis is interminable. The effect is to provoke further analysis. Susan Chitty, in her introduction, picks out three main themes that can be followed through the diary to produce some sense of fragmented narrative, an approach later taken, as we have seen, by Podnieks in her more extended study of the work. The first theme, or subject in Chitty's wording, is the guilt and hatred White felt for her father. Chitty goes on to suggest a further interpretation of White's feelings for her father in the possibility she may have been abused by her father as a child. She suggests, too, a link between this theme and the second theme of White's long-term writer's block, which White blamed on her father. Like Podnieks, Chitty also identifies White's relationship with Catholicism as a central theme of the diary, and, perhaps more importantly, she finds she can read the passages concerning this subject as an extended narrative: "In the course of the diary we see her slow return to the fold [of Catholicism] after her long lapse, a period of fervour during the Second World War, and then the equally slow return of doubts, which her painstaking reading of the Old Testament did not allay."[14]

In my own reading of the diaries I have picked out from the "miasma" of the text not so much a theme or a narrative, but a pattern of irresolution. "Irresolution" is not the "informing principle" of the diary in the New Critical sense of a theme around which the author intentionally constructed the text. It is one of a number of thematic and stylistic patterns that could be noted, but its significance for me is in the way it not only links the theme of irresolution with its stylistic expression in terms of the use of lists, questions, the conditional tense, and so on, but also links the thematic and stylistic expression of irresolution with irresolution as a structural effect of the diary form itself. There is an intriguing interplay between White's personal irresolution and the irresolution of the diary form.

The irresolution for the reader is complicated by the indeterminacy, which is another effect of the diary form, related to the diary's lack of an addressee. The indeterminacy of White's diary is increased by the amount of analysis in relation to detail, which in White's case seems related to the narrative tense of the diary since detail, in her fiction, makes sense so resolutely in the past tense. In the diary, she often gives us very few concrete details or examples on which to base her analysis of events or relationships. She does not need to, of course, as she, as her own audience, knows the details already. So, for instance, she writes:

> My father looked for security above all things. My mother wanted excitement and change . . . suffered from . . . not having enough demands made on her . . .
>
> . . . Of course I have been 'spoilt' too . . . Eric and I tried to do the impossible thing that Sue and Thomas are now attempting: have a completely pleasurable, selfish private life.[15]

This passage offers no examples or anecdotes as a basis for any of the interpretations of the six lives White analyses. Unable to turn back to examples or to any concrete details as a measure for her interpretations, a reader of the diary has only the syntax of the interpretation to analyse. The passage moves from the interpretation of the parents' desires, to an interpretation of what "Eric and I" and "Sue and Thomas" desire. But the parents are opposed in their desires, while the couples of the next two generations are united. The phrase in between, "Of course I have been 'spoilt' too," suggests that White's attempt to have a "completely pleasurable, selfish private life" is related to her mother's desire for "excitement and change" and to a lack of "demands made on her." So there is a kind of chain of spoilt daughters, who after the first generation are coupled with spoilt husbands—husbands maybe even 'spoilt' by their association with the daughters. But there are some contradictions in this pattern. While White's father and mother are opposed in terms of desires, and "Eric and I" and "Sue and Thomas" coupled, it was Eric Earnshaw Smith's marriage with White which was dissolved in divorce. There is perhaps an implication that the marriage between Sue and Thomas would be equally unlikely to succeed, being founded on the same "impossible thing" to attempt—though Earnshaw Smith's homosexuality is not mentioned as another factor in the impossibility of his marriage. Moreover, if the link between White's desires and her mother's suggested by "Of course I have been 'spoilt' too..." is to inform our interpretation of the attempt to live "a completely pleasurable, selfish private life," then it seems perhaps not impossible after all, since what she and her mother have both been spoilt by is precisely the avoidance of demands such a life entails.

This kind of syntactic analysis could be applied to any of the passages in White's diaries. At the same time, no detailed analysis is required to get a sense of the gaps covered up by phrases such as "of course" and by patterns such as the simplistic patterning of three generations of married couples.

But it is not just the absence of detail that provokes analysis. The diary has in fact been described as a peculiarly detailed genre, a claim I look at in depth in the next chapter. This chapter has been concerned with narrative tense; the following focuses on the detail as part of an examination of formal structure, but they are closely related to each other, as they are to the effects of indeterminacy. The lack of perspective that is a result of the continuous, and conditional, present tense of the narrative; the structure as a series of entries related to, yet more or less autonomous from, the sequence of entries as a whole; and the indeterminacy of missing details and facts known to the diarist all combine to destabilise the narratives and interpretations which the diary offers, and to give both concrete descriptive details, and the details of the diary syntax, a more autonomous and more central role than they have in other forms of prose.

One of White's metaphors for writing sees it as an act of digestion. The subject matter of the writing is digested to produce meaning. Meaning is what is left after processing. The narrative of revelation withholds meaning until the end of the story but the story can only be written in hindsight. The diaries, written in "midsight," leave detail undigested, petrified like a Lithopaedion:

> It has been a bad month, with Roberta's death, of which I cannot yet bring myself to write . . . This is the first death I have completely realised: even my father's death was not so real to me. I was glad at last to be able to weep for someone. I wanted to write a poem about her. I wanted to put on her grave that she was young and beautiful so that people should not remember her as she looked dead with her face swollen and yellow, cotton wool carelessly stuffed in her nostrils, her hair that used to be sleek as a spaniel's ears, dead and dull . . . She looked so majestic, so bitter, so disillusioned. Nothing could insult her body any more. She had put off all her beauty; she looked like a penitent in a white sheet . . . When I read Rilke I seem to understand her death . . . she really had carried it around with her, nourished it, achieved it . . .
>
> The Lithopaedion is a child which fails to be born and is petrified into a limestone fossil in the womb where it may remain for half a lifetime. I think that is what has happened to my creative talent, if I have one.
>
> I read voraciously the lives of painters and the journals of poets. I am nourished and nourished but I bring forth nothing . . .
>
> I wish I were a painter. I had a mad impulse two days ago: bought tubes of paint, brushes, medium, even a little palette. I felt guilty and excited. I had no right to buy these things. On a canvas board I painted the names of painters, writers and musicians who are my patron saints. Afterwards I felt very foolish and ashamed but I have left the board up . . .
>
> Someone told Phyllis [Jones] my lectures were 'brilliant.' Now, in spite of nervousness, I quite enjoy lecturing. I hate and dread the

> preparation: the reading and predigesting. I feel trapped as if I were being made a schoolmistress in spite of myself: 20 years later finding myself inexorably committed to what my father wanted me to be . . .
>
> Tom is very unhappy at the moment, very discontented with himself and his life . . . (71)

Her claim to have "realised" the death of her friend seems reflected by the prose account which "realises" the death through the details of the cotton wool and dead hair "that used to be sleek as a spaniel's ears." The details are juxtaposed with the interpretation of her death as something "achieved." There are contradictions in the account, between, for instance, White's wish to note her friend's beauty on her grave and the friend's own discarding of beauty, in White's interpretation, "like a penitent." But the diary entry allows for the kinds of contradictions she would have left out of the poem she wanted to write.

At the same time, the diary entry allows for resonance across apparent shifts in subject matter, and even the shifts themselves, to add to the meaning of an entry. The Lithopaedion, for instance, may or may not have made it into the poem about Roberta's death. Here, it is juxtaposed with it, an apparent change of subject that is inflected with its place in the sequence of the entry. It can be read as a metaphor for the death which Roberta "carried [. . .] about with her," as well as a metaphor for White's "creative talent," which she likens it to explicitly. Then White's failure to "bring forth" anything in writing is contrasted with Roberta's eventual success in achieving the death she carried around as White carries around her creative talent. Again, however, the juxtapositions do not add up. The Lithopaedion can be carried around like the death but it cannot be nourished like the death. The next paragraph seems to carry on from the Lithopaedion paragraph, "I bring forth nothing" referring to the "Lithopaedion" of her creative talent, which would be brought forth in writing, but the use of the word "nourished" refers back to the writing about the death again in a way which only works if the Lithopaedion metaphor is ignored. It sits in the way of the extended nourishment metaphor like a stone.

There is a fairly clear, if unstated, logic in the succession of paragraphs from the one about not writing, to the one about wishing she painted, to the one about enjoying lecturing. If she cannot bring forth writing, she can paint and lecture. The change of subject to Tom's unhappiness can also be read as a continuation of the theme of dissatisfaction. Tom, like White, is discontented with his life—in contrast with Roberta, who has "achieved" death. But the return to the digestion metaphor in the paragraph about lecturing relates back to the earlier "nourishment" imagery in a less linear pattern. Even the mention of her father again works as a link back to the first paragraph of the passage. There is no explicit connection made between her feeling trapped as the teacher "my father wanted me to be" and her failure to "realise" her father's death, but it is the kind of connection White's experience of psychoanalysis might have led her to make.

If writing is the product that comes *after* digestion, the diary for White seems to be too much a process to count as writing. As she writes in the diary, she claims to "bring forth nothing" as a writer. Digestion becomes the job of the reader, but remains a process, that can "bring forth" extracted meanings or interpretations but never produce a complete reading or a "grip" on the diary as a whole.[16] In White's fiction, detail is given meaning within a narrative that is only complete when it is ended. Only with the ending of the fictional narrative can interpretation take place more than provisionally. The interpretations of events and relationships that White makes in the diary veer between the provisional—"About us I do not know. I have a feeling he may within the next months really turn to me. If he does I cannot tell how I shall feel" (70)—and the prescribed: "Obviously she must have power" (105). But the diary does not prescribe the reader's interpretations, which are based not on the details of White's life but the juxtaposition of details in the text.

It is interesting to see how Chitty's editing of the diaries supports the openness of form that is characteristic of the diary as a genre and is a particularly striking feature of White's diaries. While Chitty has cut the diaries to one quarter of their original size, she has imposed no definitive closure on the volumes. The first volume could well have ended with the summary of White's life which forms the penultimate entry in the volume as it stands, but Chitty adds one further entry with White's "perfectly mad ideas" and serious resolutions for the future (321). The second volume is given closure of a sort with the note indicating White's death, yet White's own last entry, like the last entry of the first volume, looks forward to the future.

The original "forty notebooks and ring files" that White left when she died are not, yet, held in a library archive, although Chitty has been generous in allowing scholarly access to them.[17] It is interesting to observe that three of the diaries "differ from the rest," each of the three having its own thematic focus, yet Chitty has chosen to incorporate entries from these notebooks chronologically with the rest. I explore the issues raised by this kind of editorial decision more fully in the chapter on Sylvia Plath, because of all the diarists of this study it is Plath who was most interested in experimenting with different formats and thematic approaches to the diary. As Chitty points out, White herself saw the different volumes of her diaries as "all alike" and as likely to be read in a piecemeal way by readers interested "in religion. Or in psychology" who would "find things of interest to them in it" rather than read as a whole set of texts from beginning to end.[18]

Yet even readers looking across the entries for "things of interest to them," or interpreting the diaries in terms of structural and psychological patterns (a pattern of irresolution, a tendency to make lists), are still likely to find themselves caught up in the "moment of writing" that I will look at in more detail in the chapter on Katherine Mansfield. A sense of the simultaneity of thinking and writing gives White's diaries a particular emotional resonance. Her diaries have very little of the kind of scene-setting description that Cheever and Plath, for instance, excel in. Rather, White seems to write as a way of thinking. The diaries are moving to read because of the sense they give the reader of being in the presence of the diarist's thoughts. The reader shares the timing of the thinking.

An entry written when White was preoccupied with "not hoping David will ring" not only matches the time thinking with lines of writing, but uses the lines of writing to fill in the time. The reader shares the sense of impatience with which the entry was written, as the entry circles around, from character analysis to philosophy and theology, always back to the diarist's situation of sitting, writing, feeling demoralised, as she waits for a call she does not expect.

> I am tired and anxious, trying to persuade myself I am not hoping David will ring up since he is due back from Spain today. But as Djuna says, 'are you a writer or a weeping woman?' I am determined never again to be a weeping woman: no matter how much I care for a man . . . I will not let frustration reduce me to a pulp . . . I have become very deeply attached to Barker whom I have really come to know and perhaps understand a little lately . . . [there follow twenty-one lines of character description and analysis in the published diaries, with indications of more material omitted from the original.]
>
> I am so tired. I cannot write any more about Barker tonight though he is so much in my thoughts and I have so much more I want to record about him . . .
>
> I am demoralised tonight. I sit at a littered desk, smoking endlessly with itching eyes, feeling oppressed by my clothes. I am trying to behave as if I were not half-hoping for a call from David. I forced myself to spend this evening alone, to write a letter or two, to make an entry here. I kid myself that I am behaving *as if* I were free of preoccupation. I played the piano carelessly and inattentively. I pick up books, any book at hand, and read here and there a paragraph until I am dizzy . . . Yes, I am much oppressed tonight—weighed down—the old words mean something. It is like a physical weight in my head and body. For the third time lately I went into the church in Spanish Place and prayed, saying the Our Father over and over again which says all I want to say. Yet do I believe in God? I must behave *as if* I do not trust any future salvation and yet aim always at that difficult detached interior life. Yet here I am, involuntarily raising my head to listen to every taxi . . . (80–81)

Her philosophical reflections about her belief in God have a curiously ambiguous status. They can be read as one of the distractions from the waiting she is trying not to think about, a way of thinking beyond the situation she is in, a spiritual exercise undertaken in the spirit of the piano playing, perhaps undertaken equally "carelessly and inattentively." But they also read as reflections *on* her current situation, in which she is also behaving as if she expects nothing, aiming at a detached, interior life. Paradoxically, it is when they are read as reflections on her actual situation that they seem to have the seriousness and spiritual force they lack when read theologically. Even so, both the philosophical reflections and the additional descriptive passages that I cut from the passage function essentially as a "weight" of words, oppressing the passage in a way that reflects White's own feeling of oppression. Neither her stated commitment to a "detached, interior life" nor her behaviour, playing the piano and writing in her diary, really masks her palpable hope for "future salvation" in the form of a phone call.

The diary is not a genre in which White can capitalise on her skill with endings, at least not in a conventional way. But perhaps visions of the future, hopes and resolutions, are for White a way of ordering endings on speculation, or, as she would put it, on account.

2 John Cheever

"What *is* a shapely day?" John Cheever's editor, William Maxwell, wrote in the margins of a story he would publish in *The New Yorker*. It was a query Cheever ignored, and Maxwell let the story go to press still including the description of a day "as fragrant and shapely as an apple."[1] According to Cheever's biographer, Blake Bailey, "Cheever recorded every day of his adult life from 1940 on. Every day!"[2] Journal entry after journal entry seeks to give each day some form of shapeliness, whatever the disappointments, rows, financial anxieties, physical ailments and the stubborn dreariness of the suburbs in which he lived. Like Antonia White, Cheever maintained, against all the evidence, a determined faith in his own resolutions. His references to his children in the journals concern, as often as not, their failures to meet expectations: Ben's preference for his "effeminate friend" over the company of his father, Susan's bad table manners eating butter with a fork. Yet he resolves, "What fine things I will do for them. What tall things I will build," and repeats over and over again, in one form or another, his claim for "the seriousness of my wish to lead a worthy and clean life."[3]

His use of resolutions to provide a "shapeliness" to his days, however, is very different from White's way of writing resolutions in diary entries that trail off into lists, accounts, or self-doubts. An early entry in Cheever's *Journals* describing exactly the resolute frame of mind so typical of White provides a striking contrast to the entries she writes in such a mood:

> Awake before dawn, feeling tired and full of resolutions. Do not drink. Do not et cetera, et cetera. The noise of birdsong swelling: flickers, chickadees, cardinals [. . .][4]

Where White would be prescriptive, Cheever is descriptive. She would have listed the resolutions, he merely refers to them. White writes as she thinks the thoughts, from within the moment of thinking, presumably to review the writing afterwards. Cheever's writing is already a review: he writes already outside the process of thinking. There is an elegiac note to his *Journals*, as if the moment of writing is already slipping away, along with the recent past he recalls.

In comparison with the "continuous present" perspective that structures White's diaries, the perspective Cheever gives his journal entries is closer to the "past perfect" of a piece of fiction. Ted Solotaroff describes the *Journals* as they appear in the Knopf edition as "concise, lucid, moving, and brimming with implications."[5] Where a study of White's diary is useful for determining the kinds of reading practices demanded by material which is so unresolved, both at a structural level and within individual entries, Cheever's journals in contrast allow a consideration of the literary potential of the open form. Demanding though the open form can be on readers, Cheever's journals suggest that it can be liberating for the writer. Bailey's biography of Cheever emphasises the difficulty Cheever had in writing a first novel, and indeed Bailey suggests that he would "arguably never quite resolve" his problems with the novel form.[6] When Malcolm Cowley, editor of *The New Republic*, was presented in 1932 with Cheever's first attempts at sample novel chapters, he informed Cheever that "they wouldn't do...each chapter was separate and came to a dead end."[7] Cheever himself, struggling fourteen years later with another attempt at a first novel (*The Holly Tree*, never completed, but much of it reworked to be used in *The Wapshot Chronicles*), observed that it was "the work of a short-story writer: each chapter ended with a dying fall, a bit of provocative irony that went nowhere."[8] If White's problem was too many beginnings, Cheever's problem, at least as a novelist, was an excess of endings. Paradoxically, for Cheever the open-ended structure of the journal offers the possibility of concluding at the end of every entry.

Although my intention in this chapter is not to analyse the effects of editorial work on the *Journals* (I will turn to the question of the editor's role in Chapters 4, 5, and 6, looking at diaries which have been published in both a selective and a "complete" form), it should be noted that when Solotaroff praised the "concise, moving, lucid" writing of the journals as it appears in this "final draft," he is making a pointed contrast with the initial disappointment he records feeling when he first looked at the journal manuscripts, with a view to purchasing them for Harper and Row. What he was faced with, he recalls, was "badly typed, misspelled and often unstrung prose" containing "a monotonous account of the Westchester round of visits and parties and a naked but less-than-riveting one of the at-home dissipations and marital distress of a mostly depressed and money-driven man." In his review, therefore, he largely focuses on the work of the editor of the *Journals*, Robert Gottlieb. It is "the magic of editing," Solotaroff suggests, that has produced such a "coherent" text.[9]

The best description of the journal manuscripts is given in Bailey's *Slate* magazine article, which outlines the work he put into making sense of the 4,300 pages, mostly typed and single-spaced, now held in Harvard's Houghton Library. The main difficulty he faced was in determining chronology, as Cheever rarely dated entries and the volumes seem to have got hopelessly out of order; there are anomalies in the chronology of the entries published in the Knopf edition that Bailey traces back to the disarrangement of the original papers. But Bailey, like Solotaroff, describes the material itself as the representation of a "stubbornly chaotic life" in a "very messy artefact."[10] These are criticisms that recall the critical response to White's diaries in their published form. The critical response to the published edition of Cheever's *Journals* has, in contrast, largely been positive; while some critics found the material overwhelming or dispiriting (among them John Updike), it was more often praised as an "intimate self-portrait of a writer," as *The Entertainment Weekly* put it: "A stunning itinerary of a lost man intermittently saved by a change of wind or a moment of love."[11] The *New York Times* review, declaring it "A daring contribution to American letters," addressed directly the reader's role in making sense of such private material, suggesting the *Journals* "can be read as a writer's notebook, a family chronicle, a brutally honest autobiography and almost as an unfinished novel." However faceted the material is, the *Journals* does, as the review goes on to claim, read "As a book . . . adding up to more than the sum of the parts."[12]

While Solotaroff suggests the coherence of the text was given to it by Gottlieb's editing, most critics suggest its coherence comes from the quality of Cheever's writing and the recognisably Cheever style that is apparent in every entry. As Philip Roth observed in his review of the *Journals*, "[Cheever's] voice . . . is as rich and distinctive as any of the leading voices of post-war American literature."[13] Cheever's son, Ben Cheever, suggests there is less of a distinction to be made between these two positions than it might seem, describing Gottlieb as "a champion of my father's prose . . . The man has a great ear."[14] In a phone call he held with me, Gottlieb described his editorial work primarily in terms of being "honest to the material."[15] While the published edition was necessarily selective, he aimed to represent proportionately the range of entries in terms of their concerns, themes, and typical subject matter. (Given that he had, as he commented wryly, "no scarcity of material" with which to work, he did admit to limiting the number of entries concerned with relatively banal domestic duties: "This is not exciting information." He also aimed to limit the amount of repetition across entries. In this, he can be seen to be editing for literariness, and, to a certain extent, against the most distinctive aspects of the diary form.[16]) His intention, too, was never to intervene in a passage, to make no internal cuts from the beginning of a selected passage to its end, and to offer no explanations or other editorial material that would disrupt the reading of Cheever's prose. The asterisks between the passages as they appear in the *Journals* represent breaks in Cheever's own work.[17] Cheever himself provided the "shapely" form to the record he made of each day.

It is in the *Journals*, even more than in his fictional writing, that Cheever seems to "get a grip" on the material he writes about, mastering the details of his daily life by providing idealistic interpretations of them. The contrast between Cheever's diaries and his fiction is as illuminating as is the contrast between White's diaries and fiction. Surprisingly, it is Cheever's short stories which seem to resist or avoid closure, and the diary entries which are given definite conclusions. And yet the diary form itself resists closure, even when a particular diary is made up of carefully concluded entries. Cheever's diary demonstrates the peculiar power that the detail is given by the diary form.

Detail is often referred to as one of the defining characteristics of the diary. Rebecca Hogan, for instance, in her article "Engendering Autobiographies: The Diary as a Feminine Form," bases her claim that the diary should be understood as "feminine" on the importance of the detail to the diary, in terms of both the diary structure and diary content.[18] In reading the detail as feminine, she draws particularly on Naomi Schor's *Reading in Detail*, which examines the ways in which the detail has historically been defined as feminine.[19] But what does it mean to suggest the diary is more detailed than other genres? Schor herself outlines the eighteenth-century concept of the detail as ornamental and as belonging to the domestic and the everyday. Hogan makes a connection between this eighteenth-century definition of the detail and the ways in which the diary has been described. I, too, have found the eighteenth-century concept of the detail, and its position as the opposite of the sublime, particularly interesting in understanding Cheever's use of the detail. This is a very evaluative understanding of the detail, however, that substitutes associations for a precise definition, and which describes the detail as much in terms of content as in formal terms. I thought it would be useful, then, to look at dictionary definitions of the detail, to more precisely define how the term might be used.

The Chambers Concise Dictionary defines the detail in curiously evaluative terms, as "a minor or unimportant part; too much attention to particulars".[20] This is especially odd since if you look up "particular" you find it is defined as "worthy of detailed attention." I find the less evaluative definition of the Oxford Shorter more helpful in clarifying what the term "detail" might mean in relation to the diary. Based on the definition in the Oxford Shorter, if the diary is especially detailed, the whole is made up of more parts, or the parts that make up the whole are more distinct, more distinguished *from* the whole, than they would be in a less detailed genre.[21] The whole might refer to the overall structure of the work, in contrast to structural details (such as the diary entries) in the course of the work. Or, the whole might mean the overall meaning of the work, made up of an interpretation of the details. The particularity of the detail then may be distinguished by its concreteness, its reference to or description of a concrete object, in contrast with the more abstract unity given by interpretation. It is this second sense of the detail in relation to a text that is referred to in discussions of the "detailed" style of nineteenth-century realist fiction for example. And it is this second sense of the detail which seems to be suggested by claims of the detailed nature of the diary. In this chapter, I consider both senses in which the diary can be claimed to be a "detailed" genre, and how the effects of the two different ways interrelate.

A particular tension between detail and some larger interpretative framework for the detail is a marked feature of all Cheever's writing. This tension often structures Cheever's short stories: they seem to be built around this tension. Whether they end with details being given a prominence, a distinction, beyond the story's framework, or whether they end by summing up the meaning of the story as a whole, by summing up some sort of moral framework for the details of the story, the endings of the stories seem to make a claim for the importance of either the detail or the whole, in such a way that this becomes in part the point of the stories.

Typically, the short stories leave a disquieting gap between the details offered for interpretation and the interpretation we are left with by the narrator, or they give a wealth of details that don't in the end add up to an interpretation of events at all. In "The Sutton Place Story" a sense of portent is created from the beginning of the story by the amount of background detail that is given to an event not at first disclosed.[22] We are told in detail about the Tennysons and their relationship to their child, about the child's nurse, and most of all about Renee and her relationship with the family and the child. This relationship is set up so carefully, in so much detail, that the reader is led to expect that the cause of what happens next will be found here, but it isn't. The child runs away for no reason apparent in the story, then is found again. This is the simple drama that the story has been leading up to, but none of the background information turns out to have any bearing on it. The story ends with the father's questions to the child, which the father knows won't be answered and to which the reader will receive no answers either:

> He knew that she would never tell him and that as long as he lived he would never know, and against his palm he could feel the strong beating of her heart, but he went on asking, "Where have you been? Who gave you the bread? Who is Martha?" (78)

Cheever's stories often end by acknowledging an inability to come to a conclusion, even as the acknowledgement works to conclude the story formally. "The Angel of the Bridge" ends with the image it begins with, the image of the narrator's mother skating round and round the ice, a circular movement reflected by the form of the story:

> I wish I could be convinced that there will always be some merciful intercession to help me with my worries, but I don't believe in rushing my luck, so I will stay off the George Washington Bridge, although I can cross the Triborough and the Tappan Zee with ease. My brother is still afraid of elevators, and my mother, although she's grown quite stiff, still goes round and round the ice. (497)

In "The Wrysons" any sense of resolution or explanation is again momentary for the characters, and for the reader it is achieved only by a restatement of the characters' interest in a good appearance (and again you could say that the story too ends only by presenting a good appearance, an empty shapeliness):

> Some comprehension—perhaps momentary—of the complexity of life must have come to them, but it was only momentary. There were no further explanations. He threw the cake, which was burned to a cinder, into the garbage, and they turned out the lights and climbed the stairs, more mystified by life than ever, and more interested than ever in a good appearance. (324)

The characters of Cheever's stories are left with details that seem to promise meaning but fail to remain significant beyond the moment. This failure becomes the conclusion of the day-in-the-life story of "The Superintendent":

> The day had failed to have any meaning, and the sky seemed to promise a literal explanation . . . But the sky told him only that it was a long day at the end of winter, that it was late and time to go in. (177)

Not all stories end, in this way, with descriptive details that "[fail] to have any meaning." As many end with a sense of unity between the particularities of the world and the abstract values the characters strive to invest them with. The grandly titled "A Vision of the World" is one of these stories. Its ending seems to plug up the gap between detail and meaning exposed in the other stories:

> Then I sit up in bed and exclaim aloud to myself, "Valor! Love! Virtue! Compassion! Splendour! Kindness! Wisdom! Beauty!" The words seem to have the colors of the earth, and as I recite them I feel my hopefulness mount until I am contented and at peace with the night. (517)

Yet there is something unconvincing about this recital of abstractions. The words "seem to have the colors of the earth" but they remain detached from the plot of the story. Nothing has changed about the narrator's situation, the changes are all subconscious, his new mood an inexplicable response to his dreams of a foreign language. There is no connection between this internal work and the details of the narrative. In story after story of married life, a change or resolution in the relationship between the husband and wife is brought about by an effort of will, usually on the part of the husband. In "The Country Husband" the husband and wife simply move from one level of feeling to another higher level that overrides the first; the cure of "The Cure" is basically a change of heart, prompted in part by a few accidents of circumstance. The high note on which the stories end gives them the sense of a conclusion, in which abstract values transcend contingent details, and indeed the "The Cure" insists the characters are "happy ever since" (164). But the details are not a part of the conclusions and the conclusions do not cancel them out. They remain uninterpreted and autonomous, and in their particularity and concreteness they seem more "real" than the recitations of abstract virtues that are supposed to transcend them.

The *Journals* share this tension between detail and interpretation, between the contingencies of domestic life and abstract values. More than that, the tension between the two can be read as the *Journals*' central subject. Cheever grapples consciously with the problem of bringing the two to terms with each other. The passage on Easter 1959, which ends with a list of virtues similar to the list that concludes "A Vision of the World", is worth quoting in full for the way in which it shifts the relation between detail and meaning:

> Easter Eve: Dyeing eggs and stuffing the turkey, all pleasant. Easter morning sunny and cool. To church with Susie and Ben. The church for once is full. I am delighted to hear that Christ is risen. I think that it is not against God's will to have my generative powers refreshed by the face of a pretty woman in a forward pew or to wonder about the hairy and somehow limpid young man on my left. It is the combination of hairiness and wistful grace that seems to mark him. When I hear that Mary found at the tomb a man in white raiment I am incredulous. It is hard for me to believe that God expressed His will, His intent in such a specific image. But when I go to the altar I am deeply moved. The chancel is full of lilies and their fragrance seems as fresh as it is heavy; a sign of good cheer. And that this message should have been revealed to us and that we should cherish it seems to be our finest triumph. Here in the chancel we glimpse some vision of transcendent love, some willing triumph over death and all of its lewd guises. And if it is no more than willingness, how wonderful that is in itself. Walk with my youngest son in the sun. How my whole love of life seems to gather round his form; how he fills me with the finest ambitions. Birds sing. There is a little shimmer of heat. The moment of darkness is gone. He throws sticks into the water, which is a perfectly clear, shallow, and rippled scarf of light. He shuffles through the old leaves.
>
> Later we go to the B.s' for the Easter-egg hunt; but I am smitten suddenly with shyness, my smile is strained, my sensibilities are inflamed, I am round-shouldered and bent-necked and dreary and nothing but a pint of bourbon will straighten me out. I count on painkillers until ten, when I retire and, half-asleep—courage, lustiness, cleanliness, love, charity, strength, industry, intelligence, vision—I recount to myself a dozen times those virtues I admire.[23]

The passage moves back and forth between detail and transcendent meaning, between the dyed eggs and the message of Christ's ascension. The attraction Cheever feels for the pretty woman and the "hairy and somehow limpid young man" he incorporates into the religious meaning of the day, yet the image of the man in white raiment at the tomb seems too specific for Cheever to accept as a religious sign. Then again, the fragrance of the lilies Cheever is able to read as "a sign". The passage strains to read all the details of the day in terms of the values Cheever recounts to himself at the end of the day, values proper to a day of religious significance, and the effect is largely achieved. By the end of the first paragraph, the "little shimmer of heat", the sticks thrown into the water, the old leaves, all seem invested with significance.

Yet the personal, physical details of the second shorter paragraph seem to cancel out the transcendent spirituality of the first paragraph. There seems little spiritual significance in the strained smile, the round shoulders and bent neck, the bourbon and painkillers. The syntax of the last sentence is curious, with the virtues—courage, lustiness, cleanliness, love, charity, strength, industry, intelligence, vision—listed before they are given any context. The reader encounters the virtues suspended between the dashes, as if the reader too moves half-asleep from fact to faith without transition. There has been a kind of reversal: where the details in Cheever's writing typically seem to be waiting for some kind of transcendent meaning to give them context, here the abstractions are suspended waiting for the concrete details of their recital to give a context to them.

As in the stories, it seems to me the overall effect is to cast doubt on the transcendence of the abstract values, and on the significance given to the details by their investment with these values. The degrading details of the last paragraph seem to be left with a concrete particularity that has a conviction the litany of virtues lacks. Yet as Cheever says, "if it is no more than willingness" there is still something wonderful in the willingness itself to invest details with the significance of transcendent values.

In this Cheever most obviously belongs in the tradition of nineteenth-century transcendentalism, with his vision appearing closely aligned with that of Emerson. The necessary experience of life "in succession, in division, in parts, in particles" is, according to Emerson, redeemed through our understanding of our experience in terms of "the soul of the whole [. . .] the universal beauty, to which every part and particle is equally related."[24] Cheever does seem to strive throughout the *Journals* to find, as Emerson urges, "beauty and holiness in new and necessary facts, in the field and the road-side, in the shop and the mill" (II, 218), as well as in birdsong at dawn and suburban Easter-egg hunts. However, there is a strain to Cheever's spiritualising of the detail which is very different to Emerson's confident belief in the detail's significance, the "worth of the vulgar" (I, 68). Cheever's anxiety over his constant return to the detail can better be understood in terms of the earlier concept of the sublime.

Debate about the exact qualities, and relative importance of the different qualities, of the sublime was carried on in treatises and articles through the eighteenth century. The sublime was increasingly opposed to the "beautiful" and was more clearly gendered as masculine later in the century, as the Romantic taste for "rugged" and "gaunt" features in both natural landscapes and male features became widespread. But the quality of "vastness" continued throughout the eighteenth century to be considered an essential aspect of the sublime and was given, by most writers on the subject, precedence over all other aspects. Hugh Blair for instance, in his *Lectures on rhetoric and belles lettres* (1785) states, "All vastness produces the impression of sublimity" (213), and John Baillie in his *Essay on the Sublime* (1747) concludes "large objects only constitute the sublime."[25] The vastness of the object is important because of the effect it has on the viewer, as Baillie explains: "Vast objects occasion vast sensations, and vast sensations give the mind a higher idea of her own powers" (89).

The vastness of the sublime effect is contrasted with the diminishing effect of the detail. The implicit gendering of this opposition is clear in this passage from Blair's *Lectures*:

> Now when an author has brought us, or is attempting to bring us into this state; if he multiplies words unnecessarily, if he decks the sublime object which he presents to us, round and round, with glittering ornament; nay, if he throws in any one decoration that sinks in the least below the capital image, that moment he alters the key; he relaxes the tension of the mind; the strength of feeling is emasculated; the beautiful may remain but the sublime is gone. (220)

Baillie explains how the "vastness" of the sublime object is important because of its relation to infinity; vastness combined with the uniformity created by an absence of detail allows the imagination to break free of limitations:

> Where an object is vast, and at the same time uniform, there is to the imagination no limits of its vastness, and the mind runs out into infinity . . . However beautiful the hemisphere may be when curled over with little silver-tinged clouds, and the blue sky everywhere breaking through, yet the prospect is not near so grand as when in a vast and uniform heaven there is nothing to stop the eye, or limit the imagination. (90)

Perhaps the Cheever detail—or the ideal towards which the Cheever detail strives—can best be understood in relation to an ideal of the detail that Naomi Schor teases out of Hegel's *Aesthetics: Lectures on Fine Art.*[26] As Schor makes clear, Hegel's general tendency is to devalue the detail in opposition to the Ideal, or the Idea of Beauty. The Ideal, like Baillie's sublime, implies "the negation of everything particular." Hegel argues therefore against the inclusion of naturalistic details in portraits, such as "freckles, pimples, pockmarks, warts etc," because they detract from the "Ideal" form of the sitter, the form that "explicitly correspond[s] with the soul."[27]

Hegel's appreciation of Dutch genre painting, which gives detail an especial prominence, is therefore unexpected. The following passage from Hegel's lectures on aesthetics validates the detail in Dutch painting with the idea that a transference takes place onto the profane detail from the sacred detail, which itself develops from a more general treatment of the sacred:

> In general terms, the essence of painting's progress is this: a start is made with *religious* subjects, still *typically* treated . . . Next there enter more and more into the religious situations the present, the individual, the living beauty of the figures . . . until painting turns towards the world; it takes possession of nature, the everyday experiences of human life, or historically important national events, whether past or present, portraits and the like, all down to the tiniest and most insignificant detail, and it does this with the same love that had been lavished on the ideal content of religion. (35)

What makes the detail spiritual is the love lavished on it by the artist, the quality of attention given to the detail, the "willingness" to present the detail in spiritual terms.

> In this way Dutch painting, for example, has recreated, in thousands and thousands of effects, the existent and fleeting appearance of nature as something generated afresh by man . . . what at once claims our attention in matter of this kind, when art displays it to us, is precisely this pure shining and appearing of objects as something produced by the *spirit* which transforms in its inmost being the external and sensuous side of all this material. For instead of real wool and silk, instead of real hair, glass, flesh, and metal, we see only colours; instead of all the dimensions requisite for appearance in nature, we have just a surface, and yet we get the same impression which reality affords. (35–6)

This is a willingness we can recognise in Cheever's treatment of the detail. However, for Cheever there is an *effort* of will involved that is almost as different from the spirit of Dutch genre painting as it is from Emersonian transcendentalism. As Schor writes, the detail is "gendered and doubly gendered" as feminine (4). Cheever writes against a gendering of the detail as feminine, not just because it is particular as opposed to Ideal (and therefore risks being profane as opposed to spiritual), but also because it is small and therefore not "great," and because it is domestic and therefore confined. By "writes against" I do not mean he denies or deconstructs these categories. Rather he writes against the gendering of the detail as feminine in the same way Hegel values Dutch genre painting against his own devaluing of the detail as particular and opposed to the divine. Just as Hegel's appreciation of Dutch genre painting requires justification and an interpretation of the detail in spiritual terms, so does Cheever's use of the detail require constant justification and interpretation, to compensate for its femininity.

Throughout his *Journals* Cheever expresses a constant anxiety over the smallness and domesticity of his writing:

> I would like not to be vindictive or narrow. I would like to avoid phony compassion. Thinking of the midsummer night, "*Parlons français*," the drunkard said. I see that this is small. I see in the five-and-ten-cent store yesterday that my descriptions of Betsey's pleasure are small. It stinks of peanuts and cheap candy. (4)

While a historical understanding of the devaluation of the detail as feminine, and, particularly, as profane, usefully illuminates the tension between Cheever's emphasis on the detail and his more abstract, often spiritual, interpretations, his anxiety over the way his use of the detail limits his writing can only fully be understood in relation to the masculine aesthetic Cheever shared with Hemingway, Updike, Bellow, and Mailer. An intriguing passage in the later part of the journals suggests that the "spiritualising of the detail" that I have seen in Cheever's prose may be a compensation for a perceived failure of masculinity:

> I am galled at my lack of physical bulk and galled that this should concern me. There is really no evidence of this in all the photographs I have, but I fear being taken for an elderly bosun's mate, that gentle clerk in the hardware store who knows the whereabouts of all the nails, the rifle-company typist, the small museum guard in a worn uniform who says softly, "It is beautiful, isn't it?" I think of myself in West Berlin, toastmaster at Iole's wedding,—bang-bang, a dynamic, lambent flame. So, having no bulk, one counts on spirit. I skate, shovel the snow, and think that I see in some unidentified tree a trace of greenness and lightness. This seems to be what I've been looking for. But on the dark or mysterious end of things I imagine, when I lie down for my nap, that I hold in my arms some unsuitable lover. (330)

Cheever's concern about his physical size might seem irrelevant to a discussion of his evaluation of his writing. Yet his anxiety about the "greatness" of his writing is matched only by his anxiety about his physical size on the one hand, and his sexuality—his virility—on the other.

> My forty-seventh birthday and I feel neither young nor old, sprightly in the middle, and pray that I will have done a decent book by the forty-eighth. Shaving, and trying to come to terms with myself, I think that I am a small man, small feet, small p—-k, small hands, small waist, and that these are the facts. I must confine my attentions to little, little

> women, sit in tiny chairs, etc. And then I think of how I hate small men, those whose incurable youth is on them like a stain. How I hate small feet, small hands, small-waisted males who stand behind their small wives at cocktail parties in a realm of timid smallness. (111–12)

Small men are seen as less manly than larger men, and their position of dominance over women is threatened: they "stand behind their small wives at cocktail parties." Manliness is associated with "greatness". In the following passage, Hemingway is described as a great writer, and a "great man":

> Hemingway shot himself yesterday morning. There was a great man. I remember walking down a street in Boston after reading a book of his, and finding the color of the sky, the faces of strangers, and the smells of the city heightened and dramatized. The most important thing he did for me was to legitimize manly courage, a quality that I had heard, until I came on his work, extolled by Scoutmasters and others who made it seem a fraud. He put down an immense vision of love and friendship, swallows and the sound of rain. There was never, in my time, anyone to compare with him. (152)

Cheever draws on other aspects of virility besides size to provide metaphors for evaluating his writing. He desires for instance a "muscular vocabulary" (112). The coding of men as hard and muscular, and women as soft, is apparent in the following passage, though the contrast between heat and snow does not seem so obviously to fit in:

> My style seems ruminative and soft; my descriptive powers are not what I would like them to be. I want to let some air and light into this room; waking up this morning I thought that I could use a brisk fistfight. I would like to write a story but not the New Jersey night, not the man in Columbus Circle, nothing overbalanced with morbidity, something with bulk and power. Not the heat wave. The news that it was snowing in Berlin. (21)

Even the frequently evoked search for "depth," and corresponding anxiety about "shallowness" in his writing, seems in this passage possibly linked with the deeper notes of the male voice:

> I read two stories of mine and find them too breezy. They were deeply felt at the time but there seems to be a lack of deep notes; no bass clef; a lack of fundamentals. (117)

Yet Cheever does keep coming back to size, as his primary term of evaluation for literary greatness. Discussing Mailer's writing again in terms of "size", it is clear that Cheever does not mean simply the number of pages in the book:

> Very pleased and excited by Mailer's book "The Naked and the Dead." Impressed particularly with its size. Despaired, while reading it, of my own confined talents. I seem, with my autumn roses and my winter twilights, not to be in the big league. (13)

Cheever's "confinement" is a confinement of subject matter, a confinement to detail without the abstractions of "love and friendship" of Hemingway's vision, and a confinement to domesticity suggested by the "autumn roses." Detail in itself is not confining: swallows and the sound of rain are a part of Hemingway's "immense vision", and such things as "the color of the sky" are heightened for Cheever by Hemingway's writing. It is the sort of detail, and the relation of the detail to abstract and "manly" values, that determines the "size" or greatness of the writing.

Three consecutive passages from Cheever's journal of 1953 deal with his anxiety over his confinement to the suburbs, as domicile and subject matter. The suburbs are "small" and lacking in "heroes":

> Driving for seven hours, straight into the sun, tired my eyes. "How lush and green it is here," my wife said, and I saw how the lawns were shining but I was not particularly happy to be back. It was coming back to offices, back to Grand Central Station, back to the evening train home, back to the discomfort of a full suit on a hot day, back to tiredness, back to parochialism, back to a small part of the world, back to parochialism, back to a lack of excitement. That there are no heroes here does not mean that there are no heroes anywhere. I would like to keep the sense of being away from New York, away from the noise and excitement there. I would like to keep the sense of what a small part of the world this is; to master it, not to take it too seriously. (33)

The suburbs are associated with the commuting businessman, but the businessman is not seen as particularly masculine; rather he is an appendage to the confined female world of the dormitory suburb. In the next passage, he writes of the suburbs' power over him to return him "in spite of myself" to "passiveness". He compares his own subject matter in the next passage again with the "big, wild, rowdy country, full of whores and prizefighters" of which Saul Bellow writes (33). The suburbs are small, passive, and in a surprising number of passages associated with "autumn" and "twilights"—a time of day and season of year associated with closing down, drawing in.[28]

In passages like these, Cheever's anxiety over his "confined" subject matter can scarcely be distinguished from his anxiety about his own confinement in the domesticity of his life, the "smell of cooking, the sound of children's slippers on a staircase, the feeling that one is incarcerated by beautiful and hideous things" (20) as one of these entries puts it. His determination to "keep the sense of what a small part of the world this is; to master it," makes equal sense as a resolution about his writing, and as an approach to his life in the suburbs. In the passage quoted earlier, however, in which he despairs of his talents in face of the "size" of Mailer's new book, he accepts that "Eccentric I must be, gentle, soft in some ways," in his domestic life, while, as a writer, he sees himself as "forced to consider my prose by the ignobility of some of my material" (14).

Paradoxically, perhaps, he makes up for a "confinement" of subject matter, with a "mastery" of prose that he elsewhere describes as a "containment":

> I feel that I take a minor, an obscure, a dim position that is not my destiny but that is my fault, as if I had lacked, somewhere along the line, the wit and courage to contain myself competently within the shapes at hand. (7)

He uses the term "limitations" to refer to the *lack* of formal containment:

> If I am writing narrative prose, and I sometimes am, I must content myself with these limitations. Every line cannot be a cry from the heart, cut in stone. But I do rebel against common speech, against the quality of filler I find in my work. (118)

Details then can be limiting if they are the details of domestic, suburban life: they particularise and tie the prose down to a limited subject. But they can also be limiting formally, if they detract from the formal perfection of the prose. The detail always risks escaping the boundaries of formal containment. The "greatness" of great writing cannot be achieved by piling up detail, but is an overall effect which requires the sum to be greater than the parts. This is achieved by "inner logic" and "passion":

> As a part of moving I have had to go through some old manuscripts and I have been disheartened to see that my style fifteen years ago, was competent and clear and that the improvements on it are superficial. I fail to see any maturity, of increased penetration; I fail to see any deepening of my grasp. I was always in love. I was always happy to scythe a field and swim in a cold lake and put on clean clothes. I was more exuberant and naive about both this and love than I am now, but this is not a change for the better. There are thousands of notes, thousands of pages of description, thousands of striking conversations, and because they all lack an inner logic, because they lack passion, they are of no import. (25)

Cheever's criticism of his "old manuscripts"—which sound like a mixture of notes towards his fiction and more diary-like journal material—is very much the criticism which is often levelled at the diary form in general. The diary is "vast" in terms of the quantity of material many diaries amass, but fails to achieve greatness because of this lack of "an inner logic" or form.

Cheever's distinction between a negative confinement of subject matter and a positive containment of form is neat one. However, it has its own limitations. The confinement of subject matter does not seem to me the most serious limitation of Cheever's prose. There is a containment of interpretation which may be linked to the containment of form that Cheever aims for, but which often tends to shut down and limit the meaning of passages of his journals.

Much of Cheever's writing in the *Journals* seeks containment within one interpretation, resisting alternatives. He writes for instance: "I am tired, but this will pass. I love my wife's body and my children's innocence. Nothing more" (19). Of course, the very insistence that there is "nothing more" introduces the idea of extraneous desire. Perhaps it is significant that the attempt at closure is an attempt to confine himself to a heterosexual, male identity.

Repetition and continuity—features of the diary usually considered in terms of its open structure—become features of a closed identity. Cheever often summarises a life by describing a repeated pattern within it as if it represents the whole. "These Westchester Sunday nights" are described as if they are always the same, so that his own actions become a role play that he can describe himself performing in the second person: "You take a shower. You put on old clothes. You drive your wife to church and your children to Sunday school. You rake the leaves off the flower bed . . . " (4).

He more often than not refers to Mary Cheever as "my wife" and his sons and daughter as "my son", "my younger son", "my daughter", as if their roles are more important than their individuality, or as if their importance is only, or mainly, in relation to him. (Susan Cheever, in her memoir *Home Before Dark*, observes "As individuals we often displeased him, but as a unit we were cherished and indispensable . . . The three of us were, as he said, the 'roof and settle' of his existence."[29]) Although much of the *Journals* is concerned with analysing his marriage, his interpretations of his wife's behaviour towards him typically fail to consider her behaviour as a response to his own. Instead his belief that her feelings and behaviour are a set response to events in her past takes the place of examination, shuts down interpretation.

> It seems to me that she is unhappy, that she seeks the cause of this unhappiness in our marriage, and that it lies in some much earlier time of life. But that she cannot, quite understandably, face this. (103)[30]

His word for Mary's periods of unhappiness is "maldispositions", as in "Mary especially *maldiposta* on Saturday" (91), or "What I think of as 'the maldispositions' continues" (258). The word suggests a physical cause for her unhappiness. Perhaps because of his alcoholism, Cheever has a strong sense of the connection between health and mood, and between mood and interpretation. There is a contradiction between this sense of mood and interpretation as something basically determined by the body, and his attempts to raise his spirits through a willed faith in abstract virtues. Both the helplessness before the body and the insistent faith in his "litany of virtues" can shut down interpretation and give a sense of closure to a passage.

The "cafarde" is what he calls his own version of Mary's "maldispositions." Being his own mood he describes it not from the outside, in terms of behaviour, but from the inside, in terms of emotion. But the mystery of the "cafarde" can still be reduced to a physical cause: " . . . and sitting in the movie I wonder if this *cafarde*, this mysterious and stupendous melancholy from which I seem to suffer is no more than common alcoholism" (135). His interpretations of the world are dependent on his physical state, and he wonders at times if "my equilibrium is such a touchy piece of machinery that I only waste time in trying to control it" (65). Health is responsible for the "form" of daily life:

> When the beginnings of self-destruction enter the heart it seems no bigger than a grain of sand. It is a headache, a slight case of indigestion, an infected finger; but you miss the 8:20 and arrive late at the meeting of credit extensions. The old friend that you meet for lunch suddenly exhausts your patience and in an effort to be pleasant you drink three cocktails, but by now the day has lost its form, its sense and meaning. To try and restore some purpose and beauty to it you drink too much at cocktails you talk too much you make a pass at somebody's wife and you end with doing something foolish and obscene and wish in the morning you were dead. But when you try to trace back the way you came into this abyss all you find is a grain of sand. (23)

It is interesting that the happiness of the day is described in such literary terms, as "form" and "sense" and "meaning," and that the passage itself is so formal, ending neatly with the same phrase with which it began. This sense of confinement to the physical (mastered by literary containment) is at odds with the will towards faith shown in the litanies of virtues of other passages. "Bestial" man and the man with "grace" inhabit different interpretations of the world:

> After drinking two bottles of beer in the diner, I decided that man is not physical, man is bestial. I am troubled, however, by the sexual interpretation I put on everything—that the mountains should look to me like knees and clavicles—but this seems to be one of the burdens of men without grace. (19)

But the *Journals* do more than dramatise the struggle between these two interpretations of the world, one determined by the body, one willed by the soul. The most interesting passages to me hold open a moment in which the two states, physical and spiritual, meet and add meaning to each other. It is the detail which performs this function.

I have quoted the Easter Eve passage as an example of the tension between detail and interpretation. It is the willingness to give meaning, rather than the abstract meanings themselves, which matches the power of the detail in this passage. In other passages the meaning of the occasion seems invested more convincingly in the moment of the occasion. These passages often end with a detail, mundane in itself, but invested with all the undefinable significance of the occasion, just as Cheever successfully wills the sticks and water of the Easter Eve passage to be invested with the more defined significance of that day.

The two passages dealing the births of Cheever's two sons incorporate detail into the evocation of spiritual significance, not so that the detail cancels out or replaces a willed spirituality, but so that the detail is a part of the significance of the moment. The significance is both more specific and less definable than a litany of virtues can be. In the following passage, "Holiness" is left an incomplete sentence, a sentence by itself, but it is given meaning by the other more concrete details around it:

> May 4th, my son Benjamin was born. My splendid, my forgiving, my gentle wife. Both of us caught up on a tide of stronger circumstance. In the hospital the lamps blooming in the linoleum floor. The delicate lights of the distant amusement park; the city; the highway. The sense that one's heart and watch are nearly stopped. And Mary's talk of the universal subconscious, the illusions of gas and ether, the parched taste, the coronas and ridges of fire. The uprush of human greatness that answers to charity and pain. Holiness. The remote neighbourhoods of the city—the hospitals, graveyards, and wharves—that we forget. The day that you were born I broke a bottle of bay rum on the bathroom floor. The night before I'd taken your mother to hear Maggie Teyte. (13)

The fragmentary style characteristic of the diary, with the incomplete sentences, the commas, and the dashes, places the details of the event next to each other without hierarchy. "The sense that one's heart and watch are nearly stopped" also seems reflected in the grammar, the fragmentary observations belonging to a moment without the immediate context of an ongoing narrative. The beginning and end of the passage frame it with the simple temporal context of the date and two events belonging to the day of the birth and the night before, but these frame the birth rather than incorporate it into a plot. The date and the isolated events, the details of a broken bottle and a concert, take on significance only because of the timing of the birth. In the same way the significance of the birth expands geographically to invest with significance not just the hospital lamps "blooming in the linoleum floor" but also the lights of the amusement park, city, and highway; and the hospital is linked with the graveyards and wharves that are usually outside the narrative of Cheever's life.

In the passage that records the birth of Cheever's second son Federico, there is more of a disjunction between his fine feelings for his son and the details of the concrete world he travels through to get to the hospital. In this passage he is struggling again to will the right interpretation of the world. His interpretation this time does not simply have his wife's pain to "answer to," but is affected by his own cold. But the simple juxtaposition of his fine sentiments for his new son, and the uncomfortable details of his surroundings, leave the interpretation of the details open to sharing the significance of his son's birth. The birth of his son is what has prompted the record of details in the passage, and they have some of the same sort of accidental significance that is acquired by the bottle of rum and Maggie Teyte concert in the previous passage:

> On the day after my son is born, I wake up filled with good wishes for him: courage, love, virility, a healthy sense of self, and workable arrangements with God. I will climb Mount Chocorua with him. I tell the maid and then the children how fine he is. I am very excited and, still having a cold, find my eyes sore and watery. I do not go to church, finding that this observance is not necessary. I take the bus with Ben and Susie to the hospital. Walking from the bus stop to the gates, we pass through a dark turn in the streets—I mean emotional darkness. K. has told me that a murder was committed here and I think I detect an atmosphere of sexual roughhouse, the smell of piss, a cat sleeping in an ashcan, and some very dirty drawings on the walls, which I examine. In the hospital there is Mary and my fine son and all the things I plan to do for him. I don't ever remember loving a child so much. So then we go home in a bus that is crowded and smelly. I have a drink and feel very odd—the cold, I guess—and looking down from my balcony into the street I covet the freedom of young bucks in open cars going down to Ostia to raise hell, and observe how a man can be given nearly everything the world has to offer and go on yearning. We go to the Palatine after lunch and now I think the world seems very strange, perhaps through the caul of my cold . . .
>
> Back to the hospital again—I am very tired—and then to bed. I wish I could lose this cold. (80–81)

The only place that is not described in any detail in this passage is the hospital. The new baby is not described in any detail either. The passage is not about the baby but about Cheever's fatherhood, and this is described less by the announcement of the good wishes, the love and the plans for him, than it is by the details of the cat sleeping in the ashcan and the sore and watery eyes. Or rather, it is in the juxtaposition of the two that a sense of what his fatherhood means at this precise moment is conveyed. It is in the *gap* between the details and the whole. The significance of both the details and the stated emotions is held open by this gap, or absence of interpretation, and it seems to allow for a larger meaning than could have been defined more precisely.

One intriguing passage in the *Journals* goes beyond Cheever's usual complementarity of confinement of content and containment of form:

> What I am determined to get away from are set pieces, closed things, shut paragraphs.
>
> The doorways of Europe, varnished and polished and waxed, even if the houses they secure are crumbling, in this vast city that is painted the color of spoiled lemons. The high doorways of Portugal with their stained glass transoms built to accommodate a thin and a melancholy man on stilts. And the *portoni* here, built to withstand armed men on horseback and battering rams. You turn the key in the lock and the cumbersome door swings open. This is your place. You, among the many people in the street, have the key. When you close the door behind you it is dark and cold and the noise of the fountain sounds very loud. You unlock the elevator gate, part the frosted glass doors [. . .] (74)

In this passage, it is the containment of *form* which must be resisted. The passage itself demonstrates how this resistance is to be achieved. The abstract theory of the first sentence is abandoned for concrete and detailed description of actual doorways, of doorways that are increasingly particular. The way the description alternates between doors opening and closing rather nicely mirrors the alternating impulse between openness and closure, between abstraction and detail, in Cheever's prose. With the term "containment" replaced by the terms of closure "set . . . closed . . . shut" (so that the corresponding idea of "failure" could be replaced by the idea of "openness"), this paragraph brings Cheever's aesthetic much closer to a postmodern aesthetic valorising openness and disruption.

It is significant that the *Journals* were best received when published in extracts in *The New Yorker*. For a number of critics the published journals were a disappointment. The entries seem to have a sense of sufficiency and of closure in themselves, which can be better appreciated when read in isolation. Their "confinement" of subject matter is redeemed by the "containment" of form in the balance between detail and interpretation each entry achieves. The formal resolution Cheever gives many entries, where an entry might end with the image with which it began, is very different from Woolf's suturing together entries to achieve a flow between them. It is, in fact, more like the formal resolutions he gives his stories, with this same technique of beginning and ending with a single image one he uses in both genres.

As the fragmentary structure of the *Journals* breaks up the containment of form of the individual entries, however, it also disrupts the containment and constriction of Cheever's interpretations and opens up the *Journals* to a broader range of meanings. More sweeping stories emerge: the complicated narratives of his inhabitance of a masculine role, his marriage, his battle against alcoholism, his coming to terms with his sexuality, and so on. The interest and depth—the "size"—of these narratives comes from the open-endedness of them and the interaction of the different narratives with each other. The much larger selection of the published entries allows for details to be read on more levels, in more webs of significance, as parts of more stories, with greater cross references between Cheever's own semantic networks. The willed significance given to the details in so many of the passages no longer contains the details in a final resolution, but becomes part of the pattern of tension between detail and interpretation that distinguishes Cheever's prose. Each moment of resolution is perhaps like one of those stopping points that slow the eye down on its journey to the sublime—but the *will* behind the spiritualising of the detail has its own significance beyond the provisional resolution it affords. The structure of the diary produces as an overall effect the "open doorway" of those passages which allow the detail to hold the meaning open. The diary form transcends the "set pieces, closed things, shut paragraphs" of the individual entries, the small parts of the greater whole.

3 Joe Orton

The momentous month in 1950 in which Joe Orton entered the Royal Academy of Dramatic Art, met his life-long partner (and eventual murderer) Kenneth Halliwell, and moved in with him and became his lover is recorded in a diary kept over this period that amounts, in total, to 191 words, the length of one of Cheever's shortest paragraphs. Orton did not keep a diary again until December 1966. This is the diary edited by John Lahr as *The Orton Diaries,* and even this diary lasts only nine months, ending with Orton's death in August 1967.[1] Lahr's editorial role was therefore quite different from the role of the editors of the White and Cheever diaries. There was no selection required; instead Lahr provides an introduction and extensive annotation to the entries which are published intact. The nine months Orton kept the diary proved to be pretty much the exact amount of time required to produce a book-length amount of material, with the published diary running to 230 pages. The diary ends when Orton was violently murdered by Halliwell, an ending it is hard not to read as Ortonesque. Yet the diary was kept, of course, with the usual sense of it as a genre defined by its open-endedness. Orton worked creatively with the open form of the diary to create an Ortonesque diary style that is clearly related to the style of his play scripts and yet which depends for its effects on the particular ways in which details can be juxtaposed within and across diary entries.

The Ortonesque is typically defined in terms of dramatic action. Lahr defines the adjective as shorthand for "scenes of macabre outrageousness"; Maurice Charney, in his study of Joe Orton for Macmillan's Modern Dramatists series, describes the Ortonesque as "a peculiar mixture of farce and outrageousness."[2] The diary, then, might seem to be a genre antithetical to the Ortonesque, with its subject matter limited to the daily events in the diarist's life, and its structure based not around scenes, but around the daily chronicling of events and observations. Far from resisting the dailiness of the diary, Orton is remarkably faithful to diary chronology, one paragraph succeeding another paragraph in the same order that the recorded events succeeded each other in the day. There is no special emphasis given to any particular events through narrative commentary or through dramatic scene setting: the entry in which Orton is offered the job writing the Beatles script is given the same treatment as the entry about the china pig he and Halliwell bought for a friend.

Christopher Innes adds a further element to an understanding of the Ortonesque by emphasising the contrast between the "conventionally tragic or disgusting situations" presented in the plays, with their comic treatment.[3] He emphasises Orton's insistence on a realistic direction of his plays, however absurd the action. In the biography Lahr describes how Orton focused, as a developing playwright, on sharpening his skills in writing dialogue, and although Orton himself refers to the "extravagance of dialogue" in the plays, the dialogue is based on his careful attention to real speech.[4] When he first started to pay detailed attention to language, intending at this stage to become a novelist, he sought to extend his vocabulary beyond the everyday, listing adverbs such as "oxymoronically," "chrystalecently," "allergically," and experimenting with imagery in phrases and sentences such as "Trees like twisted black arms against a red landscape," "On the table top stood a large anchor of peonies," or "A cypress rose blackly out of a mist of olives."[5] Soon, however, he turned to the language that was used around him, making lists of words as he heard them spoken:

> Are both, perhaps
> In the not
> not for not
> Thus, in you I
> not less than everything
> Towards the never
> Have has what
> I can only say how (127)

Kenneth Williams later remembered Orton recounting to him "a lady who said to him 'I speak as I find.' And he answered, 'What have you found?' Another time someone said to him, '*Loot* is unnecessarily filthy.' Joe examined the phrase. 'Isn't it funny?' he said. 'As though there was a *necessary* amount of filth'" (126). In his own writing, Orton increasingly spoke as he found. The style of his plays, Orton later maintained, "isn't superimposed. It's me. You can't write stylised comedy in inverted commas, because the style must ring true of the man, and if you think in a certain way and you write true to yourself, which I hope I do, then you will get a style, a style will come out. You've only got to be sitting on a bus and you'll hear the most stylised lines . . . " (126). The Ortonesque can be defined by this style as much as by the macabre content of Orton's plays.

This stylised use of everyday language distinguishes *The Orton Diaries* as much as the plays. It is a style at once "true of the man," and, as Lahr wrote of the dialogue in the plays, "a collage of the popular culture."

Unusually for a diary, it is full of direct speech. In one entry, Orton records a three-way conversation overheard on a bus, amused at how the old woman repeats everything the bus conductress says for the benefit of her husband. Orton duly records every line twice himself:

> "It's taken us forty minutes to get from Vic to here," the conductress said. The old woman leaned across to her husband and said, "It's taken her forty minutes to get from Vic to here." A little while later the conductress said she was working on Christmas Day. "She's working on Christmas Day," the old woman shouted. (36–37)

When Orton first kept a diary as a sixteen-year-old, he was not yet writing in this stylised version of the language overheard on the bus or in the streets. Instead, he combines the diary-style recording of events, in the sentence fragments that he retained always as a marker of diary style, with an exuberant commentary, resolutions, and notes to himself:

> Playreading tonight. Three plays were read. . . . imagine to my surprise and joy when, upon picking characters Mr Atkinson said, 'I think we'll have this young man to play Davie.' I'm in a play–oh joy, oh joy. Must put all my thoughts of the Greek play out of my mind. I'm lying down in my bed now and am going to mark my part . . . (Lahr, 78)

There is an odd sense of audience conveyed by these early diary extracts. Who is he addressing when he writes "imagine . . . my surprise and joy"? This sense of audience, undefined and private, yet present, is everywhere apparent in these entries, with their carefully indicated ironies:

> 'Joy of joys' as I lay in leaden slumber this morning Mum's angel sweet voice?? floated through the air telling me there was a p.c. for me. Dressed hurriedly hoping all the time for details of a play and telling myself it could only be from the library. Got down and it was from Vaughan. It said a meeting to discuss the production of 'Aria da Capo' would be held on Friday . . . (78)

Orton experimented with a radically new form of diary keeping when he started at RADA in 1950. The diary he kept then is a much sparer diary than the one he kept from December 1966 to August 1967, the later diary depending for its effect on the accumulation and juxtaposition of inconsequential and, occasionally, consequential detail. The 1950 diary is distinguished by its remarkably dramatic form, very different from Orton's later treatment of diary chronology. In its shift away from interpretation, and, increasingly, from emotionally and historically laden language, however, it looks ahead to the later diary style. It is short enough to reproduce in full from its publication in the Lahr biography:

15 MAY 1951
Started at RADA O bliss!
16 MAY
Met Florence G. A sister. You are she.
17 MAY
An actor's life for me.
18 MAY
Digs in Gower Street. Such fun.
19 MAY
Oh the larks.
Memo
Someone in the other class keeps looking at me.
20 MAY
Did nothing.
21 MAY
Mr Constable's special movement. Was eyed.
22 MAY
Florrie at all the biscuits.
23 MAY
Florrie at all the cheese.
24 MAY
Florrie at all the eggs.
25 MAY
Met Ken and John at Charing Cross Road.
Memo
I don't quite understand Ken.
27 MAY
Did nothing.
28 MAY
Mr Constable's movement.
29 MAY
Florrie at all the nuts.
30 MAY
Florrie at all the bacon.
1 JUNE
Met Ken and John again. This time with Rex Butler.
2 JUNE
Flo rang Ken.
Memo
Am beginning to understand Ken.
3 JUNE
Did nothing.
4 JUNE
Mr Constable's movement. Well!
5 JUNE

Florrie at all the cheese.
6 JUNE
Florrie at all the cake.
7 JUNE
Fuck Florrie.
8 JUNE
Met Ken. He invites us to live with him.
9 JUNE
Went to the pictures.
Memo
I am puzzled.
10 JUNE
Did nothing.
11 JUNE
Must leave our digs.
12 JUNE
Ken offers to share flat again.
13 JUNE
I say No.
14 JUNE
Ken offers again.
15 JUNE
We accept because we must.
16 JUNE
Move into Ken's flat.
17 JUNE
Well!
18 JUNE
Well!!
19 JUNE
Well!!!
20 JUNE
The rest is silence. (90–92)

All the elements that are usually given as evidence for a diary's non-literary quality—repetition, indeterminacy, the sentence fragment, the mundane detail—are here employed by Orton to deliberate, comic effect. What does it mean to use that most typical of diary phrases (typical at least of a certain type of boy's diary) "Did nothing" in a diary which *never* records any significant action? It might, at a stretch, be read as code. But what would Orton want to hide, and from whom? When, after moving in with Halliwell, he does write in a kind of code, it is not to hide a secret but reveal one; it is not the *use* of code so much as the *performance* of code.

This sense of diary keeping as performance can be detected in Orton's later diary writing too. The narrative potential that is found in the pared-down style of diary writing of the 1950 diary is largely lost in the *Diaries* as Orton fills out the entries with overheard dialogue, conversations held with friends and acquaintances, and detailed accounts of going shopping or catching a bus, but the comic potential of the kinds of juxtapositions the early diary offered between the beady attention given to Florrie's share of the household provisions and the burgeoning romance with Ken is greatly increased. Unlike a play, a diary is limited to the record of events that actually took place, but Orton records even the more dramatic events in his life in the same dead-pan way he records the banal. The effect is both comic and disturbing. The death of his mother in December 1966 makes the disturbing potential of this aspect of diary style particularly apparent.

It is surely no coincidence that of the six recorded instances of casual sex in the first part of the diary, "London: December 1966—May 1967," one of them is recorded in the same entry that describes the viewing of his mother's corpse in the Chapel of Rest, and another is recorded in the next entry, after the description of his mother's funeral. Whether Orton made a point of recording the sex scenes, for the sake of the Ortonesque juxtaposition of death and sex, or whether the sex itself was undertaken in a spirit of Ortonesque farce, cannot be determined: either is equally likely. But equally shocking, or comic, or both, is the focus on apparently insignificant details in entries which might be expected to have a weightier focus.

The funeral took place during the West End run of Orton's play *Loot*, a farce which derives much of its humour from the central presence of a corpse, the hero Hal's mother. In *Loot*, as in the diary, the solemnity of death is juxtaposed with talk of sex. The nurse Fay propositions the new widower McLeavy in the opening scene, while by the end of the play she has given in to the demands of her usual lover, Hal's accomplice in crime, Dennis, to marry him for his money, having made it quite clear she would not accept him on account of his sexual expertise. The presence of a corpse adds humour to almost anything on the stage, as the conventions that regulate dealing with death are flouted and held up for laughs. McLeavy's conventional pieties and concern for the practical and financial details of the ceremony are seen as being more ludicrous than the other characters' lack of concern for the corpse in their concentration in pulling off the final stages of a robbery.

At the Chapel of Rest, as recorded in the diary, Orton's relatives display the same concern for trivial details that Orton satirises in *Loot*. Even the concern with the costs is similar:

> The coffin lid was propped up against the wall. It said 'Elsie Mary Orton, aged 62 years.' Betty said, 'They've got her age wrong, see. Your mum was 63. You should tell them about that. Put in a complaint.' I said, 'Why? It doesn't matter now.' 'Well,' said Betty, 'you want it done right, don't you? It's what you pay for.' (42)

Another entry records his father's mishaps alone in the house with the coffin before it was taken to the Chapel of Rest, and his own recounting of the story to his agent, Peggy Ramsay: "Peggy said how dreadfully reminiscent of *Loot* it all was" (42). Since it was Ramsay who first suggested his keeping a diary for publication, he is likely to have been writing with her suggestion in mind. Certainly he plays up the Ortonesque quality of the occasion. Considering spending a night in the house with the corpse, he declares it "A little too close to the Freudian bone for comfort" (41), improving on a line from the play in which Hal, at the prospect of burying his mother naked, combs his hair and declares it "a Freudian nightmare" (21). Later Orton affects, or shares, Hal's insouciance at handling his dead mother's bodily appurtenances, when he shocks the actor playing Hal by passing on to him his mother's false teeth. But the main technique he uses to convey his sense of the Ortonesque is the usual technique he employs in the diary: a meticulous recording of detail. The corpse, the discussion of protocol, the cups of tea, the seating of the guests are all recorded in detail. The humour of these accounts of the funeral and surrounding events is more unsettling for seeming to be the reader's own response to the detail Orton simply presents than it would be if it were more obviously directed by Orton's interpretation.

Orton in fact focuses on the same practical details that he presents as so farcical a focus on stage. In the play, this focus is seen as an absurd social ritual, unrelated to any real feeling: "Show your emotions in public or not at all." Emotion itself becomes a practical detail, part of the trappings of a funeral. The play's narrative focus on the robbery makes the death incidental to the plot. The diary never exactly has a narrative focus, and the diary entries for the days following the death of Orton's mother shift the focus within each entry between anecdotal accounts of sessions with the cast of his current play, work in progress on his next play, details of the funeral plans and ceremony, encounters with mad neighbours, overheard conversations in the street, sexual encounters and other subjects, all given much the same weight. The lack of interpretation or narrative focus becomes a shocking effect in itself, given the expectation that death should have a significance that interpretative comment would express.

Orton's treatment of his mother's death can be compared to White's treatment of her friend Roberta's death, or Cheever's treatment of his first son's birth, events which are given a momentous weight by the diarists. In these examples, it is the detail that carries significance, since detail allows for a less defined and at the same time more specific significance than any explicit explanation of significance can allow. The phrase "Holiness", given a sentence to itself, in the passage recording the birth of Cheever's first son, only has meaning in relation to the details that surround it, of "the hospital lamps blooming on the linoleum floor," and the "bottle of bay rum" broken on the bathroom floor earlier in the day. It is the detail, too, which "realises" the death of Roberta. The detailed description of the "cotton wool carelessly stuffed in her nostrils, her hair that used to be sleek as a spaniel's ears, dead and dull" support White's statement that this "is the first death I have completely realised."

However, the "will" that invests these details with significance is not manifest in the details alone. Both Cheever, writing on his son's birth, and White, writing on her friend's death, explicitly state the emotional significance of the events early in the entries. Cheever writes of the "tide of stronger circumstance" which has swept him and his wife up into the event he describes, and describes a "sense that one's heart and watch are nearly stopped," and White begins by declaring that the whole month "has been a bad month, with Roberta's death, of which I cannot yet bring myself to write." Her disclaimer at the start of the passage, that she "cannot yet" write of Roberta's death, suggests that writing of a death is a task of more magnitude than writing of, for example, new clothes or the state of her pen. Something has to be "made" of a death, the details are not enough by themselves.

The structure of the passages, too, allows the details of birth and death to have a resonance that the details in Orton's writing lack. Both Cheever and White begin their entries with the statement of the birth or death that the passage goes on to describe. The Cheever passage ends by mentioning the bottle of bay rum broken on the bathroom floor earlier and the Maggie Teyte concert of the previous evening, but both are given significance by their relation to "the day you were born." The White passage goes on to reveal apparently unrelated matters: White's wish to be a painter, her mixed enjoyment and dread of lecturing, Tom's unhappiness with his life. However, the repeated return to the "nourishment" metaphor she used to write of Roberta's death, and the mention again of her father, suggest thoughts that carry on from her reflection on Roberta's death. The subject matter too, of reflections on her purpose and progress in life, is of the same level of significance as the subject of death and again suggests a continuation of thought. Her later reflections, in fact, gain significance from being placed after the writing on the death, just as Cheever's writing about broken bottles and shiny linoleum is elevated by its context. In the same way, in personal correspondence, news of a death would always be related at the beginning of a letter, and responded to at the beginning of a reply, even if the letter went on to mention other matters. Usually, the death would become the sole topic of a letter even between two close friends or relatives whose correspondence would typically be detailed and wide-ranging. Orton's refusal to structure the entries which include details of his mother's death and funeral to give these details precedence makes the juxtaposition of details of death, theatre, sex, and everyday life farcical.

When Orton wrote to his sister Marilyn, on the death of his nephew in 1965, the contrast in tone is striking. Lahr cites the letter as evidence that Orton "had no sentimentality about family matters," but although the letter is, indeed, hardly sentimental, nevertheless it conveys real feeling, as much by what is left out as by what is stated:

> There's nothing I can write that will make any difference. I know how you must be feeling. Do understand that I would've come home if I'd known, and if there was anything I could have done . . . I haven't been told when the funeral is and I suppose it's over. I wouldn't send a wreath. I don't begrudge the money but it seems a lot of show. Nothing can bring the kid back.

There is, admittedly, a touch of the Ortonesque in the detail about the wreath, but the point he is making is how insignificant these details are beside the insurmountable fact of the child's death. Nothing can be written that measures up to this fact. While for a writer like White or Cheever detail can "realise" the insurmountable fact, for Orton the detail only diminishes.

After Orton's death, the details of his life story were dramatised for the stage and the screen. But detail is employed to very different effect in these productions, compared to the way Orton used detail in the *Diary*. Lahr's biography *Prick Up Your Ears*, much of it based on Orton's 1967 diaries, was published in 1978, and in 1987 a film was released based on the biography and given the same title. Alan Bennett's screenplay for the Stephen Frears–directed film was published the same year. Two years later, in 1989, Lahr himself produced a play, *Diary of a Somebody*, a dramatization of the diaries.[6] The diaries themselves were not published until 1986, but they provided most of the material for each one of these treatments of the Orton story. Yet the requirements of the different genres has meant the material has been used to very different effect. A comparison of Orton's diaries with Lahr's and Bennett's dramatic adaptations of the same biographical material reveals the different effects of genre. Stage and screen productions call for the construction of a plot, and even biography involves interpretation and narrative. Detail has a different role to play in supporting plot than it does in the open form of the diary.

When Lahr described Orton's dramatic dialogue as "a collage of popular culture," he may have had Orton and Halliwell's wallpaper collage in mind. The walls of the apartment shared by Orton and Halliwell were covered with images stolen from library books about art to create an extensive collage. It was while he was in prison for stealing and defacing library books that Orton adapted for the radio a novel he and Halliwell had been working on, commencing his successful solo career as a playwright. The collage wallpaper can be read as a striking image for the way Orton would continue to adapt and rework material, but it can also be seen as reflecting the design of Orton's diaries. Like the diary, wallpaper is "endless" in form, and this is just as true of Orton and Halliwell's collage of unrepeated details as it is of traditional repeated wallpaper designs. Like the diary also, their collage is a hard read. Described as contributing to the oppressiveness of the small apartment, the collage is relentlessly busy in its details, demanding in the attention for which the familiar art images compete, confusing in its juxtapositions, and unhelpful in its formlessness. There is no plot, no design, to direct the viewer's attention.

One of the main tasks of a dramatist of autobiographical material is to edit. In Bennett's screenplay for *Prick Up Your Ears*, such economy is achieved by allowing detail to be representative in a way that goes right against the way detail operates in the diary. Scenes become representative of a way of life, implicitly through context and through the absence of alternative and contradictory scenes, and explicitly through the use of commentary. A scene showing the Orton character making a pick-up in an underground station, for instance, is given a voice-over commentary with the biographer Lahr asking "Was this customary?" and Peggy replying, "Oh yes! According to the diaries practically a daily occurrence."[7] The scene itself is stripped down to its bare essentials, just a "good-looking youth" and the sound of a zip unfastening. It has, however, been given a lead-up to it which shows Halliwell being abandoned by Orton to make the pick-up, a situation which is never recorded in the diaries. Further meaning is given the scene by its context. It is placed after a scene showing Halliwell's collage exhibition to be a failure, which ends again with a voice-over commentary from Peggy: "Nobody could understand it. One of them so bright and funny and clever, the other such a plain envious failure... Oh, that's not fair... It's just that people shouldn't marry young, that's all" (13).

Bennett's way of setting a scene up and explaining its meaning by voice-over is very different from Orton's narration of one detail after another, with none given especial weighting. In the diary, when casual sex is described it is the details that Orton records: the whitewash that covers his rainmac after a session up against a wall with a Scotsman, the "navy-blue coat with leather across the shoulders" that another pick-up is wearing.[8] Orton collected detail for his diary the way he and Halliwell collected art images for their walls. The eight recorded anecdotes of casual sex in the London diaries (the Tangier diaries come closer to recording sex as a daily occurrence) are far outnumbered by anecdotes of conversations overheard on buses or in the street, of conversations held with neighbours and acquaintances. His way of recording detail is close to Andy Warhol's compulsive diary keeping as an extension of his habit of filing samples of everyday items in boxes for the future. For Andy Warhol, everything is interesting, an *objet trouvé*. For Orton, almost everything—or rather, almost everyone—is funny. Funniest of all is the way people speak.

Orton is unusual for a diarist in his recording of direct speech. The *Diary* is full of conversations, collected apparently for the aesthetic enjoyment of the speech rhythms and turns of phrase. He has a liking for the indignant incomplete sentence—"It came from Africa the material. All the way from Africa" (37)—which he uses again in his plays—"He comes in and stands by my bed in the dark. In his pyjamas."[9] Orton's friends provide him with further material for his diary. When Sheila Ballantine recounts to him one of those absurd conversations between women in a bus that he himself is always overhearing, he transcribes into the diary the direct speech she repeats to him. Often the anecdotes they tell denigrate their subjects: they poke fun at Americans, the middle class, and at "mouldy old queens." Orton's technique of recounting their anecdotes in their own words, however, can make the malice hard to place. It is not always clear whether he is laughing at the subject of the joke, or what it betrays of its *raconteur*.

Orton's use of direct speech is a powerful way of conveying character. From time to time he sharpens up a portrait by inserting an adverb here and there. Henry Budgen's fear that Orton may be "indiscreet" and acknowledge him in public, is mocked by recording the whole nervous conversation verbatim, with the addition of pauses, nervous and breathless laughs, even "over the phone [. . .] an impression of pop-eyes and a toothbrush moustache" (55). Orton's reservations about P. Willes, as he usually refers to him, apparently a close friend and producer of his plays, could be guessed from Orton's noting his use of words and phrases like "disgraceful," "my dear," and "are you still crawss?" even if it were not for the adverbs—if P. Willes is not saying something "hysterically" he is likely to be saying it "predictably." A truer friend is Kenneth Williams, who shares Orton's enjoyment of speech patterns: he is "head over heels in love" with Orton's creation Edna Welthorpe, the persona in whose voice Orton writes absurd letters to various authorities, to the extent that Orton suspects "the spirit of Edna Welthorpe is taking over his personality" (120). The evidence of this possession is a new rhythmic extravagance to Williams' expressions of indignation: "Budgen's a perfect fool. '[. . .] mind how you go.' 'Mind how you go!' Me!" (120).

Editing the detail of the diaries for dramatisation has largely meant reducing the cast. *Prick Up Your Ears* and *Diary of a Somebody* both exaggerate the concentration on Orton and Halliwell as the central characters, though they deal differently with the rest of the cast. *Diary of a Somebody* is basically, as the blurb states, a collage of Orton's own words, along with other "sources" which seem to include some fabrication by Lahr himself. The collage method is naturally suited for reworking Orton's writing, allowing Lahr to reproduce Orton's concentration on the details of people's lives and speech, as well as many of the best lines from the diaries. Lahr lifts scenes and speeches out of the diary verbatim, just as Orton copies them verbatim—or seems to—from real life. As a result, the cast of *Diary of a Somebody* is closer in its range of characters to the diaries than is the cast of the film, with the two central characters, Orton and Halliwell, dominating a cast of anonymous yet autonomous extras. However, Lahr's practical measure of having the extras all played by three other actors further exaggerates the centrality of Orton and Halliwell, the extras diminishing in reality like the backdrop of faces and figures on the wallpaper backdrop of Orton and Halliwell's flat where the dramatised diary was written.

In the film, *Prick Up Your Ears*, the secondary characters are played by individual actors, but they appear only in scenes relating to Orton and Halliwell, never in the self-contained scenes Orton observes in the diaries and Lahr reproduces in the play script. Two other characters, however, take a central position rivalling that of Orton and Halliwell: the characters of Peggy Ramsay and John Lahr. In fact, their position as interpreters and commentators on the actions of Orton and Halliwell is so central to the film that Orton and Halliwell can be seen as merely the products of their collaboration, just as the extras in *Diary of a Somebody* can be seen as merely the products of Orton's diary. Mark Finch, in his article "Business as Usual," argues that the "story's self-consciousness about telling itself ('I remember . . . and then . . . ') betrays a massive uncertainty . . . an uneasiness about providing a voice for a 1960s queer rebel."[10] The voice provided by the film to comment on Orton is consistently heterosexual. The pairing of a man and woman who are not a couple, against two men who are, suggests a lack in either situation that could be solved by a transposition, rearranging couples as in a Shakespeare comedy. The screenplay—though not the final film version—does indeed end with a scene showing a heterosexual couple now living in the flat which used to belong to Orton and Halliwell.

Orton and Halliwell are presented in the terms of a heterosexual marriage. The published screenplay has as an epigraph which is a quote from Elizabeth Hardwick's book *Seduction and Betrayal: Women and Literature*: "In the long run wives are to be paid in a peculiar coin—consideration for their feelings." Halliwell is cast as the wife in the film, and Orton is the inconsiderate husband, and their marriage is compared with the marriage of John Lahr and his wife Anthea. Early in the film, scenes showing Halliwell complaining about his life of housework, and showing him "Furiously tidying up the flat," are interspersed with scenes at the Lahr household, showing Anthea typing out the diaries for Lahr, whipping off her pinny to answer the door, preparing supper in silent fury. Yet Halliwell's male gender ultimately disqualifies him from the role. In the penultimate scene, Peggy spells out the film's contention, that "Ken was the first wife. They do all the work, the waiting, and then . . . " When Lahr suggests that makes her second wife, she replies, "Better than that, dear. The widow."[11] Finch points out the marketing advantages to this central metaphor of the film. The film was directed primarily at the larger heterosexual audience as a "relationship movie"—the term used to describe it by its US publicist speaking on *The Media Show*. "It's a universal story," insisted the producer.[12] The scenes of gay sex provide a visual shock for a heterosexual audience, but at the same time, the promiscuity is interpreted in terms of a heterosexual marriage and a heterosexual morality.

But as well as serving marketing interests, the heterosexual metaphor of the film is crucial as a structural device. If the diary has been considered a "genre without a form," this has been largely because of its "endless" structure. Of course a diary does end, with its last entry, but where it ends is not determined by any internal necessity relating to its plot or design, but instead (usually) by events—such as the death of the diarist—external to the text. Literary discussions of the relation between an ending and form often borrow from two different, though sometimes conflated, metaphors. When form is considered as a shape, from a geometrical point of view, an ending is essential to define the form, if an ending is to be read as the limits of the form. In discussing narrative, or plot, however, form is often considered in temporal terms, as a journey rather than a shape. The ending is the completion of the journey, the arrival at the destination. Again, it is possible to stop anywhere on a journey, and make an arrival of the stop. But in classic, or Hollywood cinema, the journey is supposed to be heading there from the beginning. Only this constitutes classic Hollywood closure. An "ending" must have an internal necessity to count as an ending.

The violent murder of Orton by Halliwell might seem a pretty definitive ending to Orton's diary. Lahr's edition of the diaries ends with a footnote describing the death and citing Halliwell's suicide note, and begins with an introduction largely taken up with discussing the murder and with interpreting Orton and Halliwell's relationship so as to explain its ending in murder. The play *Diary of a Somebody* works up to the end with increasingly fraught scenes between Orton and Halliwell, only to circle around the death in the last scene, by alternating lines from a scene just prior to the death with lines commenting on the death from a scene after the event. But the film confronts the scene squarely, opening first with a scene showing Halliwell "looking straight at the camera [. . .] naked and bloody," followed by the scene showing the policemen breaking and entering "very theatrically" upon the murder scene.[13] The main part of the film is all in flashback, told mostly by Peggy Ramsay. It ends, as it starts, with the murder, Bennett inventing a truly horrible last scene between Halliwell and Orton which ends by showing the actual hammering, "Orton's blood spattering over the collage" (70). The very last scenes return to the present tense of Peggy Ramsay's narrative, and the succession of the heterosexual couple.

The flashback is the simplest method to achieve closure. Starting out with the ending presented as the present tense means that the time before the ending is inevitably seen as leading up to it, and the ending is instantly recognised as the conclusion when it is reached again. The simplicity of the structural device, however, can suggest the lack of a more comprehensive closure. The need for every detail to lead to the conclusion of the plot explains the emphasis on the relationship between Orton and Halliwell that forms the basic plot structure of both the film and the play about Orton's life, and explains also the presentation of the relationship in heterosexual terms.

Halliwell's suicide note read, "If you read his diary all will be explained. K.H. P.S. Especially the last part."[14] The note sets up the murder not just as the ending to the diary, but as the puzzle to which the diary is the solution. The diary has been consistently interpreted in this way; the various treatments of Orton's life that draw on the diary pick through it for clues about his death. Orton and Halliwell's relationship is interpreted as a fatal relationship, as a relationship *leading* to death. Yet while the diary does record some arguments between Orton and Halliwell, and does show Halliwell suffering bouts of depression, it does not in any direct way explain everything as Halliwell promises. The only sign that anything is wrong is the comment Orton makes in his penultimate entry, "Kenneth was looking wan," and in his last entry, "He seemed odd" (265). Certainly, both Orton and Halliwell have been depressed for the weekend before these entries, stuck in Brighton staying with a family for a weekend. They hate family life, hate most of all not being able to make themselves a cup of tea, and go for long walks together in the rain to get away. But it is hard to see how this could lead to murder and suicide.

Both the film and the play set up two explanations for the ending. Halliwell is presented as resentful of Orton's success and of the lack of acknowledgement of his own contribution towards the plays. Even more, he is portrayed as resenting Orton's promiscuity. In addition, Orton is shown in one of the last scenes of the film (though not in the play) suggesting to Halliwell that he and Halliwell should split up. Yet there is little evidence for any of these contentions in the diary. Lahr refers to an interview with Halliwell's psychiatrist which supports the first contention. The whole issue of Orton's promiscuity, however, is radically distorted by the heterosexual morality of both film and play, and by the casting of Halliwell in both productions as the wife figure. Orton is portrayed as the errant husband, Halliwell as the suffering—and insufferable—wife. In the film, there is even an early scene showing Orton in Peggy's office with another man, and Peggy lying about where Orton is when Halliwell phones up looking for him—a classic scene of clichéd adultery. The sympathy is entirely with Orton: "I don't know how you can stand it," a minor character, Philip, comments.[15] As Simon Shepherd points out in his revisionist biography of Orton, *Because We're Queers: The Life and Crimes of Joe Orton and Kenneth Halliwell*, the character Halliwell takes the brunt not only of the anti-homosexual prejudice latent in the film but also of a good deal of misogyny.[16] In another scene from the film, Orton is shown abandoning Halliwell without compunction in order to pursue a youth he makes eye contact with in an underground station.[17] If the metaphor of errant husband and betrayed wife is to work, Halliwell must be entirely faithful—or, at least, sexually inept. In the play, Halliwell gives Orton a little lecture about love compared to physical sex, and in both the film and the play, the only time Halliwell has sex with anyone it is arranged by Orton, the film showing Halliwell reluctant to cooperate. In Orton's Tangier diary, however, it is Halliwell who organises most of the sex, for Orton as well as for himself. Neither ever discusses sexual activity in moral terms, only in terms of availability and accomplishment. Orton discusses his sexual conquests openly with Halliwell, whose responses are witty and unconcerned. When Orton describes an orgy close to home in London following their return from an unsuccessful quest for sex in Libya, Halliwell jokes, "It sounds as though eightpence and a bus down the Holloway road was more interesting than two hundred pounds and a plane to Tripoli."[18] As for Orton abandoning Halliwell in an underground, the only time in the diary Orton is propositioned when he is with Halliwell, he is surprised and not impressed: "as Kenneth Halliwell said, it's rather pointless making to pick-up when the object of your desires is clearly with someone else" (92).

Lahr and Bennett both distort the diary, and Orton and Halliwell's relationship as it is recorded in the diary, in order to shape the diary into the solution to Halliwell's riddling appendix. Technically, Halliwell's note is not a part of the diary. It was not even written into the diary book, and even if it were, it would not be a part of Orton's text. In a sense, it could be argued that Halliwell has made a collage of Orton's diary text, creating a new structure for the diary which alters the meaning of the entries Orton had already written. The invitation to read the diary for an explanation for the tragedy to which the note refers, so making an appendix to the text, is an invitation which has become part of the text, part of Halliwell's collage text. Even so, this "collage text", made up as it is from a diary, is bound to be more heterogeneous in its significance than the dramatisations of it suggest. Much of the tension and interest of this secondary, collage text is in the discrepancy between what the note implies of Halliwell's "reading" of the diary, and the reading of the diary that seems to be implied by the local effects of the text. The diary demands to be read entry by entry, in a "continuous present" tense, which offers a constantly shifting perspective on events rather than the kind of ruled-up perspective that vanishes to a single predetermined point. Reading with the predetermined point in mind only makes the multiple directions the diary runs in more obvious.

Even Lahr—whose editing of the diaries does so much to foreground the note, and who even includes several footnotes which add an interpretative comment on the content of the diary to bring it more in line with his reading of Orton and Halliwell's relationship as a relationship leading to its tragic outcome—comments in his "Editor's Note" to the diaries, "Halliwell's suicide note says that the diaries—especially the latter part—will explain everything. They don't, at least not definitively" (9). Lahr then makes a startling suggestion: that the last part of the diary that Halliwell refers to may in fact be pages that are missing from the diary. He does not describe the state of the diary, although presumably the coroner's report, which cites the entries for 1–3 May, would have noted any obvious destruction. The basis of Lahr's suggestion is that the diary is incomplete, ending in the middle of a sentence in the entry for 1 August, when Orton did not die until 9 August. Lahr suggests that this is "improbable," and yet there are entries in the diary which have been back-dated, and occasional gaps of several days between entries. He does not suggest what might have happened to the last entries. Orton cannot have removed them after his murder, and it would not make sense for Halliwell to have removed them after writing the note referring to them. There is a gap there, at the end of the diaries, and it would be neat if it could be this gap which accounts for that between the readings implied by Halliwell's note and by the text of the diary itself, but I cannot see how the gaps can be made to meet.

Even more intriguingly, Lahr includes in the Editor's Note the last entry, which he has left out of the edited diary for reasons of "dramatic symmetry." For Lahr, dramatic symmetry requires the diary to end "on Orton and Halliwell's last exchange." But this symmetry is a result of a curious placing of the mirror line, not in the centre of the text but outside it. The "symmetry" he seems to mean is a balance between Orton's exchange with Halliwell recorded in the diary and Halliwell's note as a kind of response. Even so, it is a markedly asymmetrical exchange. The final entry as it appears in the diary reads,

> Tuesday 1 August.
> Said goodbye to Kenneth this morning. He seemed odd. On the spur of the moment I asked if he wanted to come home to Leicester with me. He looked surprised and said, 'No.' (265)

If the mirror line is placed at the centre of the text, however, a different sort of pattern emerges. The very centre of the text, coincidentally, is almost exactly where the entries are that the coroner singled out as passages which might explain Orton and Halliwell's deaths, the entries of 1–3 May which include Halliwell's threats of suicide and a quarrel between them about Orton continuing an affair with the partner of the man Halliwell was trying to pick up. Soon after these entries, however, the Tangiers diary begins, which is separate enough from the London diaries before and after it to be regarded as a structural unit, still pretty much in the centre of the text. In the middle of the Tangier diary is a passage which makes a dramatic fulcrum for the text in retrospect:

> We sat talking of how happy we both felt and of how it couldn't, surely, last. We'd have to pay for it. Or we'd be struck down from afar by disaster because we were, perhaps, too happy. To be young, good-looking, healthy, famous, comparatively rich *and* happy is surely going against nature, and when to the above list one adds that daily I have the company of beautiful fifteen-year-old boys who find (for a small fee) sucking with me a delightful sensation, no man can want for more. '*Crimes of Passion* will be a disaster,' Kenneth said. 'That will be the scapegoat. We must sacrifice *Crimes of Passion* in order that we may be spared disaster more intolerable.' (186)

In this entry, the separation of Halliwell and Orton across a mirror line dissolves into a portrayal of them in which a list of adjectives applies equally to them both. Even the play is written about as if it is shared property, the failure of which would be a "disaster" for Halliwell as much as for Orton. In the diary, the conflict which structures the text is between the relationship of Orton and Halliwell and the wider gay community within which they lived, on the one hand, and the heterosexual community they rub up against, on the other. The passage quoted earlier goes on to describe Orton and Halliwell's dinner out with friends afterwards:

> [. . .] I sat next to a rather stuffy American tourist and his disapproving wife. They listened to our conversation and I, realising this, began to exaggerate the content. 'He took me right up the arse,' I said, 'and afterwards he thanked me for giving him such a good fucking. They're most polite people.' The American and his wife hardly moved a muscle. 'We've got a leopard-skin rug in the flat and he wanted me to fuck him on that,' I said in an undertone which was perfectly audible to the next table. 'Only I'm afraid of the spunk you see, it might adversely affect the spots of the leopard.' Nigel said quietly, 'Those tourists can hear what you're saying.' He looked alarmed. 'I mean them to hear,' I said. 'They have no right to be occupying chairs reserved for decent sex perverts.'[. . .]
>
> The American couple frigidly paid for their coffee and moved away. 'You shouldn't drive people like that away,' Nigel said. 'The town needs tourists.' 'Not that kind, it doesn't,' I said. 'This is *our* country, *our* civilisation. I want nothing to do with the civilisation they made. Fuck them! They'll sit and listen to buggers' talk from me and drink their coffee and piss off.' 'It seems rather a strange joke,' Frank said with an old school-teacher's smile. 'It isn't a joke,' I said, 'there's no such thing as a joke.' (187)

This sense of being "perfectly audible" to the heterosexual community is part of the drama of the diaries as a whole. There is a kind of raised voice quality to the "undertone" of the diary voice, with its apparent absence of addressee. The focus of the diaries is on the presentation of the relationship between Orton and Halliwell and on their shared lifestyle, described resolutely in their own terms, as it appears from the outside.

In keeping with the heterogeneity of the diary, though, it would be more appropriate to write "a focus," for as many passages suggest a continuity between the absurdities of Orton and Halliwell's relationship and the absurdities of people around them, straight or gay, neighbour or sister or doctor. The last entry, which Lahr left out of the edited diaries, describes Orton's visit to see his sister after the birth of her daughter. He recounts Leonie's story of her experience in the hospital with a typical unstated relish of the language and rhythms of narrative speech:

> 'I didn't know what was happening. I was on the pethidine. And then the sister came and nearly died. She screamed, "What's happening to

> this patient's hand!" And, you know, it was unbelievable. I've never seen anything like it. I had to laugh. My hand was like a balloon. Right up it was. "What've you done!" she said to the doctor—he was supposed to be a specialist. "I know what I've done," he said. "You put it in the tissue," she said—and what (10)

There is a kind of symmetry to be found in the diary ending as it begins, with a focus not on the relationship between Orton and Halliwell as some kind of subject for the diary, but on anecdotes recorded for the sake of a good story and, even more, for the sake of the language effects they allow: "My hand was like a balloon. Right up it was." The first two entries of the diary likewise record details relating to Orton's career fairly briefly before recording more detailed anecdotes about absurd uses of language:

> Sheila Ballantine said she heard a conversation between two women in a bus. One woman said, 'There's a lot of blue about lately.' After a pause the other woman said, 'Yes. And there's a lot of green about too.' There was another pause and the first woman said, 'And there's a lot of red. Have you noticed?' Sheila said they didn't mention purple which is quite in evidence. (36)

Any symmetry that is found, however, is a contingent symmetry that would have been altered had Orton, for instance, written up more of those entries between 1 August and 9 August. To edit the diary for symmetry means editing the diary as a fixed form, suggesting an inevitability to a process that is necessarily contingent on events outside the event of writing. It is another way to "get a grip" on the diary. What the treatments of the Orton diary suggest is that to fix on an interpretation means fixing the form. The open form of the diary will not allow for a rigid interpretation of a life, or even of the narrative of the life. The diary presents a collage of interpretations, and a reading of the diary which is responsive to its shifts and contradictions will be a collage of readings.

4 Katherine Mansfield

Katherine Mansfield could have claimed, with even more justification than Antonia White, to have produced a "superb collection of beginnings." Even her most substantial piece of work, in an opus of short stories, is a longer story called "Prelude." The collection of her manuscripts, held at the Alexander Turnbull Library in Wellington, New Zealand, is a huge archive of exercise books, engagement diaries, and notebooks from the 1910s and 1920s, most of them barely written in. Of a "Monster Exercise Book" of eighty pages, she used six. The number of brief entries dated January in the *Journal of Katherine Mansfield* come from her habit of filling the first few pages of her engagement diaries each year before abandoning the task. Projects she sets for herself are similarly abandoned. One exercise book is given a title page neatly set out with the date, her name, even a wax seal, and the title "Holiday Work and Reading," and inside it pages are headed up "Books Read," "Music I Have Studied," "Letters I Have Written," and so on. Under the headings are a few entries for each, then blank lines. Contents pages of other books list entire collections of poems, of which only the first few listed are transcribed. Her practise of numbering the pages of an exercise book in advance of her filling it is a particularly nice illustration of how far her resolve outdoes her industry.

The entries gathered together by John Middleton Murry and published in 1927 as the *Journal of Katherine Mansfield* are written in these exercise books, in between fragments of stories, following abandoned projects such as the lists of books read, at the back of engagement diaries.[1] These exercise books have now been transcribed and edited by Margaret Scott, and published, significantly, not as the journals or diaries of Katherine Mansfield but as *The Katherine Mansfield Notebooks*.[2] The cover design, a photograph of the forty-six notebooks held at the Turnbull, conveys a sense of the number and range of texts in the archive, and yet it still gives the impression of a series of notebooks which could together make up a regular diary. A photograph which included all the bundles and scraps of paper would not have been nearly as aesthetically pleasing but might have given a better sense of what Scott, and originally Murry, had to deal with. Each notebook is in itself a collection of beginnings of various writing projects. Exercise books that begin as diaries turn into notebooks for first drafts of stories or recipe books, or are turned to some other use, while collections of poems, notes on Shakespeare, and other projects turn into diaries, or have diary entries randomly placed within them. Apart from the sporadic attempts to keep a diary, usually at the beginning of a year, most of the entries that make up the *Journal* seem to have been written anywhere at all, on whatever piece of paper was handy at the time. In fact, it is inaccurate to call them entries, since few were "entered" into any sort of ongoing document.

Even more than the entries in Antonia White's diary, the diary passages Mansfield wrote are all beginnings, and her "diary" not only has no ending, but no real continuity either. The passages were written at different times, in different books, and are different lengths depending in part on where they were written and how much space was allotted them. She does not refer from one passage to another. She did not "keep a diary." The enormous discrepancy between the original manuscript material and the book originally edited by Murry as her *Journal* makes Mansfield's authorship of the book questionable. In an article written shortly after the manuscripts were deposited at the Alexander Turnbull Library, Ian Gordon goes so far as to argue that the *Journal* "is as much Murry's work as Katherine Mansfield's." The book readers have taken as a book written by Mansfield he describes rather as "a brilliant piece of literary synthesis and editorial patchwork by Murry."[3] He is writing in the first shock of discovery that Mansfield had not kept a document she wrote in as her "journal" as Murry had allowed readers of the *Journal* to believe, and much of his article is concerned with pointing out misleading passages and phrases in Murry's introductions to the two editions of the *Journal* and the *Scrapbook* of further material.

Almost twenty years later, assembling another "literary synthesis" of letters and material from the published *Journal*, C.K. Stead argues against Gordon's claim for dual authorship for Murry and Mansfield, claiming that despite "considerable variety, yet [Mansfield's writing in letters and notebooks] is all of a piece," and that any selection will have a coherence "more or less at random."[4] The coherence, Stead suggests, derives from the consistent quality of Mansfield's writing. I'm reminded of Ben Cheever's thoughts on Robert Gottlieb's editing of the Cheever journals: "Sometimes I think he did a magnificent job. Sometimes I think he did almost nothing." Stead, like Murry, can be said to have "a great ear" for Mansfield's prose, just as Gottlieb did for Cheever's. Yet Stead's selection of journal material is all from the published journals, for practical reasons which are easily understood given the extreme difficulty in transcribing Mansfield's pencilled scrawl, a job now completed by Margaret Scott. Had Stead selected his material from the manuscripts, however, a "more or less random" approach would have provided neither the coherence of the *Journal* nor the more biographical coherence of his volume of *Letters and Journals*. It is unlikely that he would have made his selections at random. Rather, like Murry, he would no doubt have selected the more "diary-like" passages from amongst the rest of the material. None of the shopping lists, household accounts, lines and lines from Shakespeare, lists of letters written, and other such material, all included in Scott's *The Katherine Mansfield Notebooks*, are likely to have been included in Stead's collection, and a much less readable, less literary volume would have resulted if they had been.

While Stead's claim seems overstated, Gordon's claim depends on theoretical questions concerning the nature of authorship and the diary, and concerning the relative importance of the entry and the sequential organising principle as defining features of the diary. Whether Mansfield can be said to be the author of a diary depends in part on how the requirement of periodic entries is interpreted. Each entry in a periodically kept diary is at once singular, complete in itself, written at a single setting in a combination of grammatical tenses anchored in the present tense of writing; and, at the same time, each entry belongs to a succession of entries, written at intervals, with the potential of creating narrative in their references to continuing dramas, and with the potential, arguably the requirement, of adding up to a body of work with a form of its own.

While the second aspect of the periodic entry—its place in a succession of entries—gives the genre its form, the first aspect—its anchor in the present tense of writing—gives the genre a quality particular to the diary, a particular closeness to the subjectivity of the writer. The reader has a sense not just of the present of the moment of writing, but of the "presence" of the moment. The more immediate the present tense, the stronger is this sense. Mansfield often writes "to the moment" in the sense of leading up to the moment, beginning earlier in the day and taking her narrative up to the point of writing, as in this 1918 Paris entry:

> *Later.* The table was laid for two. I dined opposite a white serviette shaped like a hand with spread fingers. Now I have dressed & am waiting for the motor. I rubbed some Genêt Fleuri on my collar just now: I look *different*—as though I were meant to be played on & not just lie in a corner with the blow in that slot opposite which fastens with two buttons. (2:136)

Just as the moment of writing is evoked all the more powerfully for its situation in relation to the immediate past (and, often, the anticipated future), so the evocation of place is all the more powerful for the reference to smells or sounds belonging just outside the scene of writing:

> It is a dark reluctant day. The fire makes a noise like a flag, & there is the familiar sound from below of someone filling buckets. I am very stiff, very unused to writing now and yet, as I sit here, its as though my dear one, my ONLY one came & sat down opposite me and gazed at me across the table. And I think suddenly of the verses which seemed so awfully good in my girlhood

> Others leave me—all things leave me
> You remain.
>
> L.M. in her turban with her one big eye & one little un—do I love her? Not really. And then, just now, I mounted to J's room, and opened the door. He was sitting at the table, working. All was in indescribable disorder & the air was thick with smoke. He held out his hand to me but it was not my place. Oh no—I came away. I came away back into my room—which really has for me a touch of fairy. Is there anything better than my room? Anything outside. The kitten says not, but then its such a hunting ground for the kitten. The sun throws the shape of the window on to the carpet, & in these four little square fields the silly flies wander, ever so spied upon by the little lion under the sommier frill . . . (2:143)

Other entries relate the feeling of being "swollen" and "hideous," and the day as being "thin, white" and "gritty," to the sounds of "people opening drawers of a cheap chest and trying to shut them again," and, even more trying, "In a house nearby someone . . . trying to tune a cheap cheap piano" (2:136) or the feeling of "decomposing a bit" as she lies sick in bed with the smell "of onion and chop bones in the house" (2:144).

A reference to the act of writing situates the diarist still more definitely in the moment of writing, and brings closer still the presence of the writer to the present tense shared by writer and reader. The diary of Virginia Woolf is full of these references. "A disgraceful confession—this is Sunday morning, & just after tea, & here I am sitting down to write a diary & not fiction or reviews, without any excuse, except perhaps a state of mind."[5] She writes about the pens she uses, and their nibs—"Yes. I will allow myself a new nib"—and about the pages she writes on—"This very large sheet which I bought at Baxter's" (5:255). The same sort of note can be found in the diary of Antonia White: "It's no good: I can't write with that pen: this isn't perfect either".[6] When Mansfield writes that she hopes her pen is working, the reader has a similar sense of the immediacy of the moment she was writing in, both increased and complicated by the command, later on, possibly intended for Murry, "*Don't* read this":

> I hope this pen works. Yes, it does.
>
> The last day in September—*immensely* cold—a kind of solid cold outside the windows. My fire has played traitor nearly all day & I have been, in the good, old fashioned way, feeling my skin *curl. Don't* read this. Do you hear that train whistle & now the leaves, the dry leaves & now the fire, flurring & breaking? Why *doesn't* she bring the lamps? So it is to be a baked meat pudding with a caper or twain and then the rusks cooked in milk with blackberry sauce. Talking of it made us quite friendly after the Fight of the Lamps. (2:144)

In this entry, the working pen writes to a moment that is itself in motion, the train whistle replaced by the leaves, the leaves replaced by the sound of the fire, and the anxiety of waiting for L.M. to bring the lamps replaced by the anticipation of the dinner L.M. is making now that the "Fight of the Lamps" is over.

Writing in the diary functions for many diarists as a way of locating themselves both in the moment of writing and in their surroundings. In Plath's diaries, this can be comforting:

> Here I sit in the deep-cushioned armchair, the crickets rasping, buzzing, chirring outside. It's the library, my favourite room, with the floor a medieval mosaic of flat square stones. The color of old book-bindings [. . .] (14)

Other entries suggest more of an unease with what can seem more like a restriction to the moment, and place, of writing, as she writes with that same sense of awareness Mansfield shows towards the world beyond the moment:

> I am alone in my room, between two worlds. Downstairs are the few girls who have come in . . . I could go down with letter paper as an excuse for my presence, but I won't yet—not yet . . . I'll stay here and try to pin that loneliness down.[7]

In an entry like this one, the act of writing has become part of the loneliness she is describing.

The negotiation of self and surroundings is a central concern of the diary as a genre.[8] For Mansfield, such a negotiation was particularly fraught, though often presented comically. She disassociates herself from her surroundings in alienated descriptions of her place in them, often dissociating herself at the same time from the symptoms of her illness, almost as if they are a part of her surroundings:

> I seem to spend half of my life arriving in strange hotels. And asking if I may go to bed immediately.
>
> "And would you mind filling my hot water bottle? . . . Thank you; that is delicious. No, I shan't require anything more."
>
> The strange door shuts upon the stranger, and then I slip down in the sheets. Waiting for the shadows to come out of the corners and spin their slow, slow web over the Ugliest Wallpaper of All.[9]

But in the paragraph that follows, her surroundings bring her symptoms home to her doubled, and her response is to imagine quite another self and surroundings:

> The man in the room next to mine has the same complaint as I. When I wake in the night I hear him turning. And then he coughs. And I cough. And after a silence I cough. And he coughs again. This goes on for a long time. Until I feel we are like two roosters calling to each other at false dawn. From far-away hidden farms. (87)

Susan Sontag prefaces her study, *Illness as Metaphor*, with a brief sally into metaphor herself, in which she imagines illness to be an "onerous citizenship" in "the kingdom of the sick," as if illness were a part of the geography which the self must negotiate.[10] The details of illness are, indeed, the most immediate of the details that are present to the diarist. For diarists such as Alice James and W.N.P. Barbellion, their illness becomes a narrative that is the focus and point of the diary, which can only be satisfactorily concluded by death.[11] Indeed, Barbellion, who described the consumptive diarist Marie Bashkirtseff as his literary "mother," saw death as so necessary a conclusion to his diary that, wishing both to publish the diary and to read the reviews on its publication, he faked an ending, with an "editorial note" stating "Barbellion died on December 31," nearly two years before he actually died. When the truth came out, he unrepentantly added *A Last Journal* to his publications, concluding this second journal shortly before his actual death with the same phrase Orton used to end his RADA diary: "The rest is silence." Mansfield's illness does not structure the *Journal* in the same way and is even less apparent as a narrative in the original manuscripts. For Mansfield, her illness is incidental to her self, in the same way the smell of food, the noises of sticking drawers and cabbage being chopped, and the other unsolicited details of the life she describes are incidental. They impinge on, but do not describe, the self.[12]

The diarist's illness does include the diarist in the scene, in the way that observations of scenery do not necessarily do. It is interesting to observe that in her letters, when Mansfield includes descriptions of the scenery, she often adds a note placing the person she is writing to in the position of the viewer, or otherwise attaching the significance of the scene to the person she is addressing. Describing her villa "on a wild hill slope, covered with olive and fig trees and long grasses and tall yellow flowers," she writes "It is nice, Koteliansky, you would like it," and to Murry she writes, "You should have seen after the rain was over yesterday, little old men appeared from nowhere in peaked hats, crawling over the wild hill looking for snails."[13] In the manuscript papers, as well as the diary-like entries which include these sorts of descriptions as part of an account of the moment in which she is writing, often Mansfield simply jots down descriptions without any context given to them at all. Sometimes it is only the inclusion of a date and, sometimes, a time, that makes a diary entry out of a piece of prose in Mansfield's *Journal*, as in the passage headed "December 31. 4.45 p.m." This brief comic passage, written in the third person, shifts from the point of view of the fly—"Oh, the times she had walked upside down on the ceiling, run up glittering panes, floated on a lake of light, flashed through a shining beam!"—to the point of view of God, who "looked upon the fly fallen into the jug of milk and saw that it was good."[14] Yet the inclusion of the date and time also includes obliquely the diarist, taking up her pen in a rapid, off-the-cuff response to a still life detail in front of her.

Many of the dates included in Mansfield's *Journal* have in fact been attributed to the passages by Murry. In the manuscripts, however, pieces of writing are placed in different ways that also pin them down to a moment in the diarist's life. Scribbled above her shopping lists, for instance, are little rhymes which incorporate items from the lists:

> Tea, the chemist & marmalade
> Far indeed today I've strayed
> Through paths untrodden, shops unbeaten
> And now the bloody stuff is eaten
> The chemist the marmalade & tea
> Lord how nice & cheap they be![15]

The *Notebooks* edited by Scott do present the rhymes with the shopping lists, yet even these accurate transcriptions do not give quite the same sense of the moment of writing that the original manuscripts do. The presentation of rhyme and list in a sequence of lists, some with, some without, rhymes, suggests more of a format that Mansfield keeps to than is indicated by the pages in the notebook, where the lists are clearly central and the rhymes scribbled into the top corners as marginalia, or textual doodling.

Each diarist negotiates differently the balance of present tense and recent past that makes up the "continuous present" of the diary, and may emphasise either the narrative continuity or the moment of writing. In all the editions of the Mansfield diary papers, and still more in the manuscript papers, the balance is shifted towards immediacy rather than continuity. There are few references from one entry to another, following up on previous entries the way Woolf does for instance when she notes that, after all, "I did not buy that dresser" (5:168). Rather, each entry exists as an independent "vignette" like the "vignettes" Mansfield wrote for literary magazines. Many have an economy to them like that of a poem, in which no word is extraneous, as in the haiku-like entry dated March 30, 1914: "'I am afraid you are too psychological, Mr Temple.' Then I went off and bought the bacon."[16] The focus of a passage shifts about to record Mansfield's shifts of thought:

> March 28. Put my clothes in order. The crocuses in Battersea reminded me of autumn in Bavaria. The ground is wet, and it looks as though winter were going—the grass long and green among the trampled flowers. Birds are far more savage-looking than the wildest beasts. Thinking of a forest of *wild* birds—or if the birds 'turned' even here. I want to get alone. The *Magnolia conspicua* is in bud. (11)

In one entry, what is probably an error of Murry's—Scott reads the phrase as "waiting for L.M."—nevertheless has the appropriateness of a Freudian slip: "I am writing for LM to come. She's very late. Everything is in a state of suspense—even birds and chimneys" (10). Mansfield is waiting for L.M., but she is also writing and her writing is a part of her waiting, recalling White's evening spent trying not to wait for a phone call. Writing both records time and fills time, and Mansfield's writing in the journals belongs very much to the time in which it was written. Because of this, paradoxically, the dates are less important rather than more important, since the moment of writing and the moment in time are so simultaneous and so complete in themselves that their place in an ongoing narrative, and their ties to a past and future chronology, has little bearing.

Yet the *Journal* is a very different document than the notebooks from which it was collated. The notebooks have qualities which are lost to a certain extent in the *Journal*. The sense of the moment of writing is still stronger in manuscript, with the conjunction of a rhyme or comment over a shopping list linking the two moments. The difference between an entry which is dated and starts a new page, and a comment scrawled in the middle of another piece of prose, gives a sense of what sort of "moment of writing" each piece was written in. Robert Fothergill, in his 1974 study of the diary *Private Chronicles*, writes of the "sort of Proustian passion" that fastens itself on a reference to the act of writing. It was this same sort of Proustian passion that, for me, fastened itself on the kowhai flower still existing pressed inside the journal of dated entries Mansfield kept in 1908.

The *Journal*, on the other hand, has a coherence and shapeliness that makes it a literary work rather than a collection of papers. Of the two requirements of the periodic entry, Mansfield provides the first, in the moment of writing creating a singular entry often without context, and Murry provides the second, placing the entries into a sequence, giving the continuous present its continuity and hence its form. Murry's contribution however remains editorial. Apart from the selection of entries of recognisable "diary" quality—passages that describe the present or recent past, as a diary entry does, or notes of ideas, thoughts, reflections, and intentions such as diary entries contain—his contribution amounts to ordering the entries according to the chronology he was able to ascertain, providing dates where possible and headings for entries he could not date. The headings have a similar effect to dates, distinguishing separate entries from one another. The basic form of the diary, with a basic continuity, is simple, if painstaking, to reconstruct. While the *Journal* is a work of dual authorship in the sense that Murry provided one of the two essential requirements of the genre, his calibre as an editor did not need to match Mansfield's calibre as a writer, as Gordon suggests, in order for the *Journal* to have become established as a minor classic.

The Scott edition is interesting in relation to the question of Murry's role in creating the *Journal*, in that it goes so far itself towards creating a text that can be read as a diary, even though Scott claims the volumes consist only of "transcriptions" of the notebooks and unbound papers she goes on to describe as a "huge, amorphous, nearly illegible mass of material."[17] The arrangement of the material is approximately chronological, beginning with the earliest kept notebooks, but without breaking up individual notebooks. Since Mansfield often kept more than one notebook simultaneously, and used different notebooks for different purposes, this creates a fair amount of chronological overlap and confusion. Scott explains the purpose of the transcriptions in terms of the scholar's need for accurately transcribed source material: "I was aware that critics, commentators, students and others were attempting to read these manuscripts and relying too much on guess-work, while at the same time Murry's misreadings were being quoted and perpetuated in other people's books" (xiv). She herself sees the appeal of the writing as source material: "This material—the whole raft of it—is so rich in reflections of, connections with, roots of, hints at, variations of her best work that to explicate it all would take more lifetimes than I have at my disposal [. . .] This is the raw material for an infinite number of investigations" (xv).

The presentation of the complete edition of the notebooks as "raw material" seems to validate Gordon's conclusion in 1959 that "detailed study of the source manuscripts and even publication of them is [not] going to make much difference to the literary importance of the *Journals*."[18] He implies here a distinction between the literary importance of the *Journals*, which would not be affected by publication of the source materials, and the biographical and critical importance of them, which would.

In the introduction to the *Notebooks*, Scott quotes a passage in which Mansfield thinks out her own case for writing such unconnected, fragmentary texts:

> Queer this habit of mine of being garrulous. And I don't mean that any eye but mine should read this. This is—*really private*. But I must say nothing affords me the same relief. What happens as a rule is, if I go on long enough I *break through*. It's rather like tossing very large flat stones into the stream. The question is, though, how long this will prove efficacious. Up till now, I own, it never has failed me.[19]

Mansfield writes a kind of "skim-writing" in order to "*break through*" into a deeper style of prose. Scott's metaphor for this writing as a "raft" of material also suggests a superficiality, a floating quality to the prose. To go deeper as a reader, she suggests firstly what her own approach would be—to "explicate" the writing in terms of its connections with, and "reflections of" (as if the "raft" has become the surface of the water itself) her other material. Later in the introduction she uses another metaphor to suggest a deeper reading of the material, referring particularly to the earlier writings, now a "goldmine", this time of "biographical and psychological information." In each case, a deeper reading involves reading past the text as a diary, or as a text in its own right, for links with other texts or for biographical information.

And yet, far more than the manuscript collection at the Turnbull, *The Katherine Mansfield Notebooks* presents itself *as* a text and by its very presentation, promotes a reading of it as if it were the diary Mansfield never really kept (although she does refer to "huge complaining diaries" she kept at an earlier date, but subsequently destroyed). By printing all the different bits of writing from the notebooks and various scraps of paper together in the two matching volumes, all in the same font and format, Scott creates a new textual "surface", even if it is not exactly seamless. The different manuscripts in the Turnbull collection seem to have little connection to one another and no continuity of purpose, to be just a random remainder of the mass of papers a writer collects. The blank pages between items, the text scribbled into the backs of exercise books clearly bought for another purpose long since abandoned, the pages numbered way past their contents, all give a very clear sense of how unrelated all these fragments of writing are to each other. Even the procedure a reader has to go through to look at the manuscripts, applying to look at each notebook as a separate item, to be returned before you apply for another, contributes to this sense. But in the *Notebooks*, the shifts between fiction, sketches, comments, shopping lists, reading notes, poems, and diary entries all seem to add up to a text which is something more than any of its parts. The shifts themselves become part of the rhythm of the text, a text of shifting attention, shifting modes of being.

Although Scott suggests we read "through" the text, "mine" the text, for biographical information or clues, because the text is autobiographical it is hard not to read the text itself as representative of the writer's life, and more than that, her "self". The identification of the writer's "self" and the diary text is one that is promoted in the introductions of both editions of Mansfield's texts, as it has been in the introductions to the editions of Plath's journals.

Murry writes in the introduction to the *Journal*:

> one element of her nature [. . .] it seems to me, was essential to a peculiar quality of her work. This peculiar quality of her work I can only describe as a kind of *purity*. It is as though the glass through which she looked upon life were crystal-clear. And this quality of her work corresponds to a quality in her life. Katherine Mansfield was natural and spontaneous as was no other human being I have ever met.[20]

The *Journal*, as edited by Murry, reflects this portrait of Katherine Mansfield as a translucent personality, someone who notices out of a whole day maybe one telling image, someone whose attention is visual, impersonal, poetic.

Mansfield did sometimes note factual details of a day's activities in the allotted space of the engagement diaries she used, as in the following entry for January 26, 1915:

> Went to London. We found BC had arrived; so D put us up. D's flat looks lovely to me. Had tea at the Criterion with C and D. Had my hands done. In the evening went to the Oxford and saw Marie Loyd, who was very good. Slept on the big divan in A.'s room. In the afternoon it was very foggy in London; but the relief to be there was wonderful.[21]

The surrounding entries, however, simply note one or two visual images:

> Jan 23. The old man breaking stones again. A thick white mist reaches the edge of the field.
>
> Jan 27. Met a woman who'd been in the cinema with me—her pink roses in her belt, and hollow lovely eyes and battered hair. I shall not forget her. *No, no.* She was wonderful.
>
> February 1. A slight attack of flu is bowling me over. There is a glimpse of sun. The trees look as though they were hanging out to dry.[22]

Although the dates confirm the place of these entries in a sequence, the way each entry is focused on a detail means they could easily be transposed without it making much difference. The detail holds each entry open to juxtaposition with any other detailed entry. The fact that they are dated and sequenced, however, affects how they are read. The meaning of the details in the *Journal* is altered by the "diaryness" of them, by the fact that they stand as records of actual days—days in which you assume the kind of theatre-going, tea-going manicured activities of the occasional more factually based entry are still going on, unreported. Like Pound's "In a Station at the Metro", which takes much of its power from its selectivity, even from Pound's account of its selectivity, the entries in the *Journal* are measured by what is left out. The chapter divisions by year suggest that the passages entered for each year are representative of the year, are what is left of a year. There is a poignancy to such selectivity, which does seem a kind of "purity."

The *Notebooks*, read as autobiography, present a different portrait of Katherine Mansfield, referred to familiarly by literary New Zealanders as KM (and we can refer to her more familiarly than ever now we have the *Notebooks*). The KM of the notebooks is far more material, a baker and eater of a range of stodgy puddings, all made with a mixture of flour and Atora—a kind of commercial suet—and sweetened with a variety of sweeteners according to the recipe, but something like spoonfuls of marmalade or golden syrup, then boiled for hours. This is a KM who moves from the poetic mode to the mundane, almost in the same breath. This is a kitchen KM, a laundry KM, a KM who scribbles flights of fancy in amongst her shopping lists, a KM who sits down to write a story but gives up halfway through to think about her wardrobe and plan new additions to it. This is a KM who wills herself to be poetic, who forces herself to write, but lapses easily into distraction: so many unfinished stories, so many plans for novels. The pudding recipes in between plans for great works suggest she left off writing to go and bake.

And yet, this portrayal is not necessarily more valid than the portrayal offered by the *Journal*, even though it is more complete. These papers are, after all, only those accidentally surviving, and the mixture of baking recipes and poem fragments is an editorial accident. Other diarists must also have recipe books, address books, gardening notes, or other practical papers which are not usually included as part of a published diary. It seems to me that the only possible editorial decision, or at least the best one Scott could have made, for the publication of Mansfield's papers, was to simply publish the entire contents of the papers without selection. But the effect is to give this random collection of material an authority that it does not have in this way in manuscript form.

The Mansfield papers and the different editions of them that have been published seem to make, in the end, an equally strong case for the authority of the entry, and the authority of the sequence. Gordon argues for dual authorship for Mansfield and Murry of the *Journal*, on the grounds that the text depends as much on the sequence of entries as on any individual entry.[21] While it is true, however, that to work as a diary the text requires a sequence, it does not require the particular sequence Murry provides. Mansfield's own dates provide some sequence for sections of the diary, but the focus on visual details characteristic of the entries allows for juxtapositions of entries, and of diary entries and fictional passages, to work in almost any order as an extension of the kinds of visual juxtapositions within entries. The combination of a focus on visual detail, and a sense of the "moment of writing" suggested by this focus in conjunction with the dates when they are given and with other references to the present tense of the writing act, gives individual entries a degree of autonomy, which is particularly striking when they are read in manuscript form, especially when you come across one entry, isolated in a notebook used for other forms of writing, which is clearly marked by date and contents as a diary entry all by itself. The *Journal*, it seems to me, is as much the *Journal of Katherine Mansfield*, as the *Notebooks* are *The Katherine Mansfield Notebooks*, the authority of the text residing in the "moment of writing" of the individual entries.

At the same time, when a sequence is provided for the entries, it inevitably affects their interpretation. The text as a whole amounts to something more than an accumulation of individual entries. The juxtapositions, continuities, and shifts between entries, and their relative representation of events, form a portrait it is hard not to identify with the writer, even though the different portraits presented by the two editions of the Mansfield diaries show how much of a construction such a portrait is. Mansfield did not keep a diary or construct a diary text as such. She did not make the kind of editorial decisions Woolf and Plath made, about the balance of material to include or the placing of material within a sequence. To publish any of Mansfield's personal writings has meant necessarily making these kinds of editorial decisions, sequencing pieces of writing to construct a text. What is remarkable is how the diary form works to give significance to the kinds of juxtapositions that arise, how the diary form knits up fragments of writing into a complete text with its own surface, its own direction and shape.

5 Virginia Woolf

Virginia Woolf's intentions for her diary, as occasionally, and variously, stated in the diary itself, seem similar to Margaret Scott's sense of how Katherine Mansfield's writings could be used, as a mine of information to be reworked into a different form, as another text. She pictures herself as her own reader, drawing on the diary as raw material for her memoirs. At other times, she describes the purpose of writing in the diary as being more to do with the process itself, as a sort of therapy, or as a "loosening of the ligatures" of writing, to allow the kind of "break through" into writing for publication that Mansfield describes. When, on Saturday, 20 March 1926, she addresses herself seriously to the question of "what is to become of all these diaries," she doesn't on this occasion look at what she might do with them, only conjectures what Leonard Woolf would be likely to do with them, after her death. "He would be disinclined to burn them; he could not publish them. Well, he should make up a book from them, I think; and then burn the body. I daresay there is a little book in them."[1]

In her chapter on Woolf's diaries in *Daily Modernism*, Elizabeth Podnieks argues persuasively that Woolf was writing with more of an eye to posterity than she often wished to let on, perhaps because of her own understanding of "privacy" as a generic requirement of the diary.[2] She points to Woolf's own reading of published diaries, as well as to indications of an implied audience suggested by Woolf's own diary writing, to support her claim that Woolf intended all along the diary to be published, making it in a sense a legacy left not just to Leonard Woolf but "to us, the readers she intended" not just for the "little book" Leonard Woolf was to edit, but for the diary as a whole.

Podnieks presents a detailed account of the diary manuscripts as further support for her argument that the diaries were taken seriously as a literary genre by Woolf herself, and should be given the same kind of critical attention as Woolf's other works by critics and scholars. The work Woolf put into covering the books and providing them with title pages, her practice of inserting diary fragments and travel notes into the larger diary volumes, and, in particular, her concern with matching up the beginnings and endings of yearly records with the beginning and end of a new diary volume (often impossible, and the "lapse" therefore requiring explanation and apology), does indeed suggest a sustained attention to the diary not just as the location for a particular mode of writing but as a literary form in itself. At the same time, it could be argued that Woolf's attention to the appearance of the diary books in their manuscript form is evidence against the claim that she was writing them for eventual publication; or, at least, that the diary volumes had a literary importance to Woolf independent of any publication possibilities.

Podnieks counters Judy Simons' suggestion that the narrative control evident in Woolf's diaries "suggests her needs of a structural principal, however slight, to assure herself of her own control over the medium of her life," with the suggestion she was "as determined to assert control over the medium of her diary as art" (107). It is interesting to compare Leonard Woolf's edition of the diaries, published as *A Writer's Diary* in 1953, with the full text of the diaries as it has been edited by Anne Olivier Bell, published between 1977 and 1984, to compare the structural principles on which the two editions were constructed. On the whole, Leonard Woolf's edition of the diary fulfils both Virginia Woolf's expectations for his treatment of the "body" of the diaries, and his own editorial policy, stated in the preface to *A Writer's Diary*, to extract "practically everything which referred to her own writing."[3] When the original diary is read as a complete text in itself, however, it seems to display a purpose of its own, implied by some of Woolf's own comments on her diary keeping and manifest in the structure of the text.

When Woolf writes "he could not publish them," she writes with a keen sense of what the requirements for publication were. Her novels, all written for publication and with publication very much in mind, push further and further the conventions of the novel. This looked like it was going to cause commercial chaos in the case of *Orlando: A Biography*, when booksellers insisted on categorising it as a biography because of its subtitle. Biographies were not selling well when *Orlando* was first published, and especially not a biography of someone completely unknown (let alone non-existent). In her diary, Woolf reflected that the commercial failure she anticipated for *Orlando* (in fact, of course, sales turned out to be "amazingly brisk") was "a high price to pay for the fun of calling it a biography."[4] And although she experiments with the style and narrative conventions of her novels, they all conform to the requirements of publication at least in terms of their word lengths. Ranging from approximately 49,000 words (*Between the Acts*) to 176,000 words (*Night and Day*), they all fall within the range of lengths that are "book size." If Woolf thought Leonard Woolf would not be able to publish her diaries as they were in 1926, one reason is likely to have been that the text did not add up to the shape or length of a "book."

A Writer's Diary, at approximately 158,000 words, has been edited into a regular "book size." It might seem that to edit a book, if it is to alter it at all without altering the writer's words, must necessarily cut it down. But

John Middleton Murry, having made the same decision to make a "book" out of Mansfield's journal material, collated a number of scanty diaries with extraneous material to come up with a volume large enough for publication. While in comparison with the Scott *Notebooks* it seems like a paring down of material, looking at the original manuscripts and the size and emptiness of the actual diary books amongst them, it seems far more like an act of expansion of genuine diary material into a book-sized book.

Reviews of *A Writer's Diary* refer to the text as a "book" or a "work", almost as if it were written as the book they are reviewing: "A work of the highest imaginative genius" (Isaiah Berlin, *Sunday Times*); "An extraordinary book" (John Raymond, B.B.C.); "a work of the first importance" (David Daiches, *Manchester Guardian*); "a most remarkable book" (B. Ifor Evans, *Truth*).[5] The short extracts make up a very readable book, with the entries most commonly alternating in length between half a page and a page. The dates head up the entries like small chapter headings or the subheadings of a newspaper article. The entries are further divided up by the year, with each year forming a chapter of around twelve to sixteen pages. The years are even listed as chapters in the contents page.

To ensure the edited diary reads like a complete book, Leonard Woolf has not indicated omissions, explaining that the "omissions and dots would have been so continual as to worry the reader." Leonard Woolf makes it quite clear in the preface that omissions are very frequent and that the edited diary is in no sense representative. Yet a reader has little sense of this when reading the diary. The impression is that while entries might be isolated from their adjoining entries in the original, they are whole in themselves. They seem in fact to have lost little in being separated from their contexts. While many entries start with "And," carrying on from the entry before, this seems quite natural reading them. It is a way of signifying "diary entry," and therefore casual, continuous, and offhand. Virginia Woolf often uses "And" to start paragraphs, particularly the last paragraphs of entries, and her use of the word is exactly that of signifying casualness and a general sort of continuity, to suggest a kind of "andness" of life.

Woolf herself left gaps between dates, so gaps do not necessarily represent entries that Leonard Woolf has left out. Occasionally Leonard Woolf disguises a gap between entries. The entry for 23 June 1929 ends abruptly: "Also, I think, one is much better able to enter into others'—" (144). In the complete diary, the next entry on 30 June begins, "I broke off; somebody I imagine interrupted" (3:236). In *A Writer's Diary*, the entries skip to Monday 19 August, which *also* follows an interruption and begins, "I suppose dinner interrupted" (144). The illusion is created that it carries straight on from the last entry included in the edited version. Almost half of the original entries are in fact included, at least in part, in *A Writer's Diary*. Most of the cuts, in fact, are made within the entries themselves, usually large chunks of the text, taken variously from the beginning, middle, or ends of the entries, sometimes from the beginning and end of the same entry.

Smaller cuts are also made. Quite often a line or two is surreptitiously cut out. Of the entry for Thursday, 31 May 1928, for instance, Leonard Woolf has selected the last third for publication, being the third that most concerns books and writing. Within this third, he cut out another half sentence it is a pity to lose. The full sentence runs "And I must tear up all that manuscript, & write a great many notes and adventure out into the world—as I shall do tomorrow, when I go to have my ears pierced with Vita" (3:185). Leonard Woolf cuts out the part about having her ears pierced, continuing straight on to the next paragraph about London and how it "perpetually attracts, stimulates, gives me a play & a story & a poem" (128). In refining the material down to the strictly literary, he edits out a modulation in tone that is literary in itself and alters the picture of how life and writing alternate.

A number of cuts break up the continuity of the original writing. He cuts out about eight lines from the middle of the entry for Sunday, 12 August 1928, which simply comment on some friends and which follow on quite arbitrarily from the opening comments on their writing. The second part of the entry, after this excised middle section, is a beautiful piece of descriptive writing ending with the plaint, "But what a little I can get down into my pen of what is so vivid to my eyes" (131). It is easy to see why he would want to include both extracts from the entry without the middle lines, but the sentence that he retains to introduce the setting of the descriptive piece—"But Clive yesterday at Charleston said that there were no class distinctions"—carries on directly from the gossipy comments before it in the original, and is quite meaningless and puzzling with his editing. If he felt he needed to keep that sentence for the sake of its scene setting, he might as well have discretely removed the "But" along with the other eight lines already excised.

Most of these cuts serve to make a book out of the diary by giving it a "subject," given in the title, *A Writer's Diary* (a title being in itself a mark of a book). Leonard Woolf explains that he has isolated one aspect of the diary, in choosing pieces that show how she used it "as a writer and artist." Many reviews discuss the book specifically as a book on writing, some even seeming to suggest it was written as such: "the most vivid exploration of the art of writing by a creative writer that has appeared in our time," runs one review quoted on the cover of the 1953 edition. Leonard Woolf outlines his editorial policy as follows:

> I have been carefully through the 26 volumes of diary and have extracted and now publish in this volume practically everything which referred to her own writing. I have included also three other kinds of extract. The first consists of a certain number of passages in which she is obviously using the diary as a method of trying out the art of writing. The second consists of a few passages, which, though not directly or indirectly concerned with her writings, I have deliberately selected

> because they give the reader an idea of the direct impact upon her mind of scenes and persons, i.e. of the raw material of her art. Thirdly I have included a certain number of passages in which she comments upon the books she was reading.
>
> The book throws light upon Virginia Woolf's intentions, objects and methods as a writer. (viii–ix)

The suggestion is that, this policy having been set up, to enact it was fairly mechanical. "Practically everything" that refers to her writing is included, along with these other types of entries. Editing within entries is going to isolate these types of passages from irrelevant passages, while preserving enough of the context to preserve sense and continuity.

Nearly all of the entries of *A Writer's Diary* address the subject of the author's writing or discuss other writing she reads. Ones that do not can easily be read as pieces of "practising or trying out the art of writing." The entry for 29 April 1921, for instance, records a conversation with Lytton Strachey. The impulse behind recording it seems to have been Woolf's usual impulse, to record all aspects of her life, her relationship with Lytton being an essential one: "I have seen him oftener these last days than for a whole year perhaps" (33–35). But the entry is also remarkable for being recorded largely in dialogue, as if verbatim. Leonard Woolf follows this entry with an entry that in fact comes five entries later in the full diary, in which Virginia Woolf remarks, "Sometimes I wish I put down what people say instead of describing them" (35). This follows on rather oddly, given that she seems to have just done that in *A Writer's Diary*, but does also lend weight to a reading of that entry as a writing exercise.

Indicators of "the raw material of her art" are a category that can cover any remaining entry. Their being placed in the context of the entries specifically on the writing process encourages such readings of the others. The entry for 17 April 1919, for instance, is simply an account of a tea with Katherine Mansfield and John Middleton Murry. Musing on Murry and men in general, Woolf observes: "what an abrupt precipice cleaves asunder the male intelligence, and how they pride themselves upon a point of view which much resembles stupidity. I find it much easier to talk to Katherine; she gives and resists as I expect her to" (12–13). Any passage with gender differences as a theme will suggest resonances with the novels. This particular passage could be read as "raw material" for the dinner scene of Woolf's 1926 novel *To the Lighthouse*, in which the women take responsibility for easing the conversation of the men.

While "practically everything" Leonard Woolf included in *A Writer's Diary* can be seen to be in some sense about writing, he did leave some significant pieces about writing out. He does not claim, it is true, to have included practically every passage in which Virginia Woolf used the diary to experiment with the art of writing. But this category seems more useful to cover otherwise inexplicable editorial selections, than as a real selection policy. The most interesting experiments in writing, which tend to be on the subject of her less stable emotions, are left out of the edited diary.

The entry for 15 September 1926 is an extraordinary piece of experimental writing. Woolf uses an expressionist prose to try to describe a terrifying depression. But what is most extraordinary about the passage is the introduction to it. After noting the date, Woolf coolly proposes to use a note form in writing the diary, methodically goes ahead and heads up the "note" with a title, then launches into the startling prose that follows, in a quite shocking change of gear:

> Wednesday 15 September.
>
> Sometimes I shall use the Note form: for instance this:
>
> *A State of Mind*
>
> Woke up perhaps at 3. Oh its beginning its coming—the horror—physically like a painful wave swelling about the heart—tossing me up. I'm unhappy unhappy! Down—God, I wish I were dead. Pause. But why am I feeling this? Let me watch the wave rise. I watch. Vanessa. Children. Failure. Yes; I detect that. Failure failure. (The wave rises). Oh they laughed at my taste in green paint! Wave crashes. I wish I were dead! I've only a few years to live I hope. I cant face this horror any more—(this is the wave spreading out over me)[. . .] (3:110)

Also remarkable are her attempts in March 1937 to graph what she calls her "spiritual temperature." In *A Writer's Diary*, Leonard Woolf includes the entry which begins, "As will be seen on the last page my spiritual temperature went up with a rush" (277), but leaves out the graph which illustrates a dramatic rush by means of a line diagram with dates and "temperatures" written in (5:65).

The extract Leonard Woolf has included from Woolf's entry for 4 January 1929 was intended to represent her attempts to express a particular mental state. Introduced by the philosophic question, "Now is life very solid or very shifting," the extract continues on as a neat little essay, in which a particular mood is translated into philosophic musing (141). In isolating this extract from the whole entry, however, he has actually cut out the part in which she does write directly about her writing. The complete entry begins by comparing her success with *Orlando* with Vanessa Bell's failure to achieve any recognition with her exhibition of paintings. "So I have something, instead of children," Woolf concludes, "& fall comparing our lives" (217). She goes on to write of her and Leonard's visit to see Koteliansky, and how they talked about Mansfield, and she notes the irrefutable solid details of his life against the impossibility of imagining what he can live on. Coming at the end of these issues, her musings seem less abstractly philosophical and more urgently grappling with real questions about what it is to live as a writer.

Leonard Woolf can hardly be expected to have included every piece of writing on the act of writing in the diary itself. Entry after entry—around half of the entries altogether—make some reference to the diary itself: noting where the entry is being recorded or when, and commenting on her habits of writing. Woolf notes a wide range of purposes for writing in the diary: "This is a note for further reference" (3:15); "This is written, as 'this' is so often written, to fill up a little jagged piece of time" (3:195); "To work off depression left by Desmond" (3:27); "This is the temperature chart of a book" (3:16). Most common of all are comments on her "lapses" and the "thinness" of the diary. This last type of comment is so frequently, variously, and urgently repeated, that it suggests a purpose above the incidental purposes she proposes.

Despite the enormous word length of the complete diaries as they are now published, Woolf always felt herself to be falling behind in her duty to her diary. "This book is badly treated again" (2:74); "Really, really—this is disgraceful—15 days of November spent and my diary none the wiser" (2:141); "*Disgraceful! Disgraceful! Disgraceful!* From the 27th day of April to this, the eleventh of June, not a word has been recorded" (2:176). While she often turns to the diary to fill in spare moments of time, when she has no spare moments she will still make time for the diary: "Only five minutes to record the merciful fact that N.S. is out" (5:149); "I will now snatch a moment from what Morgan calls 'life' to enter a hurried note" (3:164); "A rapid note about the lunch party" (3:166). What must she so urgently record? Everything, it seems: a party, a character sketch, a scene, the progress of her books, her emotions. Thomas Mallon classifies her as a "chronicler", the type of diarist whose purpose is simply to get everything on record.[6] It is as if she can preserve life by putting it on paper: "Here in a bound volume, the year has a chance of life. It can be stood on a shelf".[7]

Of course, it is not possible to record everything. But Woolf does attempt, in a number of ways, to make her notes representative of her life. A number of times, she sets herself to record in the diary what can be counted as a "specimen day." In one entry, she makes the resolution, "every day I have meant to record a state of mind" (3:111). She tries to represent fairly the characters who figure in her life, stopping her chronicles periodically to make a "sketch" of someone. She will follow up one entry on a subject with notes of any changes that occur, keeping what she calls "temperature charts" on the progress and reception of her books, like the "temperature charts" she kept of her emotions which were quite literally "charted" in one entry. She tries to give a true picture of what is really on her mind, noting for instance, "I must remember to write about my *clothes* next time I have an impulse to write. My love of clothes interests me profoundly" (3:21). Another day, "what interests me is of course my oil stove" (3:257).

The following entry suggests the effect Woolf was aiming for with all this:

> What a disgraceful lapse! nothing added to my disquisition, & life allowed to waste like a tap left running. Eleven days left unrecorded. Still I think if I were a painter I should only need a brush dipped in dun colour to give the tone of these eleven days. I should draw it evenly across the entire canvas. But painters lack sub[t]lety; there were points of light, shades beneath the surface, now, I suppose, undiscoverable. (1:239)

In her diary Woolf gives the "tone" of a life, not in bold strokes like a painter but in the details. Part of the tone of the days is expressed in the very unedited shape of the entries. When Leonard Woolf extracts a passage on one issue from the worries about her clothes and the gossip about friends that surrounds it, the quality of the thought and the tone of the day are altered.

The literal shape of the entries is in itself expressive. Short entries indicate such a rush of life or writing outside the diary that the diary misses out: "A gap: not in life, but in comment" (5:101). Often her remarks on failings to write in the diary are made in terms of the material effect on the book, in terms of "thinness" and "gaps." Diary writing is itself a part of her life, which the size of the entries records directly. It depends on regular habits and responds to changes: "By bringing this book down here to the Studio, I have rather stinted it I think, as my mornings have all been spent writing—Swift or letters" (3:34). Long entries that continue on from each other, commenting on and amending the entry before, indicate life is running in a pattern that allows regular time for reflection.

In fact, so frequent are the comments to herself about how well the diary is shaping up, that the length and frequency of the entries become in themselves almost a part of the action. Writing is not just the subject of the book but the plot. The struggle to get her life on record provides constant tension. Every entry is a life preserver. "I will signal my return to life—that is writing—by beginning a new book, & it happens to be Thoby's birthday, I remark" (3:317).

Woolf's famous metaphor for her diary as a "capacious hold-all," suggests everything can be thrown into such a genre—friends, nibs, ear-piercing, servants, philosophy—just as Louis Simpson suggests American poetry must be able to "digest / Rubber, coal, uranium, moons, poems."[8] Like Simpson, Woolf seems to be imagining not just a radically democratic lack of selection but a kind of "digestion" of the raw material, proposing that the fragmentary pieces of writing included in the "capacious hold-all" will fall into a new kind of order all by themselves over time. If that makes the "capacious hold-all" the stomach, it recalls, too, Antonia White's digestion metaphor, which implies writing in the diary does not count as the product of digestion but only as the process of digestion.

The image of a "capacious hold-all" suggests, too, a container for writing that can be opened, from which items could be removed as well as added. The diary's "open form" allows for editing, even for constructing, as Murry proved. Yet the example of the various Mansfield diary editions also suggests that the diary form can "digest" its contents in a way that is closer to Louis Simpson's image of how poetry might "digest" its contents. What is so extraordinary about the Scott edition of the *Notebooks*, which is simply a transcription of all the miscellaneous pieces of Mansfield's personal writing which have happened to survive and eventually end up in the Turnbull Library, is how it does seem to present a new textual "surface" to the reader, even to offer a kind of "reflection" of Mansfield herself. The very form of the diary, which Margaret Scott has adopted in her chronological, dated arrangement of the writing, has, in a sense, "digested" the various contents to create a new, and complete, text that reads inevitably as a kind of portrait. Leonard Woolf was very conscious of how a diary text might present a portrait of the diarist's "self." He felt that the "self" presented by Woolf's unedited diaries is not her "own" self.

It is interesting to find that the poem by Louis Simpson discussed earlier is quoted by Tom Paulin, in his introduction to *The Plain Speaker*, a collection of essays by William Hazlitt. Paulin is well known for his antagonism towards Virginia Woolf, which makes it all the more in keeping with this concept of radical digestion to find Paulin's discussion of Hazlitt's prose style so useful in illuminating Woolf's diary poetics. Paulin relates the digestion metaphor of Simpson's poem to Hazlitt's image of "the most perfect prose-style" as a chamois, browsing on the "roughest bark" (xiii–xiv). Paulin's discussion of how Hazlitt's prose carries us, by its upward motion, bounding over differences of contexts, and leaps in ideas, could apply just as well to the leaps and bounds of Woolf's diary. In the chapter on Virginia Woolf's use of the dash, later in the book, I will come back to this comparison between the prose styles of Woolf and Hazlitt, finding them surprisingly similar in their stretch and speed. The poem by Louis Simpson makes a further connection, too, however, between poetry's capacity for digestion and its "voice," the poem ending with an image of a poem-shark "uttering cries that are almost human."

The concept of "voice" further complicates the idea that a text is a reflection of "self." "Voice" most usefully refers to the imitation, or recording, in prose style of the particular rhythms of the writer's style of speech, although, as I consider in more detail in the chapter on Sylvia Plath, this sense of the term "voice" has been complicated by notions of authenticity. Paulin makes a connection between Hazlitt's chamois-like prose style, with its leaps between different subjects, and the conversational quality that makes Hazlitt's voice as a prose writer so engaging. He uses the term "indented" to describe the way Hazlitt's writing moves between subjects, a term taken from a passage by Horne Tooke, cited by Hazlitt. In this passage, Tooke makes the same argument that Paulin makes about the relation between prose style and conversational ease:

> Horne Tooke used to maintain that no one could write a good prose style, who was not accustomed to express himself *viva voce*, or to talk in company. He argued that this was the fault of Addison's prose [. . .] His style (in this view of it) was not indented, nor did it project from the surface. There was no stress laid on one word more than another—it did not hurry on or stop short, or sink of swell with the occasion.[9]

Hazlitt himself was a great conversationalist as well as a great prose writer. And yet, in the article this quotation is taken from, "On the Prose Style of Poets," Hazlitt is not citing Tooke in order to agree with him, exactly, as is implied by Paulin's use of the quotation. Rather, Hazlitt's conception of the development of such a style could fit Hughes' description of Plath's development of a "voice" in her *Journals*, which would come to serve as a poetic voice as well. This was not a voice Hughes suggests Plath ever used in conversation: "Though I spent every day with her for six years, and was rarely separated from her for more than two or three hours at a time, I never saw her show her real self to anyone [. . .] Her real self had showed itself in her writing."[10] Hazlitt likewise discusses the development of a natural, speech-*like* prose style as something to be developed by writers, writing in the genre. While prose is closer to speech than is (late eighteenth-century) poetry, it has its own poetics.

This poetics is not just concerned with the stylistics of the sentence or the texture of the prose. Paulin makes a chamois-like leap of his own when he quotes from Hazlitt's Tooke citation and from his chamois passage all in one sentence, to make one point:

> The 'lively transitions' of speech, the 'indented nature' of true prose, is imaged in the later passage by the leaping chamois clambering up a rocky cliff 'by abrupt and intricate ways.' And the image of the chamois browsing on the 'roughest bark' is another image of the indented nature of prose, as well as an image of the fact that the prose writer has to deal with 'dry matters of fact and close reasoning'—has to 'marshal' facts, as we say, like a general. (xiii)

The image of the chamois, however, depicts something rather different from the indentations of speech. The leaps the chamois is making are not within sentences, but from subject to subject. These are the kinds of leaps between ear-piercing and London plays that Woolf's complete diary is so rich in, and these are the kinds of leaps that are largely left out of *A Writer's Diary*. It is in these leaps that Woolf expresses the tone of her days, and it is the leaps themselves that give the tone of the diary.

In his construction of *A Writer's Diary*, Leonard Woolf has successfully created a book that is book-sized and has a book-sized subject. His editorial may not be so mechanical or so unproblematic as his introduction suggests, but it works. *A Writer's Diary* may even be the sort of book Virginia Woolf had in mind when she suggested that Leonard Woolf might one day "make up a book from them [. . .] & then burn the body" (3:67). But *The Diary of Virginia Woolf* as it is edited by Anne Olivier Bell is a much fuller expression of "a writer's life" and of writing as a *part* of life, and this is expressed as much in the rhythms of the shifts of content as in the balance of the content itself. Unlike Mansfield, Woolf did "keep a diary", controlling from day to day the rhythms of the text, the leaps and shifts in content counterpoised against the "ands" and "buts" of her fluid, water-surface prose style.

In one diary entry, Virginia Woolf wondered if she could get away from the category of novel to describe her attempts to capture the tone of life. "I have an idea that I will invent a new name for my books to supplant 'novel'. A new—by Virginia Woolf. But what? Elegy?" (3:34). Elegy is not an inappropriate name for the diary, written, she decides in another entry, "Partly I think from my old sense of the race of time." She reflects, "the past is beautiful because one never realises an emotion at the time. It expands later." Her diary is too expansive to be contained in a book-sized book.

6 Sylvia Plath

The publication of Sylvia Plath's journals has inevitably been caught up in the politics surrounding the interpretation of Plath as a writer and as an icon. As the critic Jacqueline Rose has written, "Execrated and idolised, Sylvia Plath hovers between the furthest poles of positive and negative appraisal."[1] By now, the Plath myth has become a text, or collection of texts, as complex and as inviting of interpretation as Plath's own oeuvre. The title of Jacqueline Rose's book, *The Haunting of Sylvia Plath*, acknowledges the way in which "Sylvia Plath haunts our culture" (1), for, as Rose observes, "What we are dealing with is, obviously enough, not Plath herself but her representations" (2). Janet Malcolm takes this approach a step further in her book of investigative journalism, *The Silent Woman*, dealing not so much with Plath's representations but with the biographers responsible for the representations, exploring the politics of the Stevenson biography through interviews with most of the main players.[2] The film-makers responsible for the most recent representation of Plath, the film *Sylvia* released in 2003, have talked of the need to get away from the polarised representations of Plath coming from the "Plath camp" or the "Hughes camp."[3] Script-writer John Brownlow has explained in interviews, and in his introduction to the published script, that he turned instead to Plath's journals and poetry, as well as to Hughes' own account in *Birthday Letters*, though even this material he found less "reliable" than the "story" produced by the researcher he employed.[4]

In this chapter I want to look at Plath's journals not so much as one more contested "representation" of Plath, but in terms of Plath's experiments with different diary forms and with the different possible effects she was able to achieve working in the diary genre. But I am interested in how editorial decisions have affected the ways the journals represent Plath. In particular, I am interested in how the 1982 edition of *The Journals of Sylvia Plath,* edited by Frances McCullough and Ted Hughes, represents Plath very much as the poet of *Ariel*, the poetry collection that made her name. In contrast, the manuscripts as they are available in the Neilson Library, in Smith College, give much more impression of Plath's strengths as a prose writer, and show more clearly, too, her engagement with the diary form, as a writer seriously engaged with the genre.

The publication in 2000 of the manuscripts held in Smith College, as *The Journals of Sylvia Plath 1950–1962*, edited by Karen Kukil, provides scholars with all of Plath's extant diaries, including the material which had been omitted from the 1982 journals edited by Hughes and McCullough.[5] This large volume contains transcripts of all the journal material lodged in the Sylvia Plath collection at Smith College, and, crucially, in contrast to the earlier edition, it clearly notes which material comes from which volume, retaining the structural integrity of each volume Plath kept. This edition also includes a complete transcript of the journals Plath kept during her marriage to Ted Hughes, which, even in the Smith collection, are available to scholars not in their original manuscript form but only in edited transcripts. But just as Podnieks found it essential to consider the "incarnation and format" of the diaries in her study, I have found seeing the actual physical volumes kept by Plath has been essential to my understanding of Plath's approach to her diary keeping. In this chapter, then, my focus is on the two different versions of the diaries that the Kukil edition might seem to have made obsolete: the manuscripts in the archives and the 1982 edition, which remains interesting as an example of the effects of editing and, therefore, the effects of form. When referring to manuscript material, however, I will provide page references to the Kukil edition, as the edition that gives readers an accessible transcript of Plath's writing.

Hughes has emphasised the connection between Plath's voice as a poet and the voice of the journals in more than one essay as well as in his foreword to the *Journals* (1982), and the journals as he and McCullough edited them clearly share the strengths of Plath's poetry.[6] The powerful visual imagery and the arresting physicality of the poetry are located in the diaries in the physicality of the writer, the physicality of writing. The descriptions of Plath's surroundings as she writes, of her own body seen as if from without—"a tan long-legged girl in a white lawn chair . . . dressed in aqua shorts and a white-and-aqua halter"—as well as felt from within—"in a locust-itchy-crawly body"—situate the entries powerfully in the "moment of writing" discussed in Chapter 4.[7] And while Plath's poems are increasingly rhetorical in tone, the *Journals* (1982) have a rhetorical force from the beginning. Many of Plath's poems are written in the second person, and Plath often addresses herself in the diary in the second person, the subjectivity of the diarist viewed from the outside as much as experienced from within, and not just viewed, but addressed, manipulated, by the writing. In his foreword to the *Journals* (1982), Hughes describes all of Plath's writing except for her later poems and the diaries as "waste products." The editing of the diaries by Hughes and McCullough has resulted in a book with a distinctive voice, a powerful style, which seems at once a fulfilment of the demands of the genre of the diary, and related to, if not the basis of, Plath's voice as a poet. In fact, not only does the 1982 edition of the *Journals* seem a useful way in to understanding Plath as a poet, this connection between Plath's strengths as a poet and as a diarist seems a useful way of approaching the diary genre more generally, suggesting a diary poetics based on concepts of physicality, the moment of writing, and a rhetorical address.

But the manuscript diaries are not so clearly, nor so singly, the diaries of the poet. Plath did not keep a consistent diary throughout the period covered by the *Journals* (1982), but a number of different diaries, different from each other in format and approach to the genre, and including a much greater variety of material and "voice." In these various diaries, Plath's strengths as a prose writer are equally apparent: her evocation of place, situation, social position, social relations and mores, her enormous interest in other people. And while the body of writing as a whole is more disparate than the edited *Journals* (1982), each individual volume or sequence of papers in the manuscript collection has its own integrity. Plath was far more concerned with structure, even in the supposedly formless genre of the diary, than the *Journals* (1982) suggest.

Plath started keeping a diary as a schoolgirl, when her mother used to give her a diary every year for Christmas. These were dated diaries, and the formal demands must have suited Plath at first, for she filled in each page to the allotted space, often finishing an entry with tiny writing to fit it all in under the right date. But her request in 1945 for an undated journal shows her approach to the genre was becoming more sophisticated, and closer to the definition of the diary by writers such as Fothergill, Spalding, and Matthews, as a form shaped by the idiosyncratic concerns of the diarist. In keeping entries of irregular lengths she fulfils Matthews' definition for instance in which he listed irregularity of entry length as an essential mark of a diarist's integrity.

In the diary she kept from 1950 to 1953 as a student of Smith College, in a hardcover volume with LAW printed on the spine, Plath extends the principle of keeping irregular length, with the practice she initiates of numbering, rather than dating, entries. This allows her to write two or more distinct entries on the same day, distinguishing entries not by the date on which they were written but by individual writing sessions or by separate trains of thought. She may even have written two entries at one sitting, the separate numbers heading them making the point at which she feels she has followed through one train of thought, narrative, or associations, and is beginning a new one. An entry will often have a distinct theme which Plath will present, expand on, and return to in closing, and the following entry or sequence of entries may expand on a point made in the preceding entry. Perhaps the hard covers and large foolscap pages of the LAW volume may have suggested the formal structure Plath gives these entries.

The care Plath takes in distinguishing and ordering the entries in the LAW volume is apparent in her careful numbering of them and in her careful concluding of each entry with three large dots, faithfully preserved in Kukil's edition of the journals.[8] In the manuscript text, it is clear how determined Plath is to squeeze in the three dots at the end of an entry even if it means writing them underneath the last ruled line on a page, or, if this is impossible, at the top of the next page before commencing the next entry. The dots start to taper out about a quarter of the way through the diary, at first being written on the same line, then taking on the usual function of ellipses at the end of a sentence—"perchance to sleep . . . perchance, perchance . . . "—and finally abandoned altogether from the 57th entry onwards. In the second half of the diary, from the 124th entry onwards, where she recommences the diary after a gap of several months, the entries are mostly dated, yet Plath continues to number the entries in addition to dating them, up to number 188. Only the last two overwrought entries are undated.

The 1950–1953 LAW diary as a whole has an integrity that has been lost in the edited excerpts from it in the *Journals* (1982). I will go on to look at the content that has been removed, but the editing has had an even more devastating effect on the form. The careful notation of a progression of ideas is lost, as entries are excerpted unnumbered, with large yet irregular gaps between them. Occasionally, extraneous material has been interspersed with the extracts, such as the "Infirmary Blues" poem, included in the *Journals* (1982) but not part of the original diary. The remarkable thematic unity of the entries is destroyed by the editorial practice of cutting the beginnings and ends of entries, excerpting passages from the middle, and sometimes even running an excerpt from one entry on to one from another, as if they are part of the same entry. Altogether, about three quarters of the original LAW diary has been cut.

The rest of the manuscript collection consists mainly of a great number of typescripts, covering distinct periods and in different styles, each typescript having its own coherence and sense of form. Plath used this format to keep temporary diaries, heading up the pages she types them on with titles such as "Cambridge Diary" and "Sketchbook of a Spanish summer." These diaries, kept up for two months or so, are headed up on nearly every page with the date and, less consistently, the title of the diary. Where the entries go on for more than a page, she usually writes the date on each page, sometimes following it " . . . con." While these scripts do not have the permanence suggested by the bound LAW volume, Plath has still taken care to maintain the diary format, and the typescripts do have the completeness of small books, or chapters. Kukil has, accordingly, included most of these typescripts as "Journals" within the main body of the text. Other entries in the *Journals* (1982) such as the "Letter to an Over-grown, Over-protected, Scared, Spoiled Baby" (81) or the "Program: to win friends and influence people" (137–38) are, in the manuscript collection, clearly quite different in kind. These were separate pages with no place in an ongoing document, simply letters to herself. Kukil has observed the differences between the types of documents by including these pieces not as part of the journals proper, but as appendices, in a separate section at the end of the volume. But in the 1982 edition, all of this material is incorporated into a single text.

Most of the second half of the *Journals* (1982) comes from three journals kept by Plath, none of which are available to readers in the form in which they were kept. Instead three typescripts have been made of excerpts from the journals, with corrections, revisions, and deletions throughout. The largest of the original journals was a volume similar in kind to the LAW volume and to the final two volumes kept by Plath, subsequently lost and destroyed by Hughes. The other two are copies of typescripts, one the notes of her analysis with psychoanalyst Ruth Beuscher, the other the journal of her stay at Yaddo in autumn 1959. Kukil is able to include the complete scripts of all of these journals, presented as "Journal 28 August 1957 –14 October 1958" and "Journals 12 December 1958—15 November 1959," with the second section combining the therapy notes with the Yaddo journal. She provides facsimiles of pages from each, which show the difference between the 1957–1958 journal, a handwritten volume like the earlier LAW volume, and the therapy notes, typed in tight little paragraphs. Even so, the difference between the handwritten material entered into hardback volumes and the typed material existing as a set of notes is very much diminished in the complete edition, printed as they are in the same font and format together in a single volume.

Of all the typescript journals Plath kept, the most significant in terms of diary poetics is the last of these sets of notes, the "Notes on Neighbours" Plath kept in Devon. In these notes, Plath keeps diaries of her relationships with her neighbours in the small village she is living in with her family in Devon. The diary of each relationship is kept chronologically, but simultaneously with the diaries of other relationships, so that they form a complete, overlapping picture of Plath's place in village society. Although Kukil gives these the title "Journal, 1962," she relegates them, like the hospital and infirmary notes, and the smaller travel journals, to the appendices at the back of the volume, as "Appendix 15" (630–74). In choosing to include the therapy notes as diary material along with the manuscript diaries, but relegating the "Notes on Neighbours" to an appendix, Kukil's organisation of material helps to support a representation of Plath as self-centred, primarily concerned with the drama of her own emotions. Although Plath's strengths as a prose writer are far more apparent in this complete edition of *The Journals 1950–1962*, than they are in the 1982 edition of the *Journals*, the greater significance given to the therapy journal, with its focus on the emotional history that Plath drew on in much of her later poetry, in comparison with the "Notes on Neighbours," which are more likely to have been kept as potential source material for fiction, continues to support a reading of the diaries in relation to Plath as the poet of *Ariel*. Tim Kendall, in his review of *The Journals 1950–1962*, singles out the "Notes on Neighbours" as being "among the finest prose she ever wrote." He notes the "precision and inclusiveness of her descriptions," and while, unlike Kendall, I don't see these pieces as "glorious exceptions" in the interest they show in other people, I certainly agree that they, perhaps more than any other journal material, suggest "the powerful novelist Plath might have become."[9]

Kukil's decision to keep the notes as an appendix, along with the other more fragmentary selections of diary writing, may be partly based on generic expectations for the diary, according to which the therapy notes might seem more properly "diary" material than the "Notes on Neighbours" might appear. But it is precisely the way in which these notes find new potential in the diary form that makes them so significant. In terms of the development of the diary, this sequence, though small, is possibly the most important in the collection. Plath's first diary included in the collection, the LAW volume, extends the idea of the periodic entry of irregular length with her numbered entries recording the development of her ideas and their context in terms of her daily life. "Notes on Neighbours" develops the diary in a new direction again. Whereas the LAW volume is very much written as a book, the "Notes on Neighbours" couldn't have taken the direction it did had Plath not become accustomed to typing diaries on loose leaves of paper. The way these notes are structured, with the diary of each relationship, or each "chapter" of the diary, having its own beginning and end, plays with the relation between sequence and chronology in a way that really opens up possibilities for the diary. A new autonomous unit is introduced into the structure of the diary, with the chronological diary "chapters" arranged thematically around particular relationships. It is interesting to note that these chapters can be arranged in any order, without really affecting the form of the complete work.

The result is a work which vindicates feminist theory of the diary in a way the traditional diary only begins to do. I have been sceptical of feminist theory that reads qualities of the diary as a genre both as feminine and as a result of female authorship, when in fact these formal responses to the genre are equally apparent in the writing of male and female diarists.[10] Despite Cheever's own anxiety about the "femininity" of the detail, the diary form gives the detail as much significance in his *Journal* as it has in the diaries Hogan cites in her article on the diary as "female autobiography." Judy Nolte Lensinck's similar argument for the diary to be considered as female autobiography is equally problematic. How are we meant to take Mary Jane Moffatt's point, which Lensinck quotes, that many of the same terms are used for women as are used for diaries—"emotional, fragmentary, interrupted" and so on? Lensinck cites French feminist Hélène Cixous' discussion of metaphor as masculine and suggests that the more metonymic structure of the diary, the structure of selection and accumulation, is "female" in its very nature. Yet the argument that the diary form is equivalent to, or representative of, aspects of the female gender, is itself a metaphorical argument.[11] Plath's "Notes on Neighbours," however, extends the formal range of the genre in a way which extends, too, the ways in which the diary can be read as a feminine genre. Not only is the sequence fragmentary in the usual way of the diary, with separate entries making up its form, Plath's "Notes on Neighbours" succeeds, in addition, in breaking up the linear chronology characteristic equally of masculine autobiography and the conventional diary. Furthermore, the "Notes" express, in terms of form, the theorising of the female self as defined in relation to another person, or other people, central to the feminist autobiographical theory of Mary Mason, Celeste Schenck, and Bella Brodzki amongst others. This need not suggest an essentialist definition of femininity. While Plath's commitment to the diary as a genre remained constant throughout her life, she constantly experimented with the formal possibilities of the diary, writing different kinds of diary texts to accommodate the particular life experiences and narratives of different periods in her life. The new form taken by the "Notes" can be seen as a response to the kinds of relationships she had with her neighbours as a housewife in the 1960s.

The writing in the "Notes" certainly has the precision and physicality of detail that is typical of Plath's writing in her poetry and evident throughout the *Journals* (1982). The confusion of metaphors in her description of the dying neighbour Percy works like the confusion of metaphors in much of her poetry to suggest an intensity of perception:

> Percy lay back on a heap of white pillows in his striped pyjamas, his face already passed from humanity, the nose a spiralling fleshless beak in the thin air, the chin fallen in a point from it, like an opposite pole, and the mouth like an inverted black heart stamped into the yellow flesh between, a great raucous breath coming and going there with great effort like an awful bird, caught, but about to depart. His eyes showed through partly open lids like dissolved soaps or a clotted pus.[12]

Yet the attention Plath gives the houses of the neighbours perhaps suggests a more prosaic interest in setting:

> Tiny rooms, bright, modernish. The typical British wallpaper—a pale beige embossed with faintly sheened white roses, the effect of cream scum patterns on weak tea. Starchy white curtains, good for peeking from behind [. . .] Upstairs, a pink bathroom, floors all sealed with new lino, flounces and mirrors and chrome. A new cooker in the kitchen (the other hire purchase item), a cage of pistachio and pale-blue budgies creaking and whistling, up a step from the living room. (672)

It is this balance between the poetic and the prosaic which is so characteristic of Plath's diary writing, but which is less apparent in the *Journals* (1982), edited, as they have been, as the journals of the *Ariel* poet.

Not only have the cuts made by the editors of the *Journals* (1982) often been of the more prosaic material, the act of editing in itself has added to the impact of the *Ariel*-like physicality and rhetoric of Plath's writing in the journals. Because editing diminishes the continuity of the periodic sequence, qualities relating to the moment of writing and the subjectivity of the writer are of more importance. The importance of the moment of writing in Katherine Mansfield's journals and notebooks suggested that the entry has an autonomy within—or even without—the succession of entries that make up the diary. In John Cheever's journals, the central role of detail gave the individual entry an autonomy that made extracts read sometimes more effectively in isolation than in the more extended form in which the journals were eventually published. Editing a diary in the sense of collating extracts from the manuscripts, as Hughes and McCullough have done with the diaries of Sylvia Plath, depends on this sense of the autonomy of individual entries. Certainly Plath, as much as any diarist, writes powerfully within the moment of writing, giving powerful expression to the subjectivity of the diarist, meeting fully these particular demands of the genre.

All of Plath's diary volumes are remarkable for the physicality of the writing, and so it is not simply an effect of editing that the *Journals* (1982) are so consistently striking in this regard. Plath writes often of physical sensations, describing in detail the sensations of sunbathing or cycling at night. One passage often quoted in writing on Plath's diaries describes in luxuriant detail the pleasures of nose-picking. Other passages dwell on physical discomforts, "eyes stuck together, a taste of winding sheets on my tongue." She writes of an itch: "My eyelid's hot stinging itch has spread, in actuality, or by sympathetic imagining nerves, to all my body—scalp, leg, stomach: as if an itch, infectious, lit and burned, lit and burned."[13] Not being able to write is described in physical terms, as a "paralysis" (251). It seems very natural for Plath to situate her writing within the "moment of writing" with detailed descriptions of location. The connection between her surroundings and the impulse to write is close. She may try to resist this: she mentions the rain in one short entry, but resists the temptation to write a poem about it, remembering what it said on one rejection slip: "After a heavy rainfall, poems titled 'Rain' pour in from across the nation" (4). But the diary provides an outlet that does not require censoring. Two years later, she describes herself "in bed, propped up comfortably by pillows—listening to it spurting and drenching—and all the different timbres of tone—and syncopation" (52). She goes on in a descriptive orgy, a good four hundred words long, starting with the present rain and then more briefly reminiscing about rain in other Augusts.

In fact the manuscripts include many more passages about rain which Hughes and McCullough have cut from the edited *Journals* (1982). The intensity of the sense of the "moment of writing" that rain seems to have given her is suggested in the LAW journal she kept at college by the number of times she dates the rain entries, in a volume that she initially intended to keep undated. The first entry on rain in the volume is also the first dated entry of the volume, and out of seven entries on rain in the volume, six of them are dated. Altogether, Plath dates only thirteen out of one hundred and twenty-three entries in the first half of the LAW journal, and of these, four of them are entries on rain. The one hundred and twenty-fourth entry, which starts the journal again after an eight-month gap, is again one that was prompted by a rainfall.

Despite the editorial cuts, the close relationship between Plath's writing and the setting for it remains very apparent in the *Journals* (1982). In some passages, location and thought have almost the same quality, the thoughts described almost as if they are part of Plath's surroundings. The entry she wrote babysitting which begins describing "the deep-cushioned armchair, the crickets rasping . . . the floor a medieval mosaic . . . " goes on to describe her thoughts as if they are similarly present, similarly removed from her enough to be observed:

> So I sit here, smiling as I think in my fragmentary way: *Woman is but an engine of ecstasy, a mimic of the earth from the ends of her curled hair to her red-lacquered nails.* Then I think, remembering the family of beautiful children that lie upstairs: *Isn't it better to give in to the pleasant cycle of reproduction, the easy comforting presence of a man around the house?* . . . Yes, I'm thinking, and so far it's all right. But then I do a flip over and reach on in my mind to E [. . .] (14)

While the diaries are very analytical, with a high proportion of abstract thought, Plath tends to present ideas in visual terms. As abstract an idea as mortality is described figuratively: "Cats have nine lives, the saying goes. You have one; and somewhere along the thin tenuous thread of your existence there is the black knot, the stopped heartbeat that spells the end of this particular individual" (24). She herself notes at one point "my leaning towards allegories, similes and metaphors [. . .] a vehicle to express a few of the many disturbing thoughts" (28). Her interest in dreams in the later diaries is an interest in an unconscious form of thinking which presents ideas and emotions in visual terms.

Ideas and facts are taken personally by Plath, imagined in physical terms. She applies her textbook knowledge of genetics to herself: "There is your dead father who is somewhere in you, interwoven in the cellular system of your long body which sprouted from one of his sperm cells uniting with an egg cell in your mother's uterus" (25–26). Emotions too are experienced in physical terms. In a depression she describes herself with "Nose podgy as a leaking sausage: big pores full of pus and dirt, red blotches, the peculiar brown mole on my underchin [. . .] Hair untrained, merely brown and childishly put up [. . .] No bone structure" (287–88), and yet she recognises that when she has "written a novel, a book of poems, a *Ladies Home Journal* or *New Yorker* story [. . .] I will be poreless and radiant. My wart will be non-malignant" (288).

At the same time, ideas are so concrete for Plath that emotions can be given definition by presenting emotions in terms of ideas: "There are times when a feeling of expectancy comes over me [. . .] I can feel it when I think of human beings, of the hints of evolution suggested by the removal of wisdom teeth" (11). The passage she wrote sitting in the library, doubting her own selfhood among so many similar girls, draws on the idea of the conditioning centre in Aldous Huxley's *Brave New World* to understand her feelings of annihilation (17).

The diaries have a rhetorical strength as powerful as their physicality. The use of figurative language is itself a rhetorical device, and Plath often uses images emotively, to press an idea further, as if she needs to persuade herself of her own ideas. Her habit of asking herself questions to further thought is similar to the use of questions in rhetoric. She does not always ask questions rhetorically; her questions may go round and round in circles, and the answers remain in doubt, or they may be reached only circuitously:

> Why am I obsessed with the idea I can justify myself by getting manuscripts published? Is it an escape, an excuse for social failure . . . Or is it an excuse for wanting to be alone [. . .] Do I like to write? Why? About what? Will I give up . . . Or will I stick to the damn stuff and practice? (33)

But at other times, questions are asked as a challenge to herself, to provoke a particular answer: "must I lose it in cooking scrambled eggs for a man . . . hearing about life at second hand, feeding my body and letting my powers of perception and subsequent articulation grow fat and lethargic with disuse?" (33)

A momentum is built up in the rhythm of a sentence like the last one, with its chain of subordinate clauses. Plath often writes in almost oratorical rhythms in the diaries, letting sentences build up force with more and more clauses, more and more adjectives piled up one after the other: "Sick with conflict, destructive negative emotions, frozen into disintegration I was, refusing to articulate, to spew forth these emotions—they festered in me, growing big, distorted, like pus-boated sores" (64). She describes herself "stifled, weak, pallid, mealy-mouthed and utterly absurd" (32). Repetitions also build up a rhetorical rhythm: "when I read, God, when I read that taut spare, lucid prose" (32). Whole paragraphs are given a structure by repetitive links, as in the babysitting passage: "Here I sit [. . .] So I sit here, smiling as I think [. . .] Then I think [. . .] I remember [. . .] Yes, I'm thinking [. . .] then I do a flip over [. . .] I spiral back to me, sitting here" (14–15).

In many entries particularly in the early, Smith College diary (the LAW volume), Plath addresses herself in the second person, giving a further rhetorical force to passages already powerful in their rhythms and intimacy:

> Again the refrain, what *have* you for your eighteen years? And you know that whatever tangible things you *do* have, they cannot be held, but, too, will decompose and slip away through your coarse-skinned and death-rigid fingers. So you will rot in the ground, and so you say, what the hell? Who cares? But *you* care, and somehow you don't want to live just one life, which could be typed, which could be tossed off in a thumbnail sketch "She was the sort of girl . . . " And end in 25 words or less. (25)

Plath's use of the second person pronoun is particularly interesting and will be returned to in the final chapter of the book which looks in some detail at the use of first and second person pronouns in the diary. Here, I want to draw attention to how this use of the second person pronoun to build up a rhetorical rythm can be seen as anticipating how important the use of the second person was to the development of Plath's later poetry. The *Ariel* poems are distinguished from the technically accomplished poems of her earlier work and even from most of *Colossus*, the last book she published before her death, by a new mastery of tone and a new power of rhetoric. In many of these poems, she uses "you" to address a genuinely second person, other than herself, though the second person takes a number of guises. She addresses poems tenderly to her son, balefully to her "love" and wrathfully to "Herr Enemy"—her father, her husband, her doctor: in many of the *Ariel* poems these characters take each other's place interchangeably, while the second person address remains constant.

The vehemence of the later poetry matches the vehemence of the diaries, in the extremity of her figurative language and the forcefulness of her use of rhythm. Generally tighter than in the diaries, her use of rhythm in the later poetry is still much closer to the diaries than it is in the more formally constructed earlier poems, and takes much of its power from the rhythm of the speaking voice. Plath was insistent that these poems were meant to be heard spoken aloud, refusing to let Alvarez read them before she had read them to him, when she revealed her new work for the first time. As in the diaries, she uses repetition compulsively to underline what she writes, in emphasis or in irony. Drafts of her poems show her frequently cutting back on repetition, which she used clearly as a first resort. Her use of repetition in the poems and in the journals creates markedly similar rhythmic effects in some passages. The sing-song rhythms of repetition in poems like "The Applicant"—"It can sew, it can cook,/ It can talk, talk, talk . . . / Will you marry it, marry it, marry it"[14]—can be found in particular in passages in the journal Plath wrote in response to sessions with her analyst, Dr Beuscher:

> Get a nice little, safe little, sweet little loving little imitation man who'll give you babies and bread and a secure roof and a green lawn and money money money every month [. . .] Be sure he's nice nice nice. (268)

The editing of Plath's diaries, then, has lost the sense of form that structured each of Plath's original diary sequences but may seem to have preserved Plath's "voice", which seems clearly the same "voice" that is evident in the poetry. But Plath considered herself a prose writer as well as a poet and was capable of writing in a different "voice" for every genre. Hughes, in his introduction to the *Journals* (1982), suggests that these other styles of writing Plath adopted for other genres were "false" voices, and only in the diary did Plath develop the "true" voice that finally allowed her "real self" to speak through the *Ariel* poems. But her concerns and her style of writing, her "voice", are various too in her diaries, alter from volume to volume, and share as many qualities of Plath's prose writing as they do of her poetry.

Even the edited *Journals* (1982) preserve plenty of evidence that Plath took her fiction seriously. She refers in the *Journals* (1982) to a "five year gap" in writing, during which time she had no short stories published, although she continued to write poetry, letters, and the diaries, and even continued to publish poems—sixteen the previous year. But an enormous, and disproportionate, amount of material relating to her prose writing has been edited out. A great many practice descriptions of scenery have been edited out of the Cambridge typescripts, presumably simply to avoid repetition and to retain narrative interest and dramatic intensity. Likewise, the pages and pages of ideas for short stories have been omitted. But passages about prose writing have been cut out even of entries that are otherwise included in the *Journals* (1982). This passage is omitted from the "Letter to an Over-grown, Over-protected, Scared, Spoiled, Baby," otherwise included in full:

> If I can't dream up plots in my own room and backyard, I won't be able to dream them up anywhere. I am, of course, as I said, afraid to try writing on my own, because of the huge possibilities of failure. But I am going to. I will read "Seventeen's" and write a story for them. Also for the "Ladies Home." Also maybe for Accent on Living, and the New Yorker. The more I think about it, the more creative I will be at home, without all the guilts and sapping jealousies if I pampered my original whim and went to Harvard now that my whole scheme is altered by not taking O'Connor's course.[15]

A long descriptive passage on fiddler crabs is included in the *Journals* (1982), but the notes that follow, of plans for more commercial writing, are omitted:

> A light vivid Harper's article on Cambridge. A couple of short colorful articles on Eastham to go with drawings of Mrs. Spaulding and beach-plums, boats beached in Rock Harbour, and two corn vases.
>
> A story: told with infinite detail, but must *move*: The corn vases. To balance long sentences, have short fluid sentences. Mrs. McFague, a stolid, good-hearted Cape Codder, indefatigable talker, memory runs back to Frisco quake, thrown together with young couple in her cottages without car, takes them shopping, to doctor's. Sense of her simplicity, yet she hides riches: antiques: two corn vases in trailer, amid poverty. Lazy, unimaginative, sickly husband: get in story of second marriage through present talk: husband with abscessed ear: visitors descend on them: Mrs. McFague's lack of willpower, contrast with Tookie, who

would consider such an invasion outrageous. Mrs. McFague comes back to find children playing with corn vases, utter weakminded will of parents. Main theme: parental weakness. Mrs. McFague sends them off. Tookie, no children, English husband. (Kukil, 297)

In one instance, the omission of material on prose writing actually misleads the reader into reading a comment Plath makes about extending her writing as meaning extending her work on poetry, whereas in the original transcript it is clear she is writing about extending her work as a prose writer. The paragraph that ends the entry for Wednesday July 9 in the published *Journals* (1982) begins with Plath's fears that "Prose writing has become a phobia with me," and her intention to put poetry aside and work on prose, and goes on to criticise the poetry she has been writing. The entry ends in the *Journals*: "I write my good poems too fast—they are on objects, not themes, thus concrete, limited. Good enough, but I must extend" (248). Despite the opening to the paragraph, Plath's attention seems to have returned to the poetry she has been working on. With the excised section of the entry restored in the Kukil edition, however, it is clear that she plans to extend her writing by returning to the roomier genre of fiction: "I must start outlining a story plot: obviously it takes time" (403). The entry continues with notes on ideas, on point of view, and her intention to write fifteen to twenty pages of fiction a week.

Prose writing was not just a commercial venture for Plath. She imagined the fiction writer's life as a fuller, deeper, more varied life because of the discipline of imagination:

> But the life of a Willa Cather, a Lillian Helman [sic], a Virginia Woolf—would it not be a series of rapid accents and probing descents into shades and meanings—into more people, ideas and conceptions? (Kukil, 44)

The "Journal 28 August 1957—14 October 1958" shows that Plath intended "this book year" to be a year in which she would take her fiction writing seriously. The typescript is full of detailed plans for stories and references to work on a novel:

> Typed old stories and verse dialogue to send off. Dug out some rough novel episodes. Some joy. Mainly despair. So single-viewed and sentimental: diary-like and vain. Will try now writing over each chapter as a story, with definite motion and climax, building up minor characters so they become actors, not just observed, like wallpaper, by the girl's eye. (Kukil, 311)

Plath's approach to imagining character is, characteristically, a combination of highbrow and lowbrow, of "indwelling with others" and reading true confessions:

> How does she live? Does she knit? Read true confessions. Oh, it is this indwelling with others, this meticulous gripping of detail to anchor the vague, unseen flaws and faults in internal geography, that must be done daily. (312)

"Indwelling with others" or at least an intense interest in the reality of other people's lives was already a habit for Plath. In the 1982 edition of the *Journals,* the miserable note Plath wrote to herself on a sheet of paper in the college infirmary is inserted chronologically into the diary. Kukil instead includes an appendix which shows that this miserable note is followed by a reverse of spirits on receiving a letter from one of her boyfriends—"Now to soaring, now to the heights!"—and then by a wonderful account of a conversation between Plath and the infirmary nurse. Plath records the nurse's conversation about her boyfriend Joe in so much detail that it reads like a dialogue in a novel, and Plath's own recorded responses reveal herself to be adept at drawing people into intimacy (533–37).

Plath's diaries are full of sketches of people who interest her. Her interest in people has many aspects. She is interested in their appearance, in their behaviour, in social relationships. The babysitting section of the LAW volume (the Smith college diary) is a marvellously multifaceted portrait of a household. The children feature in anecdotes which record their own sayings—"Clean doesn't feel good because you are all wet"—and are featured too in analyses of the psychology of the family and the different treatment given to the children according to gender and family position. The servants in the household are given equal attention, with passages recording the conversations in the kitchen and reflections on their lives and personalities. Her employers, Mr and Mrs Mayo, are closely observed preparing for a dinner party for "twenty crisp gay people" and Plath observes herself, the babysitter, almost as objectively, spreading cheese on Ritz crackers and wondering whether she is in the way. She considers her position in relation to the other members of the household, interested in particular in the complexity of her position socially in relation to the Mayos, ordered about with as little respect for her own leisure as a servant and yet spoken to as a social equal about the catering and company of the dinner party and even about her own interests, and with the advantage over the Mayos of youth in a youth-oriented society. Despite her interest in social position, her attitude is essentially democratic; she is interested in other people as an equal. She is interested in social positions not because they define people but because it is within these social positions that people interact with each other.

Gender relations are of still more intense interest to Plath. She is implicated more in her gender role than social status, to a certain extent identifying herself with the role and expectations of her sex, assuming the importance of babies to her one day and comparing herself to female role models taken from daily life—the author she meets, her tutors—as well as the literary models of Woolf, Hellman, and Cather. Her professional approach to her writing was unusual, but she married along with almost everyone else of her year. The Smith College archives include reunion books for certain years which record what happens to the girls after they leave college: at the 1960 reunion of the class of 1950, only eight women were still single, and most women counted their family as their most important achievement. (By 1980 most were working and many were divorced.) Plath's depiction and analysis of the dating scene in the LAW volume combines passionate involvement with stringent satire and imaginative reconstructions of how occasions might be perceived by the boys on the other side of the gender divide. A long entry on one date includes a discussion of the role of the movies in providing model manners and morals, and prompting sexual responses. The detailed descriptions of Plath's clothes revel in the fabrics and patterns of them, but also present her in them as a character in a movie or a magazine story, conscious that her self-image is dependent on the media for definition. Many of these entries describe herself in the third person, in contrast to the second person address to herself which asks the question of who she is in more psychological, less social, terms. Plath seems more sure of herself in the third person, in social situations, considering calmly her appearance and her effect on other people, than she does in the soul-searching second person addresses that have been retained in the *Journals* (1982).

The full journals, especially the "Journal July 1950—July 1953," are altogether more upbeat than they appear in the 1982 edition, and Plath's sensuousness has a much wider range. A great many passages on food have been omitted, often cut from entries otherwise retained, which show Plath to have had an enormous zest for eating. The entry for New Year's Eve, 1956, for example, includes in the original, as well as the night picnic described in the middle of the account, a dinner of roast beef at the beginning of the account and a wonderful description of breakfast at the end. The "Journal 28 August 1957—14 October 1958" also includes a large number of entries revealing an equal zest for sleeping, a sleep which in some entries seems more death- than life-oriented, a "sick, vinous, thick-furred sleep of exhaustion" that seems to have taken up most Saturday afternoons.

Much of the more upbeat material has been cut from the 1982 edition, probably due, in many instances, to the different shape of entry aimed for by the editors. In the LAW diary, Plath usually shapes entries very deliberately, with an introductory passage, an exploration of an idea or mood as far as she can take it, then often a modification of the mood, or a conclusion which puts the mood in context. Hughes and McCullough have edited entries down to the more intense passages at the heart of the entries.

Modifying sentences have been cut even from these central passages. The long passage in the *Journals* (1982) listing various disillusionments of growing up (20–23) has been extensively edited from the original passage of about twice the length. The complete list of disillusionments is much more varied, including political as well as personal disillusionment: "To study the futility of war, and read the UN charter, and then to hear the announcer on the radio blithely announce 'the stars and stripes march' for our courageous fighting forces" (Kukil, 36). In *The Haunting of Sylvia Plath*, Jacqueline Rose has noted the editing out of political material throughout the *Journals* (1982). Plath's moods in the original diaries are more varied, too. The portrait of the American man's ideal woman as a "sex machine . . . a painted doll," which in the edited journals dramatically concludes the entry, is followed in the full edition by the admission, "that there *are* some men who like a girl as a companion in mind as well as body, and want to take picnics in the sunlight instead of parking on a dark road at midnight after an evening of sexual stimulation while walking around a crowded dance floor and embracing breast to breast, stomach to stomach" (36). The whole entry is put into context at the end as an exercise in procrastination:

> To know that it is four twenty-three o'clock by the watch you got for graduation and that in three days you have your first exam and that you'd much rather read anything but what you have to, but you *do* have to, and you will, although you've wasted two hours writing stream of consciousness stuff in here when your stream isn't even much to brag, after all. (37)

Hughes and McCullough's editing of the journals is in some ways comparable to Leonard Woolf's editing of Woolf's diary into *A Writer's Diary*. Frances McCullough explains the principles behind their editing in the preface: "to include what seem to us the most important elements relating to her work, her inner life, and her valiant struggle to find herself and her voice. This leaves a great deal of material by the road . . . " (xii). It is significant that McCullough in this statement introduces the term "voice" which Hughes goes on to relate to Plath's "voice" as a poet, and, like Hughes, connects the struggle to find "herself" with the struggle to find a literary "voice." *The Journals* (1982) is not as consistently nor as narrowly a "writer's diary" as is the edited diary Leonard Woolf produces, but the effects of the editing are sometimes similar. Just as Leonard Woolf edits out the part of the sentence about having her ears pierced from Woolf's passage resolving to go out into the world, and so allows the resolve to seem to be filled by the subsequent mention of play-going in London, so in the *Journals* (1982) a note in the middle of a 1956 entry, "All this to stop crying" (127), seems to refer to Plath's interest in Baudelaire, Bergson, Blake, and Wallace Stevens, or possibly the act of writing in the diary itself. In the manuscript, it clearly refers to a shopping expedition in which her major purchase was a raincoat. Plath writes in a very Woolfian sentence: "Always feel happy shopping; gives me a sense of 'things' somehow: taste and color and touch, and a certain power and plenitude" (Kukil, 226). At the same time the choice of a raincoat as her "thing" to cheer her up is a very Plathian choice.

An earlier diary passage from May 1953 records another purchase of a raincoat, one which she could not afford but could not resist on account of its pink lining (183). The 1956 replacement that stopped her crying had "brazen gold buttons."

Janet Malcolm's illuminating account in *The Silent Woman: Sylvia Plath and Ted Hughes* of the politics involved in the publishing of various material relating to Plath's life explains Aurelia Plath's decision to publish the *Letters Home* as an attempt to counter what she felt was the negative portrayal of Plath in the *Journals* (1982) with the more positive self-portrait she produced for her mother in the letters she wrote.[16] The decision of course backfired, as most readers have seen in the discrepancy between the tone of the *Journals* (1982) and the *Letters Home* evidence of a false, even pathological, relationship between mother and daughter, and the letters are largely discredited. Ironically, the journals in manuscript form and as they appear now in Kukil's complete edition present Plath more as Aurelia Plath might have intended her to appear: socially assured, with an intense interest in other people, as well as her own life.

The distortions of the *Journals* (1982) are not just biographical. The editing of diaries into a selection of extracts preserves the authority of the moment against the integrity of the body of writing. The effect such editing has depends very much on the nature of the diary edited. The pieces of writing from which Katherine Mansfield's *Journal* was put together are little more than a collection of autonomous passages, and this remains the case even after they have been published in full. In editing Virginia Woolf's diary into the selection of extracts that Leonard Woolf published as *A Writer's Diary*, on the other hand, a continuity was lost that is an essential quality of the original writing. The *Journals* (1982) work as well as they do largely because of the qualities of detailed description and rhetorical syntax which belong so much to the moment of writing, and which can be preserved in a collection of extracts. To a certain extent all of Plath's writing has these qualities, but the much greater physicality and forceful rhetoric of the diaries compared, for example, to the letters, is a response too to the demands of the diary as a genre, and a response in particular to the demands of the singular entry and its location in a moment of writing. Yet Plath responded to other demands—or further potential—of the diary as well.

Plath's commercial approach to writing gave her an acute consciousness of genre. She subdivided genres according to her own categories, based on likely opportunities for publication, and magazine house styles: aiming to write a *Ladies Home Journal* or a *Seventeen* story, or, most ambitiously, after an anticipated five years work on it, a *New Yorker* story. Her poetry too she categorised, her main distinction being between what she called a "book poem" and a "non-book poem", a book poem being one worth including in her continually revised projected collection. In poetry too, however, she also recognised house styles, deciding in her diary that it "means something" to describe a poem as "The *New Yorker* sort."

All of Plath's writing shows a sensitivity to genre, whether intended for publication or not. An 'autobiography' written in high school as a school project, already shows a mastery of tone appropriate for the piece. She has chosen a style similar to the style of a magazine aimed at the teenage consumer, clichéd, romantic, gently ironic:

> And so there comes a time in your senior year of high school when, because you like the ocean and the wind and the sand, someone grins and drives you down to the sea; and because you like poetry, someone gives you a poetry anthology for graduation [. . .] And no matter how you change or grow up, there was a time when someone was terribly important.[17]

The letters she wrote to her mother, published in Aurelia Plath's selection *Letters Home*, show a similar awareness, and enjoyment, of genre. She plays on the formalities of the letter the way she plays with the strict poetic forms like the villanelle or the sonnet she frequently chooses for her early poetry. She varies her standard opening "Dear Mum" or "Dear Mother" with more effusive versions, like her confection of March 17, 1952, "Dearest-Mother-whom-I love-better-than-anyone" (84). At other times, her mother becomes her "Dearest Progenitor" (106, 114). When her mother received her driving license, she addressed her as her "Dear licensed mother" (189). She is just as inventive in closing her letters. The absence of such playful variations in the later letters may reflect a less playful state of mind, but also accompanies a move in her writing of poetry away from the use of more formal poetic forms to find her own rhythmic line.

The most important quality of the letter as a genre is a tone of intimacy, and Plath has a range of strategies for achieving this. She often opens a letter by establishing contact: "Your Saturday letter arrived today, and I felt the impulse to sit down and answer it" (197). She maintains the intimacy throughout the letters, guiding her mother's responses—"don't get *too* excited" (65)—or asking for advice or an opinion—"tell me what you think of my schemes" (90). The sense of the correspondence as a dialogue, a conversation, is supported by the references to Aurelia Plath's letters, and by the conversational language Plath uses: using italics to convey the stresses of spoken language, imitating a spoken drawl—"So-o-o, only about twelve more days" (74)—and using conversational phrases like "speaking again of Henry and Liz" (88), "needless to say" (146), and "as you may have gathered" (63). The impression is given of letters written with spontaneity, with the ease of conversation.

It seems likely they *were* written easily. She could not have written so many—649 in the 13 years between her beginning college and her death, often long letters of a thousand words or so—had she written them in the painstaking way she is described as writing her early poetry, thesaurus on hand. But the ease with which she wrote them doesn't mean they weren't written with skill; rather the letters were easy for her to write *because* of her skill at writing in the genre of correspondence. At the same time, that it is a skill to convey intimacy and spontaneity doesn't mean the intimacy and spontaneity aren't real.

Plath's journal writing differs in style as much as in material, and her sense of the demands both of genre and style are likely to have determined the contents of her diaries as much as of the letters: "style will determine material." The *Journals* (1982) or even the manuscript diaries do not necessarily present the true picture of her life as opposed to the false, censored picture she presented in the letters to her mother. The enthusiastic, determinedly rational plans for the future that make up so much of the *Letters Home* probably fulfil a similar function to the plans for the future that fill Antonia White's diary, but they do not fit the more intense narrative and analysis of Plath's journal writing the way they do the looser, more fragmented style of White's diary or the eager spontaneity of *Letters Home*. Both the style and content of Plath's diaries must have been formed partly in opposition to the letters, or to complement the letters. The letters in fact fulfil some of the functions of a diary. Aurelia Plath saw the letters as fulfilling, potentially, the same function as Woolf anticipated her diary as fulfilling. Both Woolf and Plath regularly, almost daily, recorded personal news in considerable detail, and just as Woolf anticipated rereading the diary when she was older and drawing on it for her memoirs, so did Aurelia Plath keep all Sylvia Plath's letters with "the dream of one day handing Sylvia the huge packet of letters [. . .] [to] make use of them in stories, in a novel, and through them meet herself at the varied stages of her development."[18]

Plath's use of genre, even in her personal and apparently spontaneous writing, is accomplished, deliberate, and responsive to the effects that the genre allows. Her request for undated journals in 1945 represents the beginning of her exploration of the possibilities of the genre of the diary, which continued to take different forms up to the last remaining extant material, the "Notes for Neighbours" she kept in 1962. The more formal structure she gave the early LAW volume reflects her enjoyment of formal structures in personal correspondence and her early poetry, but she continued to experiment with form in the many distinct diaries and journals she kept. The different volumes she kept have purposes and styles distinct from her other private writing and distinct from each other. In the mid-1950s diaries are often brief, covering a specific period in her life, such as the twenty-four page typescript diary of her visit to Paris in 1956, the thirty-three page typescript describing her life in Cambridge and the first meeting with Ted Hughes, and her typescripts from her stay in Spain after her marriage. Later volumes are more inclusive and sprawling but continue to take on a style distinctive to each volume which, to a certain extent, determines the content of the entries. Diaries such as the notes made in response to her analysis with Dr Ruth Beuscher in 1959, and the journal she kept at Yaddo, the writers' retreat, address specific concerns and the style is adapted correspondingly.

Introducing the 1982 edition of The *Journals*, Hughes presents the writing in terms of the "voice" Plath writes in and the "real self" from which that voice comes. This is not the ordinary self of Plath's everyday life. Hughes claims, "I never saw her show her real self to anyone." He distinguishes, too, between the "self" expressed in the journal and the poetry and the "false selves," the "many masks," that he felt her prose writing expressed. Hughes' reading of Plath's development as a writer in terms of "a drive" or "process of alchemy" towards this "rebirth" of a "real self" is remarkably consistent, from an essay he wrote as early as 1965 for the Poetry Book Society Bulletin, to his account of Plath's life and writing he gives in his 1998 auto/biographical poetry collection *Birthday Letters*. Plath's poems, he consistently argues, should be read together, as together they make up a single work. In a 1970 article on "The Chronological Order of Sylvia Plath's Poems," Hughes stresses that "the separate poems build up into one long poem. She faced a task in herself and her poetry is the record of her progress in the task. The poems are chapters in a mythology . . . "[18] To Hughes, the interpretation of the *Journals* (1982) as a supporting document charting the same "task in herself" that Plath underwent as a poet seemed obvious. Just as Aurelia Plath assumed that readers would recognise in the *Letters Home* a more complex and more empathetic Sylvia Plath than she saw presented by the increasingly rigid Plath myth, so Hughes assumed that readers would recognise the *Journals* (1982) as supporting, along with the poetry, the single interpretation of the Plath "mythology" as he understood it.

But just as the "self" from which Plath writes belongs to a physical body, as Plath in her writing is so vividly aware, so too does the "voice" of Plath's prose belong to a body of writing, from which it cannot be extracted without altering the nature of the work. While Hughes' interpretation of the *Journals* (1982) as the charting of a "process of alchemy" reduces it to a single function shared with the poetry, at the same time he reads each single entry as an autonomous entry supporting this overall interpretation, without any regard to the significance of the sequence and the formal integrity of each individual diary Plath kept. Similarly, as the editor of *Ariel*, Hughes showed little regard to Plath's original ordering sequence for the poems, making his selection according to his own criteria for publication, judging each poem as an autonomous work. Plath, however, frequently withheld poems from one collection for publication, in order to publish them later in a different context. The original ordering of *Ariel*, as Marjorie Perloff revealed in 1979 and Linda Bundzten examined in detail in *The Other Ariel* (2001), carefully orchestrated an emotional arc that would lead the reader back from the difficult material at the heart of the collection. As is now well known, Plath's arrangement of the collection saw it beginning with the word "love" and ending with the word "spring."

A diary, of course, does not lend itself to the same kind of organisation and rearrangement of material that is involved in putting together a collection of poetry, and it is difficult to control in the same way a diary's narrative arc. Despite Plath's attention to the structure of each diary she kept, she never formally concluded any of her diaries. The closest any of Plath's diaries come to concluding is with the entry she wrote for Saturday, September 27, 1958. Coming towards the end of journal she kept from August 1957 to October 1958, the entry begins "I shall end these pages, I hope, in a more placid, optimistic mind that heretofore," and ends, "I have worked hard today on my bird story—words come right, rhythms come right, here, there & it is the beginning of a new life" (423). But it is followed by another entry which begins, "A moment snatched, two and a half weeks later, chicken & squash ready in the oven for Ted's return from the library, back achey, eyes bleary from new job," and ends with a list of fears and a quote from Defoe. The rest of the volume is taken up with a list of names, most of them presumably intended as potential names for fictional characters, the list of names for boys and girls potential names for her own children. Each one of Plath's journal volumes simply leaves off, stopping in mid-structure with its final entry. But Plath began new journals again and again. The "voice" of Plath's diary writing is different in every journal she keeps, while belonging in every volume very much to the genre of the diary, even as the genre is manipulated, explored, and extended to create, finally, a new form of the diary, with a new form of continuity.

7 The Dash

"I love this book, black point of pen skidding over smooth paper," writes Sylvia Plath in 1954 (Kukil, 322). Keeping a diary had become at this stage in her marriage a matter of "moments snatched, & wildly snatched, between duty and duty," a description lent conviction by the way the previous entry leaves off: "Class notes tomorrow: must—& dinner—" (339). Virginia Woolf similarly describes her entries in the diary as "hurried notes" that she writes when she can "snatch a moment from what Morgan calls 'life'" (3:164). Ben Cheever, questioning whether there would be patterns to be found in John Cheever's journal entries, cautioned me that it is "important to remember that usually, my father just sat down at the typewriter and typed until he was done."[1]

However rushed the writing, the form of the diary has its own effects. A diarist like Woolf or Plath consciously manipulates these effects, Woolf drawing attention to the "andness" of life as it is recorded in the diaries, Plath trying out different formal structures in different kinds of volumes or arrangements of papers. Other diarists write as if the diary really is a "formless" genre, using it as Antonia White does as a way of filling in time while waiting for real communication with another person, or as a way of putting off the writing that would count for her as real work: "Have wasted a whole morning in this stupid repetitious stuff about E" (2:107). Mansfield scribbled notes on shopping lists, in old exercise books, on scraps of paper, making the distinction between diary material and other kinds of writing problematic. Yet there is a coherence to both Murry's publication of her journal as a "journal intime" and Scott's edition of the papers as a writer's working papers. Cheever too may have just sat down and typed without regard to the formal structure within which he was working; indeed he may not have been working "within" a formal structure at all, simply accumulating journal entries on sheets of paper; yet the body of work which accrued was something he recognised towards the end of his life as a literary achievement.

Form has a powerful effect even on aspects of literary style which distinguish the work of a writer across genres. Cheever's use of abstractions both to enlarge the significance of material detail and to provide closure at the level of form or rhetoric, Orton's juxtaposition of mundane trivia with narratives of sex and death, and Plath's use of repetition for rhetorical effect are characteristic enough of each writer's style as to be understood in terms of "voice." It is the power and distinction of the writer's voice which is most readily recognised as giving a diary text its coherence. As a result, the importance of the diary form, and the role of the editor, can be easily overlooked. In the previous chapters I have aimed to address this by examining in detail the effects of diary form, the significance of the autonomous entry, and the effects of sequence. Yet Woolf's description of dashing off "hurried notes" and White's distinction between the real work of writing fiction and the wasted time of diary writing suggest that diarists might write differently in the diary at the level of the sentence as well as at the level of form. It is not just later, in the editing process, that writing a novel or other literary work involves a different kind of work, though obviously the process of revision is one of the crucial steps involved in writing a literary work and one that is not, usually, involved in keeping a diary. In this chapter and the two that follow, I look more closely at diary style, focusing on what is distinctive about the way the six writers in this study write in the diary genre.

Writing on diary style has tended to make little distinction between structural effects and style at the level of the sentence. The fragmentary, interrupted narrative that is constructed through an accumulation of individual entries is assumed to require a fragmentary, interrupted style of writing. Judy Nolte Lensinck suggests "we can look at diary language," to find a specifically female "private, plain-speaking voice," and yet her analysis of the 4,000 word diary she studies as a test case for her proposal to "expand the boundaries of criticism" by including the diary focuses not on language so much as on imagery and narrative as it is constructed over time. Rebecca Hogan's useful discussion of the detail in the diary, which takes its significance from the diary's "dailiness" (and more particularly, I argue, from the diary structure as a succession of independent passages), makes a similar connection to a more general "feminine" style of writing that is fragmented and fluid, and, she suggests, again citing Cixous, "potentially subversive of the structures, logic, and syntax of masculine language." Elizabeth Podnieks cites many of these same critics while making a further connection between the diary's "fragmentary" style and the similarly "fragmented" writing found in modernist writing.

Is "diary language" actually any different, at the level of the sentence, from language as it is written in any other genre? Is it more "plain-speaking," as Lensinck suggests, more "fragmented," as most theorists suggest, more "fluid," and different from a more "masculine" writing in its syntax? The most systematic study of diary style has, unfortunately, not been published in monograph form, but Andrew Hassam's 1983 PhD thesis "Style and Convention in the Diary: An Investigation with Reference to the Reader" does usefully survey what he argues are the definitive features of the diary. Hassam's concern is to shift readings of the diary away from the "evaluative," and particularly away from readings that focus on questions of authenticity and sincerity, which often involve assumptions about the diarist's sense of privacy on the one hand or audience on the other. Determined to read the diary "not as a product of an essential human nature in contact with the spirit of an age, but as a rule-governed reading process" he redefines every stylistic feature in terms of a "reader convention," so that, for instance, the "abbreviation, ellipsis and lexical repetition" he finds in the text equates to the reader convention that "The style is free from organised exposition and is written quickly." In fact, what he insistently terms "reader conventions" could equally be called "reader assumptions" about the writer's intentions or methods—here, he attributes to the "reader" an assumption about the speed of writing. Indeed, each reader convention he lists could as reasonably be called a *writer* convention, since each is based on stylistic features which a writer has written. Hassam's identification of key features of the diary such as indeterminacy, abbreviation, and ellipsis does, however, provide a useful starting point for further work on diary stylistics. It is interesting to note that while these diary features are similar to those mentioned by the feminist theorists as characteristic of women's writing, Hassam takes for his examples the diaries of George Gissing, Evelyn Waugh, and George Orwell.

In the next chapter I look at the sentence fragment, which for Hassam is a key feature distinguishing the diary from other genres, and distinguishing the genuine diary from the fake diary. This chapter looks at the dash, listed by Hassam as just more feature correlated with the casual style and rapid writing typical of the diary. While the sentence fragment, along with the short entry, might be the most obvious marker of an "ordinary" diary, so that a notebook could be recognised as a diary through the length of the sentences and length of entries before a word has been read, it is the dash which has a similar prominence on the page of more literary diaries from the eighteenth century onwards. Anne Olivier Bell explains in the preface to Woolf's diary that "her almost invariable use of the ampersand has been retained" as it "suggests the pace of her writing,"[2] and indeed the number of ampersands in Woolf's sentences makes a distinct impact on the typography of the published diary. But more typical of the typography of the diary is the scattering of dashes, almost as thick on the pages of Woolf's diary as they are in the diaries of Fanny Burney, B. R. Haydon, Eugenia Wynne, and Lord Byron.

The dash, like the ampersand, suggests a rapid pace of writing, the name of the mark itself suggesting speed—Woolf herself often writes of "dashing off" a piece of writing. It is a mark that is quick to make, just a dash of the pen across the page, and it permits a looser syntactic interpretation than is permitted by punctuation marks such as the colon, semi-colon, comma, or period, all of which define the relations of one clause to another with more specificity than the dash. The dash allows a quickness of thought which moves from one idea to another without syntactic analysis. Writing about Shakespeare in her diary, Woolf links his "stretch and speed" as if the "pliancy" she goes on to mention and the speed of writing are naturally to be found together. She describes the "genius" of Shakespeare's writing using the kinds of terms that might more usually describe a star athlete, commenting on how his power "utterly outpace[s] and outrace[s] my own." She goes on to suppose, making the kind of assumptions Hassam suggests readers make of diary writing, that "Even the less known & worser plays are written at a speed that is quicker than anyone else's quickest; & the words drop so fast one can't pick them up" (3:301). Writing fast, for Woolf, then, did not mean writing less well than writing at a more considered pace; rather "speed" gives writing "stretch." This was a quality she often describes herself seeking for her diary, worrying at one point that she might have "worked through the layer of style which suited it—suited the comfortable bright hour after tea, & the thing I've reached now is less pliable" (2:24).

In her essay "Women and Fiction," Woolf writes of "the technical difficulty—so simple, apparently; in reality, so baffling—that the very form of the sentence does not fit her. It is a sentence made by men; it is too loose, too heavy, too pompous for a woman's use."[3] Woolf must have been very conscious of her own legacy of male writing, choosing as a girl to take up the tradition of three generations of (male) Stephen writers. Her father Leslie Stephen's sentences in his collected essays (with the very masculine title *Men, Books and Mountains*) are relatively taut—short and to the point—but they are weighty, each building on the sentence before and leading up to the sentence that follows.[4] Conjunctive adverbs like *however, moreover,* and *therefore* clarify the links between each sentence, and explanatory phrases clarify his train of thought further: "My reason is simply that..." (17); "this leads to a further inquiry" (24); "To explain myself more clearly, let me take a particular instance" (27); "To that question I think that an answer may be suggested by one fact" (27). The punctuation defines the relation of the clauses to one another with commas, semi-colons, colons, and full stops. So vague a piece of punctuation as the dash has little place in his writing.

Woolf uses all the punctuation marks of her inheritance, but to her own effect. She moves easily from one kind of sentence to another. In her last entry before a trip to Cornwall in March 1921, she sums up the gossip she heard at tea with Vanessa in short sentences of one or two short clauses. She ends the entry with a final paragraph of one sentence: "As for other news, I think I have never said that Lytton stays at home with Lady Strachey, who has taken to fainting on the floor."[5] The next entry in the diary, written on the last day of the Cornwall holiday, is very different in tone and in style:

> This is the last evening, & L. is packing, & I'm not in the mood for writing, but feel superstitiously that I should like to read something actually written in Cornwall. By looking over my left shoulder I see gorse

> yellow against the Atlantic blue, running up, a little ruffled, to the sky, today hazy blue. And we've been lying on Gurnard's Head, on beds of samphire among grey rocks with buttons of yellow lichen on them. How can I pick out the scene? You look down onto the semi-transparent water—the waves all scrambled into white around the rocks—gulls swaying on bits of seaweed—rocks now dry now drenched with white waterfalls pouring down crevices. (2:105)

The long lazy sentences, full of pauses, give way easily to the run of dashes in the last, more conscientiously descriptive sentence. The dashes between each item of description suggest each detail is seen complete and autonomous in itself. The details no longer shape the sentence or the scene, but could be added to indefinitely, altering only the length of the sentence. Rather than describing a scene already complete in the mind's eye, Woolf seems to be scanning the scene as she writes, the focus shifting with each dash. In contrast, the formal punctuation of the sentence about Lytton and Lady Strachey, which concludes the previous entry in the diary, sets the focus on a scene that encapsulates a situation with a single image.

The same contrast between description and narrative, informal and formal punctuation, can be found within a single sentence later in the same volume in the diary:

> Again I have a gallery of little bright portraits hanging against the wall of my mind—Nessa—Bobo—Bob—Kot—Pippa—to be exact; Nessa just back from France, alighting for a fortnight, & then off again, leaving the children, who have meanwhile got influenza, to Paris. (2:156)

The dash is a democratic punctuation mark, giving an equal spacing to everyone on her mind. More formal punctuation with commas resumes in the second half of the sentence, as the narrative gets going again.

The dash can be used to more expressive effect. Writing on a "cold dull day after all this blaze," Woolf describes her state of mind as "10 miles distant—far away—detached—very jaded now" (4:244). The dash is used here in a way quite similar to the previous two instances, as she describes phrase by phrase aspects of her mood. But the rephrasing of "distant" as "far away" and then as "detached" does not really add detail to the image so much as it adds to the sense of distance, with the dashes further contributing to a sense of strung-out spaciousness and distance. In a more agitated passage earlier in the diary, the dash cuts up sentences into a "tremor" like the tremor in which she finds herself:

> I'm in such a tremor that I've botched the last—penultimate chapter of Flush—is it worth writing that book—& can scarcely sit still, & must therefore scribble here, making myself form my letters, because—oh ridiculous crumpled petal—Wishart is publishing L.'s snap shot of me

> instead of the Lenare photograph [. . .] Now I'm all of a quiver—can't read or write [. . .] What an ill joined web of nerves—to be kind—my being is! (4:123–24)

And later in the passage, the prose quivers even more:

> on my walk—too long—I was tired—& leapt in my bed dreaming that Angelica was dead—what a dream—how vivid—on my walk I almost felt my mind glow like hot iron—so complete & holy was the old habitual beauty of England. (4:124)

Yet Woolf also uses conventional punctuation with unconventional expressiveness. In a remarkable passage describing a faint she writes "my heart leapt; & stopped; & leapt again;" using the semi-colon to stop the sentence after each clause, with a juddering like the stopping of her heart. The whole passage mixes short clauses, long clauses, short sentences, long sentences, heavy punctuation, with stretches without any punctuation, to mirror the curious rhythms and spatial and temporal distortions of the "faint" (4:121).

Woolf has not just stretch and speed, but stretch and speeds. Her use of punctuation is remarkable for the way she slows down and speeds up the prose, either in a way expressive of what she describes or to keep pace with the rhythm of her thoughts. The dash itself can be used either to speed up or slow down her writing. When she describes "the pounding straining horses with red faced jockeys lashing them pound by" at the Lewes races, the dashes seem to add to the sense of speed and weight: "What a noise they made—what a sense of muscle hard & stretched—& beyond the downs this windy sunny day looked wild & remote" (4:120). Another time the dash is used to imitate the slowest of speech, "like a heavy wardrobe; all heavy angular sentences. I noted how my own rushing pace, seemed too rushing, & after 10 minutes had adapted itself to Bunny. How—do—you—start—an—aeroplane?" (4:246). Her sense that her own pace is naturally a "rushing pace" seems true too of the pace of the diary. Although she slows the pace down in places for effect, the overall pace is a rapid one. Even the changes in speed are rapid changes, like sudden yet smooth changes of gear.

She was very conscious of her differing speeds of composition and the effects of others on her pace. She complains that "Vita's prose is too fluent" and "makes my pen run" whereas on reading the classics "I am curbed &—not castrated: no, the opposite" (3:126). On the whole, though, she presents fluency as something to be desired. She exults over the speed with which she wrote *To the Lighthouse*:

> I rush at it, & at once scatter out two pages. Is it nonsense, is it brilliance? Why am I so flown with words, & apparently free to do exactly

> what I like? When I read a bit it seems spirited too; needs compressing, but not much else. Compare this dashing fluency with the excruciating hard wrung battles I had with Mrs Dalloway. (3:75)

And her pleasure in "dashing in" *Orlando*, another novel which "came with a rush" (3:161), contrasts with her anxiety over the slow progress of "Waves or Moths or whatever it is to be called":

> One thinks one has learnt to write quickly, & one hasn't. And what is odd, I'm not writing with gusto or pleasure: because of the concentration. I am not reeling it off; but sticking it down. (3:259)

The pace of White's diary is as different as her punctuation. Her use of the dash is infrequent and conventional. She rarely uses it except to separate a subordinate clause from the main clause of a sentence, either at the end of the sentence or in the middle in place of parentheses. The effect is more democratic than that of parentheses, giving the subordinate clause a more equal weight with the main clause. She does in fact usually prefer parentheses to the dash. Indeed her frequent use of parentheses is one of the distinctive features of her punctuation, along with the frequent use of commas and colons and full stops. The effect is a much slower, more ponderous pace than is produced by Woolf's diary prose. She writes a prose full of pauses and stops, a reflective prose. The number of short sentences in many entries does not give an impression of haste, but of weight; sentences such as "I wish I loved my children more" leave no more to be said, but are not easily hurried on from either.[6] In other instances, the short sentence provides a pause for her to rebound from: "I am sorry for Frances. She is married to a conceited, egotistic fool who is too vain and sure of himself even to mind being cuckolded."

Where clauses are joined together in a more complex sentence, often it is through the use of a colon, the punctuation mark closest to a full stop. The clause following a colon in White's diary will give a consequence of the first clause, or explain it, or elaborate on it: "She was completely different: like her old self: warm and friendly" (191); "Lyndall is like me: she withers without stimulus" (286). There is always more to be said on further thought. White's habit of writing lists allows for the possibility of adding more indefinitely. Her sentences are often extended by subordinate clauses in parentheses. She is always modifying what she writes, or pausing to comment on it within the sentence: "Getting supper for him (rather unexpected)" (35); "Acute pleasure (tinged with envy)" (35); "From Carroll (who after all is not omniscient and whom I may have misunderstood) I do not get that impression" (127). Susan Chitty, in the introduction, describes the diary as "internal" with its focus always on internal events, on White's own emotions, rather than on external events that happen in the world.

Her punctuation, too, could be described as "internal," enclosing clauses within clauses, as her sentences probe deeper and deeper into her feelings.

While Woolf also writes in detail about her emotional states, with punctiliously detailed passages annotating her mental states in illness and incipient insanity, the effect is not "internal" in the same way. Her different prose style and punctuation, with the bubbling dashes, ampersands, commas, and semicolons, keep the descriptions of her emotions on the surface along with her brilliant, exacting descriptions of landscapes, parties, and people. She imagines the days she fails to record as "allowed to waste like a tap left running."[7] There is something of the fluidity of a running tap in the days she records, as well. It is this fluidity which is expressed through her use of the dash.

Yet the dash can work to slow pace down, and to open up an interior, emotional space. In returning to the dash, I want to turn for a moment away from the diary to look at the work of Emily Dickinson, of all writers surely the first to come to mind when thinking about the dash. In her poetry, we can see most clearly the effects of abandoning formal punctuation almost entirely in favour of the dash. Dickinson herself described her poetry as her "letter to the world," a phrase which could describe the diary as a genre, especially the published diary, and one of the most useful studies of the stylistic features most typical of the diary, including the dash, can be found not in diary criticism or even autobiography studies but in Cristanne Miller's book *Emily Dickinson: A Poet's Grammar.* Dickinson's "poet's grammar" is shown to be surprisingly close to what could be called a diarist's grammar.

In Dickinson's poetry, as in Woolf's prose, the dash is used more often for expressive effect than for syntactic clarification. Unusually, Dickinson uses the dash to separate not clauses within sentences, but words within clauses. Like Woolf she uses the dash to manipulate pace: "Tell Her just how the fingers—hurried—/Then—how they—stammered—slow—slow—"[8] Characteristic of Dickinson's writing in particular is her use of the dash to emphasise a word. The effect is different from the emphasis of italics; it is less forceful, less emphatic, more reflective and yet weighty: "Its bright impossibility/To dwell—delicious—on—" (245). Her use of the dash at the end of a poem leaves a similar space for reflection, which seems to add a retrospective weight to what has gone before.

Another stylistic feature shared with Woolf is Dickinson's unusually frequent use of the conjunction *and*, along with the other co-ordinate conjunctions *or*, *but*, and *so*. Dickinson's style is paratactic: an idea or story is not built up in a clearly laid out progression of stages, as in a Leslie Stephen essay, for example; rather it must be constructed out of statements and images in simple juxtaposition. Words such as *however, indeed, thus, therefore, rather, instead*, which form the backbone of Leslie Stephen's prose, and which in English prose in general are, together, almost as frequent as the co-ordinate conjunctions Dickinson prefers, are almost entirely missing from Dickinson's poetry. Just as the dash is both characteristic of diary style and seems to reflect at the level of punctuation the lack of closure which characterises the diary at the level of form, so the paratactic construction of sentences in the diary, with the frequent use in particular of the conjunction *and,* seems to reflect the parataxis of the diary form with its juxtapositions of entries.

Miller's analysis of Dickinson's grammar focuses particularly on the parallels between her poetry and patterns of speech on the one hand, and between her poetry and "feminine" language patterns on the other.[9] Spoken language is similarly paratactic in its connections, relying on juxtaposition rather than defining the logic of its progression. The connection this suggests with diary style is underlined by Miller's emphasis on the sentence fragment, as a key marker of parataxis in spoken language. A further characteristic of spoken language is the use of questions and exclamations. Again, while Miller points to the number of questions and exclamations in Dickinson's poetry, diaries too are typically punctuated more than other prose by question and exclamation marks. "Cant I expand & embalm & become a sentient living creature! Lord how I suffer!" Woolf exclaims in the diary, and "By God!—what stuff I'm writing!"[10] Questions may be used to continue a narrative—"I said that Richmond was enthusiastic over my James article? Well, two days ago, little elderly Walkley attacked it" (2:29)—or they may stop narrative—"But why do I say this? Now I say it, I don't feel it" (2:72). The effect is indeed like speech, as if Woolf were having a conversation with herself. The dialogic quality of diary prose is explored further in Chapter 9, on the use of the first and second personal pronouns in the diary.

Writing of Dickinson's use of feminine language conventions in her poetry, Miller phrases her thesis carefully, suggesting that Dickinson "uses at least to some extent a 'women's language,' that is, a language that American culture associates with the feminine, and therefore usually with women."[11] Such careful phrasing acknowledges linguistic evidence about other factors which also influence language conventions, such as race and class, as well as Miller's own study of language conventions in magazines. This fascinating study of men's and women's magazines found that the written prose of the magazines was differentiated according to the projected audience of the magazines, so that the women's magazines were written in a style conforming to the notion of a woman's language, whether the article was written by a male or female journalist. Miller found a similarity between the language of these women's magazines and the language of Dickinson's poetry, as well as with some of the features of language that empirical studies have shown to distinguish women's speech, such as the increased use of sentence fragments, questions, and exclamations, already discussed as common features of spoken language in general. Women's speech, then, shows more markers of spoken language than does men's speech, as does writing for women's magazines and writing in the diary.

If the same collection of features appear together in Dickinson's poetry, the diary as a genre, and "a language that American culture associates with the feminine, and therefore usually with women," this does not necessarily support a reading of diary style in terms of an essentialist idea of an écriture féminine. These features are associated with each other in part because of effects they have in common with each other, each of these features contributing to an open-endedness, an indefiniteness, a multi-directional quality to the logic of the prose: what Woolf calls "pliancy." The closeness of diary language to spoken language can be considered in terms of the relation between the diary and the familiar letter, and the dialogic quality of a genre which can be seen as a form of telling oneself about oneself, as Julien Green puts it.[12] Yet diary language is not just spoken language written down. Orton's diary is conventional in its punctuation, with only infrequent and conventional use of the dash, but it is full of sentence fragments. These are sentence fragments used, however, to a deliberately literary effect, owing very little to spoken conventions and far more to written conventions of the postcard, the telegram, and of course the diary itself: diarists as far back as Pepys have tended to write in sentence fragments: "And so to bed." The dash itself cannot be a feature of spoken language, since it is only apparent on the page. While it can be used to reflect the rhythms of spoken language, and its replacement of more formal punctuation also suggests the parataxis of spoken language, it is often used in the diary to a far more stylised and heightened effect. The dash does, however, express the openness associated with an informal use of language, an openness particularly suited to the diary which is structured around an openness of form. The dash avoids closure, holding open gaps in sentences and paragraphs.

Dickinson's most distinctive use of the dash is in the place of a full stop at the end of a sentence, a strikingly odd use of a punctuation mark which is more conventionally used in the place of parentheses. Yet it is fitting in poems that are so often about openness, and which suggest perfection is lost in definition and expression:

> What I see not, I better see—
> Through Faith—my Hazel Eye
> Has periods of shutting—
> But, No lid has Memory—(440)

The dash can leave a poem open quite simply like a door left open:

> Noon—is the Hinge of Day—
> Evening—the Tissue Door—
> Morning—the East compelling the sill
> Till all the World is ajar—(437)

The poem left open is larger in a sense than a poem ending with a full stop, as if it goes on beyond its own form. Dickinson is interested in what cannot be contained. A poem about the smallness of a coffin, in contrast to the immeasurability of the life contained in it, describes the amplitude of its contents to the mourner as "Circumference without Relief—/ Or Estimate—or End—" ending appropriately with a dash, and attributing to the coffin a circularity and formlessness like that of the diary.

The use of the dash to suggest what cannot be contained is characteristic of the diary, and accounts for how favoured the dash is in the diaries of the Romantic period. Byron even uses the dash as if it were a noun: "I feel most things, but I know nothing except - - -" with the three dashes drawn on top of each other. One of the diaries most heavily scored with dashes is the diary of Benjamin Haydon, whose diary was literally left open when he died, and whose writing in the diary constantly gestures towards the emotions that lie beyond written language. These gestures towards openness typically accompany endings, as, for instance, when he plays off the ending of a year and the ending of an entry against the uncontainability of his sentiments:

> This is the last night of the year 1809—a year perhaps of greater Idleness and folly, disappointment and anxiety I have not experienced since I commenced my Studies— . . . my mind is pregnant with hopes, & wishes, plans and schemes & industry & ambition. O God, I humbly ask thee to pardon my past wickedness, on condition of future virtue— . . . O God, listen to me, listen to my last prayer, uttered in the sincerity of pungent repentance. Amen—Amen—Amen—[13]

The diary even ends with a dash, with a final entry remarkable in its ambivalence between openness and closure:

> God forgive—me—Amen.
> Finis
> of
> B.R. Haydon
> 'Stretch me no longer on this tough World'—Lear.
> End—(223)

As a young girl, Mansfield set herself to reading Byron's poetry and the three volumes of his *Life and Letters* as an act of self-definition (the character Juliet in her autobiographical fiction hides Byron in her shirt before committing several acts of defiance). In her diary she uses the dash frequently for the same reason Byron and Haydon use it, to evoke what cannot be expressed in words, what cannot be contained in prose: "Let me remember when I write about the fiddle how it runs up lightly and swings down sorrowful; how it *searches*—" (170) She will often end a paragraph or an entry with a dash, holding open the intensity of feeling and the sense of uncontainable sentiment—the sublime—that the entry has evoked. The dash evokes the indefinable, yet she uses it to precise effect. The dash holds the prose poised: "When you lean over the edge of the rock and see something lovely and brilliant flashing at the bottom of the sea it is only the clear, trembling water that dances—but—can you be quite sure?" (78).

Whereas Woolf looked for a sentence "capable [. . .] of enveloping the vaguest shapes," Mansfield describes herself as "a powerful stickler for form," and she declares, "I hate the sort of licence that English people give themselves . . . to spread over and flop and roll about. I feel as fastidious as though I write with acid."[14] The dash might be supposed to be too imprecise a punctuation mark for Mansfield to make so much use of. Yet Mansfield uses the dash to precise effect. It is interesting to compare her use of the dash with her use of ellipses, both of which are used frequently, and both of which are used to avoid closure and suggest more left unsaid. She uses the ellipses often when writing of the state of her soul: "What dread to live in! But what's the use of saying aught? No, my soul, be quiet . . . " (181); "Shall I get through this, too? It is not easy still to find the courage to cope with these onslaughts . . . " (181); "There is nothing worse for the soul than egoism. Therefore . . . " (226). The ellipses give a dreamier effect than does the dash. The absence of definition is less definite a gap, less forceful, less felt. Ellipses cannot be used as a noun, the way Byron uses the dash, or the way Mansfield could be said to use the dash in this sentence: "To go to Sierre, if it goes on like this . . . or to—or to—" (197).

The ellipses would be unlikely, too, to follow an italicised word, as the dash does, to add emphasis and weight to the word, in the same way Dickinson uses the dash to emphasis a capitalised word. Mansfield uses a dash before *le mot juste*: "they are in the good old English parlance—*monkeys*" (91). A whole phrase can be given a subtle stress with a suspenseful dash: "A. came—and did not ring" (86). Often, the dash gives the sense of the "moment of writing" that structures the *Journal*, as if she jots down a dash as she stops to think of the best word: "I like the temper of that extremely—and does it not reveal the man? Disillusioned and yet—amused—worldly, and yet he has feeling" (199). She pauses sometimes too on finding the right word, to repeat it, and savour it: "My despair simply disappeared—yes, simply" (131). Mansfield's precise choice of words, her "fastidious" choice not just of the form but of the content of her prose, is matched by the precision of her punctuation which gives her prose the pliancy to follow the rhythms of her thought and achieve exact emotional effects.

Woolf writes in "Women and Fiction" of the need for the woman writer to find "an ordinary and usual type of sentence [. . .] one that takes the natural shape of her thought without crushing or distorting it."[15] The diary, written on a regular basis over a number of years, is a natural place to practise "an ordinary and usual type of sentence." The subject of the diary being the thoughts of the writer, every diarist must work to develop a style that "takes the natural shape" of his or her thoughts. The styles developed by individual diarists vary considerably, and all diarists have their own idiosyncratic grammar and use of punctuation. Punctuation that is typical of the diary then is paradoxically that which can be used in atypical and various ways. Characteristic grammatical constructions such as the sentence fragment, and punctuation such as the dash, suggest the hurried pace at which the diary is generally written, and to write at this pace "an ordinary and usual type of sentence [. . .] that takes the natural shape of her thought" is essential, although to take the natural shape of his or her thought, the type of sentence that becomes ordinary and usual to the individual writer may be highly unusual and innovative. The dash allows for innovation, with its loose definition of syntax and the range of effects it gives depending on where it is placed within a sentence.

When the diarist is also writing for publication, the innovations made in the diary may be taken up in their literary work. H. Porter Abbott argues that "Woolf's modernist oeuvre was deeply inflected by her personal writing—in particular by her habit of keeping a diary."[16] He notes the similarity between the intention for a new kind of literary writing Woolf described in her diary of 1920—a form of writing in which "one thing should open out of another" in a way that would "give the looseness and lightness I want," that would "keep form & speed, & enclose everything, everything"—and her intention already formulated three months earlier to find a new way of using the form of the diary to create something "loose knit, & yet not slovenly, so elastic it will embrace anything" (241). The "looseness and lightness" that can be found in the diary depends, like Woolf's fiction, on both "form & speed." When Virginia Woolf praises Dorothy Richardson's development of "the psychological sentence of the feminine gender," she might be describing the sentence she herself developed in the diary, a sentence "of a more elastic fibre than the old, capable of stretching to the extreme."[17]

8 Sentence Fragments

In a poem he calls "Diary Cows", young Adult author Ronald Koertge plays on the conventions of diary prose:

> Got up early, waited for the farmer.
> He hooked us all to the machines as
> usual. Typical trip to the pasture,
> typical day grazing and ruminating.
> About 5:00 back to the machines. What
> relief! Listened to the radio
> during dinner. Lights out at 7:00.
> More tomorrow.[1]

Here the sentence fragment is used mainly as a joke, as a marker of the diary genre along with the references to repeated events which require no description. These two features of the diary are of course connected, the shorthand of the sentence fragment suggesting not only that pronouns are unnecessary because the identity of the diarist as the protagonist is understood, but also a kind of impatience with recording narrative events which are repeated every day: "More tomorrow." While the structure of a day gives an entry its form, the repetition of daily routines require a shorthand contraction of their narrative to allow the focus of the entry, and the form it takes, to be determined by what is singular about a day. There is just nothing singular about the day of a Diary Cow.

Joe Orton's use of the sentence fragment is at once that of the Diary Cows and that of Ronald Koertge himself. That is, he uses the sentence fragment to contract the narration of repeated daily events or circumstances, but also as a marker of diaryness, which he uses, like Koertge, to comic effect. Typically, Orton's diary entries start with sentence fragments, then ease into narrative: "Met Miss Boynes on the stairs. She said [. . .]"; "Spent the morning writing *The Erpingham Camp*. I've now mapped a complete new middle to the play [. . .]."[2] Often he works his way into an entry with notes on the weather: "Weather very bad. Cloudy. Pleasant to walk around. We met Bill sitting on the boulevard [. . .]" (161); "Fine day. Sunlight. A little wind. Kenneth told me that Freddie Bartman had refused to hang two of the collage pictures [. . .]" (123). In a variation on this pattern, the entry for 27 December 1966 ends with a note on the weather, directly after the mention of his mother's corpse:

> And I don't fancy spending the night in the house with the corpse. A little too near the Freudian bone for comfort.
>
> Dreary weather. Pissing continually with rain. (41)

To end with the mention of the corpse would give the comment the kind of significance Orton's diary poetics insistently denies, even as the denial of significance plays off against the conventions of significance in the first place. The mention of the weather frames the comment about the corpse as one discomfort amongst others, as if the presence of his mother's corpse in the house where he might otherwise have stayed the night is the same sort of annoyance as the rain, and yet of course if it were really the same sort of annoyance there would be no need to add on the mention of the weather to put the comment about the corpse in its place.

The sentence fragment in Orton's prose is anti-narrative, and anti-sentiment. It restricts the significance of events to a diurnal frame. In the diary, his mother's death or Halliwell's anxieties are presented as significant mainly in how they affect the day's events, or as a kind of weather, a background to events:

> Sunday 19 March.
>
> Kenneth is quite different since he has started taking tablets. So tranquil. I'm shagged out. Like a limp rag. The Sundays have given Muggeridge horrible notices. But if the D.A. is determined to bring him in that won't stop him. Walked through the city, past the Barbican development area. How nice it was ruined.
>
> Monday 20 March.
>
> I've had a pain in my arm since the doctor's typhus injection. It's subsiding now. Long walk through Regent's park. Sunshine and the first ghastliness of Spring. Found that the café in the park was partially open. Bought an orangeade and a Coca-cola. Sat in the blazing sun and noticed how hideous the bright sunshine made everyone (including myself) appear. Like blanched and unsavoury apes. Felt scratchy and soiled. We walked from the park to Oxford Street where we had a cup of tea and a cake at Woolworth's. And then we went to see a Japanese film called *An Actor's Revenge*. Breathtaking direction and photography. Wasn't too keen on the acting. And the storyline wobbled a bit. But I liked it. Not an afternoon wasted. (118–19)

In these entries, Halliwell's state of mind and Orton's pain in his arm take the place of the weather as opening remarks for an entry. Like the weather, they are ongoing states that create a background for the day's events. While the second entry begins to move into narrative, both alternate complete sentences and sentence fragments in a note-like way. The rhythm is jerky, but it is the jerkiness of conversation, where the stops and starts are part of the ongoing easiness of it; the first entry shifts from one subject to another, but they run on together in one easy paragraph. The phrasing of the more dramatic similes as sentence fragments—"Like blanched and unsavoury apes"—at once draws attention to them, allows them to stand out from the surrounding prose, and, at the same time, maintains a casual, conversational tone, in which the overstatement is the overstatement of conversation. A more formal essay might build up to the ape simile with an increasingly expressionist presentation of the scene, and the scene would come to represent more than itself, to stand for a state of mind or the condition of the times. In the diary, such effects are local, the ape simile is thrown in, and the diarist is "scratchy and soiled" for an instant, then goes to a Japanese film.

The diary is the ideal genre for an insistence on the local and on local effects. It allows Orton to build up an extended, periodic portrait of characters such as his neighbours the Boynes and the Cordens, without having to establish a narrative significance for them. They are presented anecdotally, each anecdote included not for any purpose of portraiture, but for its own comic moment. If the sentence fragment and a paratactic narrative grammar are both characteristic speech patterns, they are characteristic, too, of a particular diary convention parodied in "Diary Cows" which breaks down narrative rhythms, structures of narrative significance, into a flatness which subordinates all significance to the rhythm of dailiness. This flatness nevertheless works to effect some sort of tension, some sort of drama, in Orton's diary, because it is played off against the refusal to dramatise narratives that are nevertheless present: the narrative of Orton's relationship with Halliwell, narratives of death, success and failure.

But just as the dash can express both a vagueness, a lack of definition, and a precision, an emphasis, as when Mansfield uses it to emphasise her discovery of the *mot juste*, so can the sentence fragment be used by different writers to opposite effect. The sentence fragment in Orton's prose presents even quite dramatic figurative phrases as ordinary, conversational hyperbole with the flatness of a weather report. It suppresses narrative significance, gives every anecdote the frame of dailiness. Yet other diarists use the sentence fragment to open up significance. Cheever's aesthetic seems at times to be almost precisely the opposite of Orton's, rejecting writing he feels "stinks of peanuts and cheap candy," the very smells Orton would savour, and his use of the sentence fragment, too, is the opposite of Orton's.[3]

Unlike Orton's, Cheever's diary prose is at once fluid and relatively formal, a literary prose. Sentences are often complex, linking clauses with formal punctuation such as the colon and semi-colon. When he does use a sentence fragment, it is to suggest an expansion of significance, as if the added meaning replaces the need to complete the sentence, or as if the meaning expands the phrase beyond its usual place in a sentence's syntax. The passage about his son Benjamin's birth, quoted previously in Chapter 2 in relation to the role of the detail, is framed by complete sentences which take the place of the incomplete sentences which frame Orton's entries. Like Orton's sentence fragments, the complete sentences in this passage date the passage, giving the context for the content of the passage.

> May 4th, my son Benjamin was born. My splendid, my forgiving, my gentle wife. Both of us caught up on a tide of stronger circumstance. In the hospital the lamps blooming in the linoleum floor. The delicate lights of the distant amusement park; the city; the highway [. . .] The uprush of human greatness that answers to charity and pain. Holiness. The remote neighbourhoods of the city—the hospitals, graveyards, and wharves—that we forget. The day that you were born I broke a bottle of bay rum on the bathroom floor. The night before I'd taken your mother to hear Maggie Teyte. (13)

Where Orton's use of the sentence fragment emphasises the local, Cheever uses sentence fragments at precisely the moment when the "uprush" of feeling the sentence fragments evoke makes him conscious of the "remote neighbourhoods of the city" beyond the hospital ward.

For Andrew Hassam, the importance of the sentence fragment as a defining feature of the diary depends on its non-literary status. The sentence fragment is casual, informal, quick to note. It shifts the focus of the writing from literary style to content, conveyed in as few words as possible, with no regard for formal prose grammar. It suggests not only the speed with which the diary is typically written, but also, Hassam argues, the lack of an addressee: "to say that a norm of the diary is that diarists write only for themselves is to expect to find an abbreviated style and a fragmented structure; conversely, a discursive style and unified structure suggest that the diary has been written for publication." Taking the private nature of the diary as itself a defining feature of the diary, Hassam examines the diaries of his study for the abbreviated sentences that imply privacy, listing sentence fragments as key evidence for the case he makes for the authenticity of Orwell's Wigan Pier diaries. While Hassam resists the evaluative, even moral, judgements that terms such as "authenticity" might imply, intending only to determine a set of stylistic features that can be checked off to establish a text's genre status, he nevertheless makes the same assumptions about the sentence fragment's relation to speed of composition, non-literary status, and a sense of privacy made by commentators of the diary it seems since diary commentary began.

But Cheever's more literary use of the sentence fragment is equally characteristic of the diaries in this study, diaries kept by writers, whose poetics continue to inform their writing even in such informal genres as the diary. At the same time, the conventions of the diary genre also inform their writing style: all of these writers have a higher proportion of incomplete sentences in their diary writing than in their published prose. To look at the literary potential of the sentence fragment in diary prose, I want to look at two diarists whose work has not been the focus of this study but whose use of the sentence fragment is particularly illuminating. Anaïs Nin, a writer whose major work was her diary, uses the sentence fragment in a similar way to the way Cheever uses it in the hospital extract, to poetic effect:

> Always too much seriousness! The smallest pretext to plunge into tragedy. But I know why. The pretext is inconsequential, but the need of tragedy is a deep necessity. It is the descent into coal mines, the exploration. I let myself get drowned merely to reach Atlantis. Old Habit. My lead weight. My ball and Chain. My compass. My barometer. It makes me laugh.[4]

Nin's tendency is to write sentence fragments made up of nouns, often abstract nouns, or nouns symbolic of abstract states, separated in their sentence fragments from the surrounding prose in the way Dickinson's nouns are separated within their sentences by dashes. The relative lack of verbs in Nin's prose suggests a lack of interest in narrative. She describes states rather than action, with nouns acting as symbols for inner states.

Elizabeth Smart, whose first novel *By Grand Central Station I Sat Down and Wept* is a masterpiece of poetic prose, and is largely drawn from her diaries, uses the sentence fragment in her diaries both in the Diary Cows, weather report manner and in the heightened, prose poetry manner of Anaïs Nin. Alice Van Wart, the editor of the diaries (published in two volumes, as *Necessary Secrets* and *On the Side of Angels*), notes that many of these entries are from appointment books and are little more than a jotted record of engagements and travel dates, so that Joy, for instance, is a person rather than an emotion:

> October 1, 1954
>
> Joy at lunchtime. Ill in bed and Joy and Geoff and Derek but got up and went to Canad House (Mike Pearson and Charlie Ritchie). Dinner.[5]

Longer entries relax into complete sentences:

> June 10, 1944.
>
> News from Ave dated May 21. I expected George (sort of) yesterday. At teatime I waited, thinking he might come. I lit the fire for the first

> time since he'd left. The coachman hasn't come and there's no fuel. When I went to see the time it was ten to eight. So I just dumped the children in bed. Alfred had gone by on his cart and said Didy would like to see me tonight. (23)

But in the long entries of the meditative journals of the 1970s, Smart writes in sentence fragments again, now with a probing precision and a rhetorical force:

> I'm tangled up in various layers of the mother thought. From pretty and superficial to the deep ugly, murderous.
>
> The smug mother love walking around so self-congratulatory, so sure it won't be shot at. Sacred, known to be sacred, scaring the jeerers, touching the toughies, committing acts of super-egotism under the guise of unselfishness, and with the approval of the world.
>
> Oh but we were so cosy. We were all-in-all to each other. A total understanding. (111)

The sentence fragment here has more conviction than correct grammar would give. "From pretty and superficial to the deep ugly, murderous" and "A total understanding" could both have been run on to the sentence before with just a comma, altering the syntax very little, but the effect would be to subordinate them somewhat to the sentences they would join, to make them qualifying clauses rather than statements with their own force. In the middle paragraph, the present participle "walking" could be made into a finite verb, "walks," but now the sentence is narrating an action rather than sticking with the "smug mother love," the state made concrete as a noun, stuck in its subordinate clause as if permanently perambulating on the spot. The sentence fragment suggests a kind of fixedness of attention, as if every part of a sentence has its own fascination, or as if the mind tracking the mind stops to watch itself watch.

Alice Van Wart's treatment of Smart's diaries resembles Murry's treatment of the Mansfield manuscripts. The different kinds of entries, with their different kinds of sentence fragments, come from different kinds of diary notebooks. The Literary Manuscript Division of the National Library of Canada, in Ottawa, holds in all 158 notebooks kept by Smart, from which Van Wart has compiled the two, fairly small journals *Necessary Secrets* and *On the Side of the Angels*. Yet, while Van Wart refers in the introduction to *On the Side of the Angels* to "notebooks full of lists, recipes, appointments, ideas, notes for commercial writing, drafts of articles, and book reviews," there is little of this range of material represented in the edited volume.[6] She explains her editing principles later in the introduction:

> My cutting has been extensive and my focus remains on the literary. Again, I have cut the poetry, the lists (Smart was a compulsive list-maker), all rough notes for her extensive commercial writing and book reviews. Consequently the journals lose much of their texture. (10)

Significantly though, where writing crosses over from one of these categories to another, it can count as a diary entry again. While poetry is too literary for the diary, and the list is too mundane to include, when the list crosses over into poetry it can be included in the edited volume:

> October 19, 1942
> Therapeutics
> Healing Games
> This way. That way—madness lies.
> Pamper.
> Humser. The madman.
> But take away his tools.
> (O for the touch of his salty lip.)
> And he lay arced above her unclean core.
> And in how many shitholes has he buried the key to my fulfilment.[7]

Or even:

> New Year's Resolutions 1945
> 1) Keep a diary or Daily Notebook.
> 2) Keep Accounts and *never* spend more than £20 a month on living (and partly living).
> 3) Keep children Prettily dressed always.
> 4) Keep Everything *Clean.*
> 5) Answer all letters within three days.
> 6) Keep bowels open.
> 7) Have a baby. [checked] Sebastian 16 April 1945
> 8) Learn to play Chess.
> 9) Write Canadian History Book.
> 10) Acquire a Radio, Piano, Dulcitone, Harpsichord, Clavichord, gramophone or Alto as means of obtaining music, and teach children to listen.
> 11) Translate Canadian Folksongs and acquire all available books and information on them.
> 12) Make a final decision about George, if he won't about me, and stick to it. The years roll on and the freezing wind. (25–26)

It is interesting to see Smart's list ending with the weather, in a sentence fragment of course, but as a figurative reference that lifts the list from prose to poetry.

Although the edited journal is, like *The Journal of Katherine Mansfield* (and even *The Notebooks*), an editorial construction, it too starts to make its own sort of sense out of its accident of form. The alternation between the brief entries of the engagement diaries and the longer, more reflective entries and, in particular, the kind of bursting through into the long entries of the 1970s, becomes textually significant. The brevity of the engagement diaries takes on, variously, suggestions of repression, haste, concision, and the withheld. The force of the sentence fragments of the longer, more reflective entries seems all the more forceful for the way the long entries appear to have finally broken out from the crabbed entries that surround them.

But even within the separate notebooks, some of this alternation in the mode of writing is apparent, and even seems to be played against by the writer. After a terse note, "GB left at 12," there is the capitalised cry, "(WHY?)" (33); a plaintive note can be introduced into the briefest note with a single word, as with the "nevertheless" of "My birthday in bed, nevertheless cooked a duck" (43). In the more substantial journals of the 1970s the pattern is reversed, with descriptive, lyrical prose, and reflective, abstract prose, still grounded at intervals in records of people seen, places visited, things done. In these journals, it is the weather which is treated at length, and often in complete sentences, while the terse sentence fragments are all that record the most emotionally significant events of 1971–1973, her daughter Rose's drug overdose, the births of three grandchildren, the marriage of her son Christopher. Again, this reflects changes in diary-keeping practice, which the events recorded may have had a lot to do with, but the effect is rather like the Orton effect in reverse. Where Orton writes of his mother's death in exactly the same style as he writes about the weather, referring to both in the same entry, the dramatic shift in style in Smart's diary underlines the difference in the kind of event being recorded, and gives a gravity to the terseness of the records of these events.

The incomplete sentence then represents both extremes of diary prose, the non-literary extreme in which the diary is used to simply record events, jotted down in the sparest shorthand to prompt the diarist-reader's own more extensive memory at a later date, and, on the other hand, what could almost be called the extra-literary, in which grammatically correct syntax is abandoned for a free play of words, which revise, rewrite, rephrase memories or thoughts as they are written, or which jab at a thought to try and pin it down, which come and go at a thought to find the right word to think it up, and which come to represent not only the thought itself but the jabbing, circling, revising process of thinking it. The location of the sentence fragment most frequently, and consistently, firstly in descriptions of weather, and secondly in lists, roughly relates to memory, in the first instance, and thought, in the second.

The association of the sentence fragment with descriptions of the weather seems to be a diary convention that is shared by most diarists, even diarists who normally otherwise write in complete sentences. Woolf's prose, for instance, while experimental in syntax and punctuation, is usually in complete sentences, although the proportion of incomplete sentences gradually increases from volume to volume. The sentence fragment would not, as a rule, fit the fluidity and continuity of her prose style. Fragmentary phrases are more likely to be included within a sentence, often suspended between dashes. Even a note on the weather can be slipped in to a narrative sentence in this way: "Today—dreary wet—I may go to Matthew Smith's pictures; or may not."[8] But the weather, more than any other subject, is likely to have a sentence fragment all of its own, even in a passage as fragmented and disrupted as the following:

> A thunderstorm, still further to distract my already distracted brain. How am I to calm & contract back again to Roger? We returned on Saturday. Now this morning I settled to a difficult passage in P.H. Pippa rings up. 20 minutes with her about 3 Gs. L. comes in & asks me to choose 3 quotes for the Observer. Nessa brings Maynard on Julian. Lightning. Torrents. Yet I must slide beneath all this if I'm to make a job of the summer lap. (5:154–55)

Curiously enough, the other subject, which in the fifth volume is written of with a higher proportion of sentence fragments than most, is the war. It is almost as if the war is another kind of weather, contrasted in the following entry with the regular weather:

> I have been sorting old cuttings out here. Molly & Q. will soon come. A very fine clear spruce blue day. The news as black as possible. Hitler has at any rate cursed, & Goering spat: nothing said till tomorrow. And now in to the house to tidy rooms & hair. (5:168)

In her biography of Virginia Woolf, Hermione Lee gives a detailed analysis of Woolf's complex attitudes towards the First World War, Woolf's own divided feelings about the war reflecting her sense of how the war divided society. The First World War was a "complete break," which Lee finds reflected in many of Woolf's novels: not only in the air-raid scene of *The Years*, from which the phrase comes, but in the complete break that divides the structure of *To the Lighthouse* and in the "violent moment[s] of destruction or obliteration" that recur as a feature of her fiction.[9] With the Second World War, division entered the Woolfs' marriage. Rose Macauley summed up the situation as it was in 1939: "She is for Peace, Leonard for the war."[10] In the diary entry, the casual shifts from noting the weather, to noting war news, to discussing "rooms & hair" again, present a kind of division or opposition between two types of "weather," the good weather of the fine clear day and the bad weather of the political situation. But the similar sentence construction she uses for both weathers suggests the kind of merging of politics into daily life that other diary entries remark on: "It all seems in keeping: my drudgery; our unsociability; the crisis; meetings; dark—" (5:305).

The rain statistics of Chapter 6 have already established the importance of weather for Sylvia Plath. She, too, tends to write of the weather in sentence fragments, often, like Orton, opening an entry with a note of the weather. But weather is no Diary Cow for Plath. Weather for Plath is "soul weather":

> A beautiful blue day. Pure soul weather. Frosty, and my Harcourt form rejection. Ted says: You are so negative.[11]

"Frosty, and my Harcourt form rejection": it is an exemplary diary sentence.

Again and again, the weather is tied up with Plath's feelings. Usually there is no need to spell this out; the two are simply juxtaposed:

> A chill clear morning. Yesterday's anger has clearer, finer edges now. (416)

> A heavenly, clear, cool, Sunday, a clean calendar for the week ahead, and a magnificent sense of space, creative power, and virtue. (486)

> A good walk this morning. Got up in time for breakfast at 8 and the mail came early as if to reward us. Warm blowy gray weather. Odd elation. Note this. Whenever we are about to move, this stirring and excitement comes. (528)

While the reference to the weather locates the entry in the present tense of the moment, weather references recall, too, earlier moments. The permanent presence of memory, which the present tense of the diary entry fixes, fixes in turn weather, and the emotions tied to it. Plath's sense of the presence of weather is complicated by her sense of its cyclical nature. While particular rainfalls prompt her to write again and again, the remembered, recurring "tinsel rains" of April inspire her first sonnet, written in September 1951, "the first thing I've written for a year that has tasted wholly good to my eyes, ears and intellect" (96). The description of the "bland vanilla moon" and "honeyflavored morning" seem to be derived from the vowel sounds and "supple *l*s" as much as from any particular memory, according to Plath's own description of how the sonnet was written. The syntax of the sonnet is complex, with many clauses connected by colons and semicolons, and the structure of its argument is complex too, with the "deception" mentioned in the first line only revealed in the final couplet: "Again we are deluded and infer/ that somehow we are younger than we were."[12] But the idea behind the sonnet, that the return of a season's weather returns us, too, to the thoughts and emotions that were connected with the weather before, is an idea she comes back to in the journals. In the following extract from the journals, the memory of the August rain is written up in complete sentences, while the present rain is evoked with a fragment:

> In bed, bathed, and the good rain coming down again—liquidly slopping down the shingled roof outside my window [. . .] And it seems always in August I am more aware of the rain. A year ago it came down on my porch and the lawn and the flat gray sea beyond at the Mayos [. . .] Two years ago August rain fell on me and Ilo, walking side by side, wordless toward the barn [. . .] Three years ago, the hot sticky August rain fell big and wet as I sat listlessly on my porch at home, crying over the way summer would not come again—never the same. The first story in print came from that "never again" refrain beat out by the rain. August rain: the best of the summer gone, and the new fall not yet born. The odd uneven time. (123–24)

Here the memories of rain become a list, though a prose list with proper syntax, and of course memory is a kind of thinking. Plath uses a list construction frequently to remember events, to note down the particulars of an event or occasion for future reference. Her lists are almost always prose lists, unlike White's tabulated lists that list dreams (225), likes and hates (32–33), "things worth noticing with D[orothy] K[ingsmill]" (204), "things I have been fearing to lose" (158), like shopping lists. The list, for Plath, is a genre that seems at times close to the genre of the essay. Her list of disillusionments, rounded off with its neat conclusion that sets the whole exercise in perspective as an instance of procrastination, is almost like a magazine essay in form and style. The entry about the August rains, too, has a formal quality to it, a neatness to its construction with its return at the end from the memory of August rains to a reflection on August rains in general.

The kind of formality Plath gives the list is extended, in the "Journal July 1950—July 1953" (the LAW volume), to the very structure of the diary itself, with the numbers given the extracts making a kind of grand list out of the whole volume. The diary becomes a kind of list of thoughts, or something between a list of thoughts and a list of days. In a sense, every diary is a kind of list of days, sharing with the list the open-ended structure, the paratactic relationship of its units, the days of the diary or items on the list. Plath's numbering of the entries in this volume emphasises the similarity in structure between the diary and the list, and makes the diary more list-like, by suggesting a common ground between the entries beyond their dailiness, beyond their shared reference to her life. The numbering of a list is normally pretty insignificant, depending on the order the items were thought up rather than any intrinsic order of the items themselves, so that usually the items on a list could be rearranged with no significant alteration of effect. Might the numbering of the "Journal July 1950—July 1953" be similarly read as suggesting that this is a list of things Plath has thought, that together add up to a representation of her thoughts at that time, and which could be rearranged in any order, with little effect on their total significance? Hughes and McCullough's editing seems to have been undertaken on that principle. If, on the other hand, the numbering might be read as insisting on the development of the entries, each in order one after the other, its meaning depending partly on its place in an ordered sequence, the "Journal July 1950—July 1953" can be read as not only extending the form of the diary but also extending the form of the list.

The *Notes on Neighbours* can also be read as a sort of a list, this time stretched in the opposite direction, away from sequence, numbering and tabulation. In this list, the typically inessential, interchangeable order of items on the list—if the neighbours are read as items on a list of neighbours—is given structural expression in the "list" of neighbours being typed up on loose-leaf papers that can be shuffled into any arrangement. The association of the list with "notes" is the more common association, and the one that most fits the flexible, unhierarchical form of the diary, and it is the list of notes that is most likely to be written in sentence fragments. Plath's diary prose frequently falls into a kind of list structure, as she develops a thought or as she describes a place or person (and she often describes a person in terms of place, as in *Notes on Neighbours*). The list structure allows for an attention to detail, allows detail the autonomy essential to detail in the diary. When Plath visited an author as a young student, she fixed on all the minute details of living as a way of realising a writer's life:

> I sit down in small kitchen. Wallpaper is brown background—colored Pennsylvania-Dutch-looking pattern. Dirty dishes on floor. Two cats: Prudence, a snooty black, sultry green-eyed Persian blood, and O'Hara. Ashtrays full of cigarettes. She smokes 2 cartons of Wings (cheap, non-advertised) a week. Can't taste, no palate left.
>
> So I look around. She likes to cook—stews and ragouts especially. Things with wine. There is a shelf of cookbooks over the refrigerator. Also a shelf of spices. She unscrews them and I smell each as she says, "Thyme, basil, marjoram . . . " and so on. There is also a preserving closet—jams, jellies, apple butter, beach plums. She picks and cans. Wild, sweet, tart, clear in glasses. (131)

The writing moves in and out of lists, in and out of correct grammar, to fix the memory in the details. Like the sentence fragments in Orton's diary prose, the sentence fragments in Plath's writing insist on the equal significance of narrative and detail, on narrative's local effects. Unlike the effect of Orton's sentence fragments, this does not imply a reduction of significance for the narrative; rather, the focus of the significance in the details heightens the overall significance of the narrative.

It is not so much the sentence fragment itself which is characteristic of diary prose, but the movement in and out of complete sentences, and in-between narrative and descriptive lists. The movement within a paragraph or an extract between complete sentences and sentence fragments is reflected at the level of structure by the movement between narrative prose, note-like analysis and lists, including even the shopping lists of Mansfield's notebooks. While the list itself as a "genre" is surprisingly fluid in its boundaries, so that passages in Plath's journals seem to straddle the boundaries of the list and the literary essay, in its propensity to lapse into list-making the diary seems to risk dissolution as a genre, to dissolve itself out of the diary form. As in the case of Mansfield's personal writings, the lapse of diary notebooks into lists and other note-like forms can present an editor with a problem of determining where the diary ends, and where it dissolves into "miscellaneous." Van Wart edited out of Smart's journals the considerable number of lists she made, as something other than diary material, while also adding as an editorial policy the work of "tighten[ing] up the syntax and writ[ing] out all ampersands."[13] Yet the diary-like result of Margaret Scott's editing of the Mansfield notebooks demonstrates how easily the diary form can accommodate the list.

Even more than the dash, the sentence fragment seems to be an essential feature of the diary, and like the dash, it is a convention of diary prose at the level of the sentence which is reflected in, and reflects, the structure of the diary. Curiously, Woolf, whose prose poetics were so extensively developed within the practice of keeping a diary, and who so extensively developed the prose poetics of the diary in particular with her creative use of the dash, wrote relatively few incomplete sentences, in or out of the diary. In fact, however, it is her very facility with the dash which replaces the need to develop the literary sentence fragment. In Woolf's diary prose, too, narrative often gives way to description, and description often gives way to lists, in note form. But Woolf's flexible grammar encompasses these lists, these sentence fragments, within her pliant diary sentence, through her use of the dash:

> You look down onto the semi-transparent water—the waves all scrambled into white around the rocks—gulls swaying on bits of seaweed—rocks now dry now drenched with white waterfalls pouring down crevices.[14]

9 "I" and "you"

As Sylvia Plath wrote in her college diary, "there has always furthermore in addition inescapably and forever got to be a thou. otherwise there is no i because i am what other people interpret me as being and am nothing if there were no people" (168). The question of audience has been a central concern of diary criticism, often one of the main issues raised in introductions to published diaries. Before Robert Fothergill's 1974 study of the diary, the most serious book-length study of the diary was P.A. Spalding's 1949 *Self-Harvest: A Study of Diaries and the Diarist*, less a "study" of the diary form than an appreciation of the diary as "artless chronicle." Similarly Arthur Ponsonby, who compiled several bibliographies of the English diary, regarded diary writers "at their best when they are just scribbling down with effortless frankness the little incidents which they are honest enough to record as having caught their attention at the moment."[1] Both Spalding and Ponsonby emphasise the importance of the frankness, honesty, and authenticity which they consider dependent on the diarist's belief in the privacy of his or her writing, the absence of an addressee. Indeed, Ponsonby suggests that the value of a diary "need not in any way suffer from . . . literary incapacity. On the contrary, literary talent may be a barrier to complete sincerity" (1).

In the 1980s, privacy and the absence of an addressee received renewed attention as part of the project of theorising the diary as a female genre. The word "private" is frequently included in the title of books on women's diaries, such as Elizabeth Hampsten's *"Read This Only to Yourself": The Private Writings of Midwestern Women, 1880–1920* and Penelope Franklin's *Private Pages: Diaries of American Women 1830s-1970s*.[2] Judy Simons presents a more complicated account of the importance of privacy in her study *Diaries and Journals of Literary Women from Fanny Burney to Virginia Woolf*, acknowledging the common practice of keeping shared diaries and diaries as family histories as well as the awareness of audience for diarists of more apparently private diaries. Yet she also argues, as have other writers on women's diaries, that private writing was permissible for women as public writing was not, and further, that "privacy became a precondition of women's literary development."[3] Katie Holmes, bringing this assumption to her research on Australian women's diaries, was disappointed by the "petty details" she encountered, rather than the description of "private life." In her preface to the anthology, *Spaces in Her Day: Australian Women's Diaries in the 1920s and 1930s,* she explains how she had to *learn* to read "silences" in order to read the diary as "a place of resistance [. . .] or [. . .] a place of rapprochement or accommodation."[4]

Yet the 1980s also saw the dominance of theory that questioned such connections between "private life" and "authenticity." Andrew Hassam counters such terms as "integrity," "authenticity," and "lack of style" with his strict focus on stylistic features that can be measured against a checklist of features that define the diary, arguing that the lack of style earlier diarists read as an effect of the diarist's spontaneity and authenticity should rather be regarded as a "stylistic convention," fulfilling reader expectations of what constitutes a diary. While taking the absence of an addressee as one of the defining qualities of the diary, Hassam looks for evidence of this absence not in the diarist's own claims about the privacy or audience imagined for the diary, nor in any extra-textual evidence about the actual readership of the text, but in textual features such as indeterminacies caused by missing information and an informal writing style characterised by the use of sentence fragments, contractions, and ellipses. His insistence on disregarding writers' own statements of their intentions, and on measuring a diary's indeterminacies with reference only to textual features, disregarding any historical information or other texts that might point to information missing from the diary, reflects the problematising of notions of "self" particularly in relation to textual referentiality in autobiography studies more generally in this period. Domna Stanton's move to excise the "bio" from autobiography in *The Female Autograph* reflects a similar concern to deny any "facile presumption of referentiality."[5]

Lawrence Rosenwald, in his 1988 study *Emerson and the Art of the Diary,* similarly refuses to presume referentiality when considering Emerson's use of the personal pronouns "I" and "you":

> We are first tempted to ask *what* Emerson's "you" refers to: himself, God, Margaret Fuller? But that question proves futile, and is based on a misconception.[6]

Rosenwald quotes the theory of Émile Benveniste on the status of the first- and second-person pronouns, a theory which not only denies reference to a life, but denies a stable and objective existence of even a textual self:

> The instances of the use of "I" do not constitute a referential class, because there is no "object" definable as "I" to which the instances uniformly direct us. Every "I" has its own reference, and corresponds on each occasion to a unique being posited as such.
>
> To what reality then does "I" or "you" refer? Only a "reality of discourse," a very odd thing. "I" can be defined only in terms of "locution,"

> not in terms of object . . . "I" means "the person uttering the present instance of discourse containing 'I.'" . . . The point has to be stressed: "I" can only be identified through the instance of discourse containing it, and not otherwise. (95)

In the first six chapters of this book, in which I was concerned primarily with the structure of the diary, I was struck by how readily the text of a diary can be read as representative of a "self," a "self" constituted by the structure, or symmetry, of the text. This textual "self" is more than simply the sum of the "instances of the use of 'I'." It includes shopping lists, descriptions of neighbours, anecdotes repeated by a friend, even fragments of fiction. Significantly different textual "selves" can be constructed by different editorial policies of selection and arrangement, and even by the different "symmetries" that can be constructed by differently contextualised readings. Clearly this textual "self" that can be constructed so variously by different editors cannot be, in any direct or facile sense, equivalent to the historical "self" of the diarist who wrote the text. However, to argue against equivalence is not the same thing as to argue against referentiality.

The reference of the diary "I" to the author of the diary is, in fact, axiomatic: our first aspect of the definition of the diary. It is the autobiographic aspect of the diary which includes the diarist in Lejeune's autobiographical "pact," and allows Fothergill, for instance, to read the diary as a "serial autobiography." A "facile" presumption of referentiality might conflate referentiality with equivalence, but it is also possible to acknowledge referentiality while focusing on the stylistic effects of the pronoun "I" within the text, whether constructing, or failing to construct, a protean textual self.

It is interesting that Fothergill considers the effects of audience not, as I expected, under the chapter heading "Motive and Manner," but as his starting point for a chapter on "Style, Tone, and Self-Projection." As Plath was aware, it takes a "thou" for the construction of the self. Fothergill quotes William Jones, writing in a diary entry from 1800, " . . . yet I had nothing to do, but to submit, & that peaceably too, I assure you. I have just observed that I ended the last sentence with 'I assure you.' I suppose I may have frequently used the same form of expression, as if appealing to some listening friend."[7] While the "listening friend" suggests the importance of audience, however, it is qualified by the phrase "as if." As Fothergill suggests, typically "a diary is addressed not to a specific figure but to a certain kind of responsiveness."[8]

This chapter takes an approach somewhere between Hassam's focus on stylistic features without reference to diarist or audience but only to "reader conventions," and Fothergill's suggestive but impressionistic accounts of the kinds of "responsiveness" evoked by diarists and their autobiographical selves. My focus is on the use of "I" and "you" in particular sentences and passages, and on the paradoxical shifts between "I" and "you" in diary writing in which the first- and second-person pronouns swap effects. If, indeed, the diary is a text without an addressee, it is not a text without a great deal of addressing. This chapter examines the poetics of the diary address, the way the "thou" of the diary functions in relation to the diary "I".

Rosenwald compares Emerson's diary with "the Transcendentalist diary" in which "the first person is normally historical; that is, 'I' is made use of in sentences of historical narrative." In Emerson's diary, on the other hand, "the first person is not strictly associated with sentences of historical narrative and makes its way more easily into the discourse of fine thoughts" (96). This "I," Rosenwald argues, is disembodied, disconnected from Emerson's "*person*." Emerson refers to the historical facts of self as "weeds" to be cast off:

> That which is individual & remains individual in my experience is of no value. What is fit to engage me & so engage others permanently, is what has put off its weeds of time & place & personal relation. (96)

In Plath's diary, her frequent descriptions of the clothes she is wearing serve precisely to refer the "I" of the diary to the facts of "time & place," embodying the textual "I" by reference to the physical self of the writer as "a tan long-legged girl in a white lawn chair [. . .] dressed in aqua shorts and a white-and-aqua halter" (108). And yet, while the textual "I" is embodied in the reference, the historical person she describes herself as slips away from the text, as the reader becomes conscious of the gap between the reader's incomplete picture of the "tan long-legged girl" (we cannot look up from the legs to the face, or out from the face to the lawn beyond the white lawn chair) and the diarist's own vision she picks the references out of. It is only the textual self that can be counted as, in Montaigne's phrase, "consubstantial" with the book, allowing even essays to be read as autobiography.

In fact it is not just the first and second persons which swap places in the diary, but the first and third persons. Taking another look at Plath's "tan long-legged girl in a white lawn chair," it turns out she is writing of herself here in the third person, aware even of the gap between this image and the facts of her own life that can't be observed from the outside:

> Outwardly, all one could see on passing by is a tan, long-legged girl in a white lawn chair, drying her light brown hair in the late afternoon July sun, dressed in aqua shorts and a white-and-aqua halter. The sweat stands out in wet shining drops on her lean bare midriff, and trickles periodically in sticky streams down under her armpits and in the back of her legs. To look at her, you couldn't tell much . . . (108)

Even Lejeune, who insists on referentiality as a condition of autobiography, argues that "the first person [. . .] always conceals a hidden third person." The relation between first and second persons, however, is more intriguing, for if the relation between first and third persons only seems to confirm Lejeune's definition of autobiography, which is also the first defining aspect of the diary, the involvement of the second-person pronoun in the diary seems to contradict, or at least complicate, the second defining aspect of the diary: that the diary is a text without an addressee.

Occasionally a diarist will address a specific "second person." Katherine Mansfield, for instance, addresses a sequence of passages directly to her dead brother:

> Dear brother, as I jot these notes, I am speaking to you. To whom did I always write when I kept those huge complaining diaries? Was it to myself? But now as I write these words and talk of getting down to the New Zealand atmosphere, I see you opposite me, I see your thoughtful, seeing eyes. Yes, it is to you. We were travelling—sitting opposite to each other and moving very fast. Ah, my darling, how have I kept away from this tremendous joy? Each time I take up my pen *you* are with me. You are mine. You are my playfellow, my brother, and we shall range all over our country together. It is with you that I see, and that is why I see so clearly.[9]

It is this address to her brother which carries over into her fiction writing:

> It is the idea (it has always been there, but never as it is with me to-night) that I do not write alone. That in every word I write and every place I visit I carry you with me. Indeed that might be the motto of my book. (46)

Writing to her brother is a way of thinking how to write the book:

> And now I know what the last chapter is. It is your birth—your coming in the autumn . . . And you must mean the world to Linda; and before ever you are born Kezia must play with you—her little Bogey. Oh, Bogey, I must hurry. All of them must have this book. (48)

For the book is addressed not just to her brother: "Oh, I want this book to be written. It MUST be done. It must be bound and wrapped and sent to New Zealand" (48). The subject of the book becomes the audience of the book, "sent to New Zealand." The need for an audience for the fiction compels the diary writing, the address to the brother in the diary making more direct the relation, and the audience more specific, even visualised as if present. Eventually, however, the fiction's demands for audience extend beyond the audience addressed in the diary, and the passages addressed to the brother cease.

In the Murry edition, the passages addressed to the brother are followed by the account of the birth of the baby sister Gwen, and the death too, although she does not actually state in the diary that the baby is dead. This could be read as the kind of indeterminacy Hassam seeks as textual evidence of the absence of an addressee: Mansfield does not need to tell herself that the baby is dead, since she knows this already. Yet she also knows everything else she recounts, and in this instance the indeterminacy, or ambiguity, has another function as a kind of textual correlative of the comment she makes at the beginning of the passage, that "Things happened so simply then, without preparation and without shock." The story is told from the perspective of the child she was, as an accumulation of details and moments, not fully understood at the time. But the effect of the telling—tender and chilling at once—depends on the simultaneous remove from the perspective of the child. The control of the telling of the story, the controlled limits of the perspective, are present as a gift of attention, enacted in narrative, to the dead baby sister and also to the memory of the writer's own self. If the brother's hand is held by the diarist's imagined self—"I will come quite close to you, take your hand"—so is the diarist's imagined self given the hand of a brother to hold in the writing of the passages, and when the dead sister is remembered, the imagined self is hand-held through the process of remembering.

In the *Notebooks*, the inclusion of much more miscellaneous genres of writing means this kind of fictionalised autobiographical account is read less as diary and more as fiction, or as proto-fiction, material to be worked into fiction. Even the passages addressed to the brother, which do not seem to have been written as fiction, or not as material ever to be worked up for publication, seem to be not so simply diary passages in this context. Mansfield constantly shifts genres, even working up shopping lists with rhymes, as if writing is something she can hardly do without working it up aesthetically. The passages addressed to the brother, coming before the story of the dead sister and being occasioned by the need to think through her fiction writing, have not just the control, but the ironic consciousness of control, of fiction. There is something almost public about this holding hands with her dead brother.

As convincing as a hand-hold are the more purely diary gestures towards an addressee in other passages of the journals. The passages addressed to her brother are full of questions, as letters are, as is appropriate for writing with an addressee. But other passages in the diary also contain questions. Who is asking whom? There is an addressing of the self going on with these questions very different from the posed address to the brother:

> Isaiah (or was it Elisha?) was caught up into Heaven in a chariot of fire *once*. (110)

> The tops of the flowers were burnt; the stooks (are they stooks?) were like small heaps of half-burned tobacco. (157)

Often she answers her own questions, the questions prompting the answers as a way of thinking:

> Well, J. doesn't want money and won't earn money. I must. How? First, get this book finished. That is a start. When? At the end of January. If you do that, you are saved. If I wrote night and day I could do it. Yes, I could. Right O! (17–18)

In this passage, Mansfield moves from the first to second person and back to first from sentence to sentence, not so much as if one were in dialogue with the other, but as if they are the same "person." The sense of doubling, of dialogue, comes more from the pattern of question and response than from the back and forth of the pronouns. Comments in parentheses also double, or split, the subject of the text, the "one" of the following passage:

> And yet one has these 'glimpses', before which all that one ever has written (what has one written?)—all (yes, all) that one has ever read, pales . . . The waves, as I drove home this afternoon, and the high foam, how it was suspended in the air before it fell . . . What is it that happens in that moment of suspension? It is timeless. In that moment (what *do* I mean?) the whole of life is contained. (148)

Here she is not so much prompting words, as questioning or confirming them. And questioning or confirming are not quite opposites; she is not quite doubting, and not quite denying, the queried phrases. Both queries and confirmations seem to suggest an ironic acknowledgement that the writing is as much—and inevitably—a display of tone as a way of thinking. And irony, even private irony, is by its nature dialogic.

The same sense of irony is present in her use of questions in diary passages not to prompt thought but to leave thought open. In these instances, the question is used to similar effect to the dash, as she uses the dash, both to leave the text open to the ineffable, and to give the ineffable a very definite emphasis:

> read Tchechov aloud. I had read one of the stories myself and it seemed to me nothing. But read aloud, it was a masterpiece. How was that? (230–31)

> Oh, what will this beloved month bring? (233)

Each of the diarists in the study has a quite different style of questioning which seems related to the different sense of an addressee each diary evokes. I have suggested that the number of questions in White's diary is related to her sense of the conditional nature of the present tense, while at the same time, the question and answer dialogue the questions prompt is linked to her tendency in response towards prescriptiveness. Her concept of the self is influenced by psychoanalytic theory, in which the self is split into a conscious and a subconscious self. Her dialogues with herself in the diary, however, seem less dialogues between conscious and unconscious selves than dialogues between a split consciousness trying to pin down the unconscious between the two of it, like two exasperated parents trying to pin down a child. The "I" becomes the third person.

> I am supposed to be sitting here writing my Mirror article. Why do I not begin since it would be good to have the tiresome thing over? I feel raw and humiliated after yesterday's analysis as if everything I did were done from some vile and self-seeking motive. Now, why will I not get my article done? Because I would have a little time left and could get on with my work?[10]

> Why is it I can't be natural. And what *is* natural for me? (163)

> I have turned 40 now. Is there *nothing* I won't do for money and admiration? (163)

In the following extract she even gives herself quotation marks:

> My first thought—on hearing of the revolution—would be 'shall I still be able to get face powder?' (28)

Cheever's questions, on the other hand, even when concerning the self, seem to be addressed beyond the self. Where White's questions are full of italics, and might begin conversationally, "Now . . . ," Cheever's are more likely to begin, "Oh . . . ":

> Only after drinking a little whiskey do I feel the simple pleasures of travelling through the tag end of this rainy day. Oh, where are all my claims of wholeness? Where are all my gifts of judicious self-admiration? [11]

More concrete questions are often attributed to a generalised "we" and are included in order to make a more abstract point:

> On our knees in church we are face to face with the bare facts of our humanity [. . .] The door at the back creaks open and we wonder, Who has just come in? Arthur? Charlie? Henry Penrose? Who is the boy in the plaid shirt? When was he confirmed? (62)

> That was the year everybody in the United States was worried about homosexuality [. . .] Is he? Was he? Did they? Am I? Could I? seemed to be at the back of everyone's mind. (117)

The questions gesture towards a very large, very diffuse addressee, indicated by the enlargement of "I" to "we," by the overstatement of emotion, by the long words, and in the following passage, by the sublime landscape proposed as the fitting setting for these kinds of questions:

> What has gone wrong, that we should all seem to be made of paper and straw? What is the world I wish to achieve for myself and my sons? What would be a better scene for this discourse? God knows. A mountain pass, a long beach, the darkness just before a storm. (142)

And yet, in the actual, conversational addresses reported in the journals, questions are so wonderfully pointed:

> "Can I make a piece of toast?" "Would you mind waiting until I've made mine?" [. . .] "All I want [. . .] is a boiled egg. Is that too much to ask?" (152–53)

> "Can I do anything to help you, short of dropping dead?" (152)

Significantly, Orton's diary contains questions *only* in reported speech, only narrates questions but never poses them. Is this because Orton's diary does not, in fact, become its own addressee? In the chapter on his diary, I suggest that Lahr's effort to find a "symmetry" in the diary leads him to read the diary as a kind of extended "note" to Halliwell, to mirror the suicide note Halliwell wrote in response. I place the line between writer and reader elsewhere, reading the diary as, in Orton's words, "perfectly audible" to the heterosexual audience for which he was accustomed to write. The diary is written in the past tense, narrated like anecdotes already rehearsed, with commentary but without analysis. There is no explicit "addressing" in the diary, and no use of the second person. Even the first-person pronoun is often elided, which only confirms, through its transparency, the role of the first-person pronoun as referent to the narrator of the diary. The narrator becomes invisible because narrator and protagonist are so completely merged, without the split consciousness typical of the diary.

When White, in contrast, questions "why will I not get my article done," the "I" is distanced from the writer querying the motives of the "I." Plath's writing is remarkable for her use of the second-person pronoun, but her use of the first-person pronoun is also complex. The passage about dreaming up plots at home, for instance, which I looked at earlier in terms of her ambitions as a prose writer, is interesting to analyse in terms of its use of the first-person pronoun:

> If I can't dream up plots in my own room and backyard, I won't be able to dream them up anywhere. I am, of course, as I said, afraid to try writing on my own, because of the huge possibilities of failure. But I am

> going to. I will read "Seventeen's" and write a story for them [. . .] The more I think about it, the more creative I will be at home, without all the guilts and sapping jealousies if I pampered my original whim and went to Harvard now that my whole scheme is altered by not taking O'Connor's course.[12]

If the first-person pronoun refers to a "reality of discourse," the "reality" of Plath's "I" is changing with every sentence in this passage, in fact is changing within sentences. There is, for a start, a present tense I, a past tense I, a future I, and a conditional I. There is the I who has already spoken, "as I said," the I who is speaking, and, presumably, an I who is listening and knows what has already been said and needs that knowledge acknowledged. In fact, it is this "I" who is deferred to in the phrase "as I said" who intrigues me the most. It is this "I," conscious of what has been said already, who insists on narrative in the diary, on continuity, on all those "determinacies" which are at least as interesting, and in fact far more prevalent, than the indeterminacies that, for Hassam, prove a diary is a diary.

This passage is from the piece of writing Plath headed "Letter to an Over-grown, Over-protected, Scared, Spoiled, Baby," which, as the title indicates, was written as an address to herself, but to a self that has been distanced, described in the third person, in order for the writing self to have control over the self described. The self is controlled too by the emotive language of the piece: her previous decision is described as a "whim" which she would be "pampering" if she followed through.

When this same controlling, rhetorical language is used to address herself in the second person, as it is in passage asking "what *have* you for your eighteen years" quoted in Chapter 6 of the book, paradoxically the "you" is more closely identified with the diarist's self, than is the "I" of the passage from the "Letter." The "you" she addresses herself as, when she replies to the question "Who cares?" with an adament "*you* care, and somehow you don't want to live just one life," seems to me closer to herself than the "I" she describes herself as, perhaps because of this distinction between address and description. And it is the self addressing herself as "you," the writing self, which seems somehow separate. Unlike the Orton narrator, who needs no personal pronoun, the narrator here with no pronoun at all is nevertheless implied as "the person uttering the present instance of discourse" and in fact is not just implied but very apparent in the controlling of the second person.

It is this paradoxical reversing of reference that I referred to earlier when I wrote that the first- and second-person pronouns swap effects in the diary. When the diarist addresses herself as "you," as a *second* person, it is not the self addressed as "you" who seems distanced from the diarist, but the self addressing "you." Whereas, when the self is "addressed" as "I," the first-person pronoun can refer to a self that is indeed distanced from the diarist, held at remove, with the diarist identified with the writer rather than the addressee.

By now, however, it is becoming clear that any characteristic feature of the diary that can be distinguished will have different stylistic effects depending on the particular poetics of each diarist. The enlarged "I" of Cheever's diary is matched by a similarly enlarged "you," which functions quite differently from the "you" of Plath's diary. Occasionally, Cheever uses the impersonal "one," although he seems to shift more easily from "one" back to the first person:

> The strain of debt; the difficulty of trying to write one's way out of it. There are seven more days, six more days, etc. Once in New Hampshire for three months I tried unsuccessfully to rip a story out of my brain or to patch together a series of incisive notes with no success at all.[13]

Passages in the second person, on the other hand, remain in the second person even when they include apparently particular references to Cheever's own life:

> These Westchester Sunday nights [. . .] You put on old clothes. You drive your wife to church and your children to Sunday school. You rake the leaves off the flower bed. They are too wet to burn. You put a chemical fertilizer on the lawn and examine the bulbs. The Rockinhams, on their way to a Sunday-lunch party at the Armstrongs', shout their good mornings from the sidewalk. "Isn't it a glorious day; glorious, glorious." Your wife and children return from church. (4–5)

It is not quite clear whether the Rockinhams and the Armstrongs are real names, or fictional, and it makes very little difference. There is an arbitrariness about detail in Cheever's writing, even when the detail is very particular, and essential to the texture of the prose. It is essential *as* texture, rather than as a record of fact.

The particularities of Cheever's life illustrate general principles. His very particular experiences in Rome, described in detail, illustrate a general sense of Rome's dangers. Cheever becomes "the visitor to Rome":

> What the travel books don't mention is the sense of danger experienced by the visitor to Rome. Driving back into the city after a long weekend you see at the gates of the Campo Verano a long line of hearses [. . .] You ask one of the drivers what the occasion is, and he says it is the epidemic [. . .] You park your car and lock the ignition switch, the steering wheel, and all the doors, since car thefts go on every night in this quarter. You go into a bar to buy a package of cigarettes and the place is so damp and cold that the poor girl who waits on you—she wears three sweaters and fur-lined boots—is shivering [. . .] You might fly, like your friends, to Switzerland or Majorca, but how can you flee until you know what it is you are fleeing? (87)

The last sentence at once opens the passage out to still more general significance, with its almost aphoristic quality—"how can you flee until you know what it is you are fleeing"—and concludes the passage with a formal neatness, the friends fleeing to Switzerland and Majorca having been mentioned earlier, and incidentally, in the passage. The formal neatness of Cheever's diary passages adds to the sense of distance between the "self" of the diary discourse, the self referred to with the diary "you" or "I," and the "objective" self of the diarist, the self Plath describes as the "tan long-legged girl," the self Benveniste argues cannot in fact be referred to with the first- or second-person pronoun. Many of Cheever's passages in the second person seem in fact to be fictional, or so generalised that it would make little difference whether they were fictional or factual. The passage in which he traces "the beginnings of self-destruction" that lead to a day's loss of form, discussed in the chapter on his work earlier in the thesis, seems to fit the picture of his life the diary evokes, with the over-indulgence in cocktail drinking a typical route to self-destruction, but he deliberately avoids reference to a particular occasion. Phrases such as "a headache, a slight case of indigestion, an infected finger" insist on the arbitrariness of detail. Detail is necessary formally, but also destructive to form, unless it is insistently generalised to make an abstract point, a point belonging not just to the first person but to every "one."

In arguing that the first and second person cannot be referential outside the reality of the discourse they function within, Benveniste insists on the referentiality, in contrast, of the third person. Without quite wanting to claim for Virginia Woolf a position as the Shakespeare of the diary genre, I will conclude this chapter once again by looking at Woolf's diary poetics.[14] Woolf's diary certainly assumes a referentiality for the third person, distinguishing "life" and "comment" only to regret that the commentary has not kept up with the life to which it refers. A similar referentiality seems to be assumed for the first person:

> I am distressed by my failure to make cigarettes. I had a lesson from a man in Francis Street—cant do a thing with my fingers. Angelica is expert with hers already. Nessa says all painters are: this is a perquisite they get thrown in with their gift.[15]

It does not seem to me to make any sense to distinguish between degrees of referentiality in the reference to Angelica's expertise and the reference to Woolf's own clumsiness. It seems to me that one of the functions of the first-person pronoun is to refer to a self who is as much a "*notion lexicale*"—a "fixed and 'objective' idea, capable [. . .] of being realised in a unique object"—as is the "himself" or "herself" referred to by the third-person pronoun, who, after all, is hardly going to remain "identical in whatever representation it evokes," any more than is a first-person pronoun reference to the self in the world.[16]

On the other hand, the first-person pronoun—and the second-person pronoun—also has a range of functions beyond the function of reference, and it is the function of address with which this chapter has been primarily concerned, a function which belongs particularly to these two pronouns. Woolf's diary, while spectacularly referential, is distinguished above all by its extraordinarily cohesive patterns of address.

Woolf very rarely uses the second person in the diaries, although she does on occasion:

> This is written at Rodmell; oh yes, & it is the best, the freest, the comfortablest summer we have ever had. Figure to yourself feet swollen in boots. One takes them off—that is my state without poor dear Nelly; with nice bright Annie.[17]

But the whole diary is saturated with the conversational mode of address that prompts the use of the second person in this instance. "Figuring to herself" is a good description of the projected reader reading these diaries, and the writing does not just address this projected reader but guides her through the recorded days, and the recording of the days. Helpful pieces of information are included in parentheses, rather like editorial footnotes:

> The Waves is I think resolving itself (I am at page 100) into a series of dramatic soliloquies. (3:312)

> I sat surveying the whole book complete, & quarrelled with L. (about Ethel Smyth) & walked it off. (3:297)

The reader is everywhere gestured towards with conversational asides, "to tell the truth," "sketchily I admit," which enact a mode of confession as a social gesture. Sentences, especially at the start of entries, tend to open conversationally with a word or phrase like "and," "but," "well," "so," "oh," "sure enough."

This reader is the same kind of reading "I" Plath defers to with the phrase "as I said"; a reader keeping pace with the diary, reading each entry in sequence, as a narrative, missing nothing, looking for connections, requiring determinacy; a reader responsive to his or her own construction by the text, responsive enough to the relationship between reader and writer constructed by the text to need careful handling. The reader's expectations are acknowledged when they are met, and when they are frustrated: "Just back from Rodmell—to use again the stock opening. And I should explain why I've let a month slip perhaps" (3:57).

Entries frequently refer back to the previous entry. Woolf's tendency to open an entry with the conjunctions "and" or "but" suggests a continual sense of narrative coherence, which some entries make more explicit:

> Oh—yesterday we made an offer for 47 Gordon Sqre—a house where we may die; for it's a 24 years lease [. . .]
>
> Monday 16 November
>
> But we are not to live & die in 47. The Bedford Estate wont house a publisher; would create a precedent; vans would stop at the door. (4:52)

Woolf uses "oh" frequently to introduce a change of topic, which, like the explanations offered to the reader for lapses in writing, acknowledges the reader's expectations of narrative continuity at the point where continuity is broken, in a casual, conversational manner. The pliancy of Woolf's prose not only allows her attention to flit from topic to topic with unbroken continuity, but guides the reader's attention with it, "figuring" to the reader; and the reader beholds: "But behold, I think the spirit of delight is hovering over me" (3:324).[18]

Conclusion
"And coming here this morning . . . "

The more obvious title for the conclusion of a book on diaries would be Samuel Pepys's "And so to bed." Yet one of the clearest points to emerge from a study of the diary is the importance of its open form as a defining principle, and the particular kinds of significance that details can hold within a narrative which has no predetermined ending. I want to conclude by returning to a considering of the diary's open form, to make more than paratactic connections between the diary's open form and the other features of diary writing I have examined. And so I take for my chapter title a phrase opening rather than closing a diary entry, written in the morning rather than at the end of a day.

The phrase comes from a passage from Cheever's journal, written in 1956:

> And coming here this morning, out of idleness and habit, I am face-to-face with the fact that this is, at times, a kind of retirement from the excellence of life. Any search for truth or beauty is perilous and this is a common peril. There is a world of difference between taking out a sailboat and filling in the pages of a journal and I would like to bring these worlds together . . . (64)

Despite the reservation he expresses here about his "retirement from the excellence of life" to write in his journal, he continued to give every day some sort of shapely form in his journal for the rest of his life. The entry in which he was forced to confess that "For the first time in forty years I have failed to keep the journal with any care. I am sick. That seems to be my only message . . . " is the second to last entry he ever wrote. It is followed by one final entry, which conveys his dedication to journal keeping like no other. This final entry begins, "I have climbed from a bed on the second floor to reach this typewriter. This was an achievement . . . " (394).

Critics reviewing Cheever's *Journals* have understood this achievement as autobiographical, describing the *Journals*, as we have seen, as "an intimate self-portrait" or "brutally honest autobiography." Fothergill's evaluation of the diary as a genre with literary potential is made on the basis of his reading of the diary as "serial autobiography," and he selected for his study only those diaries "whose prime subject is the life of the writer, valued for its own sake," foregrounding "the individual consciousness," and amounting to, in his own concluding words, a "book of the self."[1] His chapters are arranged around such concerns as "the ways in which certain long-kept diaries give to their contents the literary character of 'A Life'; . . . the preoccupation apparent in certain diaries with developing the self according to preconceived models; . . . how a diary's style and tone contribute to the projection of a self-image" (7). Just over a decade later, the project of "theorising diary," as Felicity Nussbaum puts it, involves a further re-evaluation of the diary as "an important and often unpublished site of contest between the ideologies of the unitary self and the more discontinuous subject."[2] Like Fothergill, Nussbaum quotes William Matthews' argument against reading the diary as a literary genre on the grounds that "if he is a true diarist, one day is likely to be at odds with another for any reader who thinks of people as having fixed characters," but where Fothergill argues against Matthews' reading of a less structured, less self-conscious diary as more "true" than the coherent, self-conscious diaries Fothergill prefers, Nussbaum's argument is with Matthews' assumption that their lack of fixed character makes these "true" diaries less literary than those "articulating a multiplicity of contestatory selves, of unstable and incoherent selves" (132). After reading Althusser, Derrida, Lacan, and Foucault, it is precisely this incoherence Nussbaum finds most important about the diary representation of "self." The assumption remains, however, that "self" is what a diary is about.

Cheever, however, describes finding himself as he writes in his journal "face-to-face" not with "self" but with the "search for truth and beauty" that, he fears, is a retirement from "life." His achievement might be understood as he represents it, as the successful "bring[ing] together of these worlds" of everyday living and the everyday writing that records it. While the reader of a diary might see it as a book of the self, diarists are often more concerned with writing about the "world" or "life," worrying that the life unrecorded is wasted, in Woolf's phrase, "like a tap left running." One of the most suggestive passages of Nussbaum's essay concerns the relationship between self and memory. She nicely cites Hume on the relationship between self and memory—"For how few of our past actions are there, of which we have any memory? Who can tell me, for instance, what were his thoughts and actions on the first of January 1715, the eleventh of March 1719, and the third of August 1733?"—pointing out that this is exactly the kind of information a diarist will have recorded and will be able to look up (133). While the diarist's attention is directed towards the present, paradoxically it is this attention which creates the memoranda that give the diarist access to the past. But should access to the past necessarily be understood as access to the "self", rather than to the remembered world?

Certainly for Hume, the loss of memory raises questions about "the most established notions of personal identity" that he understands as predicated on a coherent memory. For Nussbaum, in contrast, it is not memory loss so much as memory which is likely to raise such questions, because of the discontinuity she argues memory reveals between the self of the past and the self of the present. The case of Jill Price suggests that the loss of memory should indeed be considered essential to establishing a coherent sense of identity. In her memoir *The Woman Who Can't Forget*, Price describes the effects of living with an extraordinarily rich autobiographical memory.[3] One of the greatest difficulties for her was in shaping a sense of self, which she understands through her own experience as well as extensive reading in psychology as depending less on *accruing* memory than on the *selection* of memories to retain. Perhaps surprisingly for someone who is unable to forget any of her own memories, Price is an obsessive diarist, who records the details of almost every day of her life in a journal format. When she, like Woolf, "lapses," she is able, unlike Woolf, to fill in the missing days in as much detail as she would have recorded had she written the entries up from day to day, even once filling a five-year gap in the record. Yet she does not feel her journal keeping assists in shaping a sense of self, but rather serves to "contain" what otherwise feels like a "swirl" of memory. Her attempt to reduce her voluminous journals and shape her memories into some kind of form, her "version of the story of my life" as she calls it, is an extraordinarily strange document: no more than a lengthy list of dates, arranged in an arcane layering of headings and sub-headings representing time periods divided into smaller blocks of time. This oddly opaque "life story" felt to her so private that before writing this memoir, she reveals, "I have never shared the time line with anyone before, including the UCI scientists [the scientists investigating her memory]" (138). Her journals, in contrast, she writes in public, and shares with others. She regards keeping them as fulfilling the same function as the obsessive hoarding she does of everyday objects, keepsakes, and personal items she has outgrown. It is the world, not the self, she sees the journals as containing.

The study of the six diaries examined in this book suggests, of course, that diaries do contain "self" as well as "world," though "contain" might not be the most accurate word. Rather, diaries *construct* a presentation of self as much through the selection, combination, and accumulation of entries as through the writing of individual prose passages. The different versions of Katherine Mansfield presented in the different editions of her journals reveal the role an editor can play in the construction of the diary-self. Given how constructed the diary-self is, Leonard Woolf's suggestion that in editing Virginia Woolf's diary he was presenting a more truthful portrait of Woolf than the diaries present can be given more consideration than it might initially seem to warrant. If her diary is understood as a record of a life otherwise left running like a tap unrecorded, rather than as a self-portrait, the lack of selection might indeed make it misleading if it is read as autobiography. The different kinds of diary Sylvia Plath kept in different periods of her life, or sometimes even in the same periods, as when she kept a separate journal for her therapy notes, might each offer a very different version of her "self" if they were read as self-contained documents, separate each from the other as well as from the politics of the Plath myth. Each version of the diary-self is at once referential and a construction, just as any autobiographical writing is at once referential and a construction. But where the construction of an autobiographical or biographical portrait involves, as Hermione Lee puts it, giving "a quasi-fictional, story-like shape" to the material—"making up, or making over" a life—the "shaping" involved in a diary's construction of its subject may be less evident.[4] It is easier to understand how a story is made up, or made over, after the fact, but the diary constructs its biographical portrait cumulatively, and in the present tense. Yet form still plays an essential role, as the different versions of the Mansfield diary dramatically reveal.

The world or "worlds" the diarist writes about is equally a construction, made up and made over in every entry. Cheever gives each day its own "shapely" form, in a search for "truth and beauty." The raw material for the entry comes from the daily events and observations, but the shape of each entry is arranged to allow the detail to take on a willed significance. Cheever's description of his intention as a diarist as an endeavour "to bring together these worlds" of everyday, outdoor pursuits and the private practice of writing calls to mind Rebecca Hogan's description of the diary as a genre in which "Things happen *between*—between entries, between events, between diarist as writer and diarist as reader."[5] The chapter on Cheever's diaries focused on what happens between the detail and its context, the particular and the abstract, world and willed significance; but what happens between world and willed significance within any particular entry is complicated and transformed by what happens between entries.

The spareness of the version of Mansfield's diary as it was edited by Murry throws the juxtaposition of entries, often simply a juxtaposition of images, into striking relief. Mansfield's diary is not one that Podnieks discusses in *Daily Modernism*, perhaps because her emphasis on the diarist's deliberate self-fashioning makes the editorial work involved in fashioning the diaries problematic, though her discussion of modernism in terms of a negotiation between high and low culture, aesthetics and the everyday, and in terms of the fragmentation and multiplicity of the self, could be applied rather well to a reading of the Mansfield *Notebooks* edited by Scott. More obviously modernist, at least in terms of the "aesthetic, directed, monological" and "masculine" modernism that Podnieks sees the work of the modernist women diarists as disrupting and complicating, is the version edited by Murry. The spareness of the entries and the emphasis on the visual image give the juxtaposition of entries a similar effect to the collision of images in an Imagist poem. The juxtaposition of images such as the "slow building-up" of an idea in her mind described in the entry for April 2, 1914, and the walk by the river described in the entry for April 3, a description which leads to musing on her fear "of people closing over me" and her wish that "I lived on a barge," builds up an emotional charge that might be best understood in terms of modernist theories of montage.

Parataxis in the diary is usually written about as a levelling or democratising feature of the diary, related to the diary concern with "dailiness." Even Podniek's brief description of juxtaposition in the diary as a modernist feature comparable to Eliot's removal of transitional and connective material from *The Waste Land* takes no account of the emotional and dramatic effects of juxtaposition in modernist poetry, but reads it as a "failing to privilege one event over another," and a reflection of "the real fragmentation of lived experience which modernism sought to emulate."[6] Like a number of other writers on the diary, she refers to Rachel Blau DuPlessis' 1979 article, "For the Etruscans: Sexual Difference and Artistic Production—The Debate over a Female Aesthetic," citing DuPlessis' description of Monique Wittig's *Les Guérillères* as "a form of verbal quilt. We hear her lists, her unstressed series, no punctuation even, no pauses, no setting apart, and so everything joined with no subordination, no ranking. It is radical parataxis."[7] In *The Extraordinary Work of Ordinary Writing*, Sinor refers to Hogan's elaboration of DuPlessis' notion of "radical parataxis" in "Engendered Autobiographies," citing Hogan's description of parataxis as "the piling up of unsubordinated and repetitive sentence patterns" and relating this to the "dailiness" that for Sinor defines the diary. Parataxis, she suggests, "eliminates perspective based on distance and creates immersion."[8] The examples she gives of diary entries that are little more than a list of tasks achieved, and accounts of the weather, certainly convey this sense of dailiness as levelling and lacking in perspective. For Sinor, parataxis involves "a spacing" but "not a melding" (158). Each action or event is given equal weight and separate consideration. In Annie Ray's diary, this levelling parataxis operates similarly within and across entries. Each entry is made up of a number of separate sentences or sentence fragments, which sit next to each other in the same way the entry for one day takes its place after the entry for the day before. Chronology provides an order which takes the place of connection.

Though his subversive use of parataxis goes against the grain of the "ordinary" writing Sinor celebrates, Orton's diary certainly highlights the power of parataxis to produce radically flattening emotional effects, with its juxtaposition of the description of his mother's corpse with details of the tea served and the sexual encounter that followed the funeral. Yet DuPlessis' account of "radical parataxis" suggests other ways of thinking about how parataxis might operate in and out of the diary. DuPlessis' article is written in a radically paratactic form itself, each paragraph introducing a new quotation, idea, description or reflection on another text, piece of autobiographical memoir, or even jotted notes. While the passage on radical parataxis with its description of a text as a quilt is often quoted, other sections such as a tiny piece of autobiography ("The general feeling of the dream was that I was free of the testers; however, I was entirely obligated to take and pass their test" (128)) only accrue meaning gradually and associatively, in relation to the passages on literary evaluation, feminist scholarship in academia, distinctions between masculine and feminine ways of knowing and writing, institutionalisation, and so on. Citing Woolf's description of the diary as a capacious hold-all, or deep old desk, she goes on to consider the connections made in re-reading a journal, suggesting in similar terms to Hogan that "The writing is in the interstices, the meaning is between. It is created in the relationship between, between the elements" (137). Parataxis does not only create an emotional charge but also meaning. When DuPlessis writes, "I knew more, said more than I knew," we might recall the second part of Woolf's description of the deep, old desk in which she imagines opening it up some time later to find "that the collection had sorted itself & refined itself & coalesced"—and she does indeed describe her own experience re-reading the diaries as one of finding "the significance where I never saw it at the time."[9] We might also think of the role of the reader in finding the significance in White's diary where she said more than she knew.

While Hogan's use of DuPlessis' account of parataxis to support her concept of the diary as a feminine genre makes the common assumption that it will have a levelling effect that reduces "anything out of the ordinary" to a common pattern, her description of parataxis includes both "a sentence structure in which related clauses are placed in a series without the use of connecting words (I came, I saw, I conquered) or clauses related only by the coordinating conjunctions."[10] Leaving aside the surprising choice of example for a feminist poetics of parataxis, she introduces a distinction here between two kinds of parataxis which could be taken further. The examples of parataxis she gives demonstrate the gap between entries (the date that heads an entry in place of "any articulated link to the previous entry") and within entries (she cites Hampsten's description of the way "No one event appears to color or displace another" in the nineteenth to early twentieth century diary kept by Grace DeCou). But she goes on to discuss the "paradoxical nature of parataxis" which can also be understood, she suggests, in terms of "elasticity," a term which allows her to connect the parataxis of diary writing to Nancy Chodorow's description of the feminine ego. She quotes the diarist Etty Hillesum writing, on the one hand, of her use of the diary to record "many unconnected thoughts," and on the other hand, as a genre which allows her to "continue to spin one and the same thread, where one can gradually create a continuum" (104). The chapter in this book on Woolf's diary is concerned precisely with the kind of continuity that allows one event to colour another. In November 1918 for instance she writes, "I am overwhelmed with things that I ought to have written about; peace dropped like a great stone into my pool, & the eddies are still rippling out to the further bank." Into her account of peacetime events must be worked the tripe and leeks shared with Roger, "Harry Stephen who sat like a frog with his legs akimbo," and "poor James Strachey . . . soft as moss, lethargic as an earthworm" along with the threat of Revolution and the possibility of Leonard representing England on the League of Nations Peace Conference (1:219–20). When she writes of the death of her friend Kitty Maxse, she begins by listing exactly the same kind of incidental details that DeCou gave before recording the death of T.H.: she opens the entry with a description of the fire they have going, which chapter she has reached in the book she is reading, the cat Grizzel sitting on Leonard's knee, the kitten Boxall having jumped off her own. Instead of continuing straight on with Kitty Maxse's death as one more detail, however, she gives the diary entry a paragraph break and opens the next paragraph not with an "and" but a "but," as she writes, "But the day has been spoilt for me—so strangely—by Kitty Maxse's death; & now I think of her lying in her grave at Gunby . . . " (2:206). The rest of the diary entry is taken up with recollections about Kitty Maxse, the length of the entry—like the length of White's entry about her friend Roberta—reflecting the importance of this relationship to her. Woolf's interest is in the kinds of continuities that make up a life, and the connections between impressions, events, and emotions, expressed in her diary through her frequent use of the word "and," often even to begin a new entry.

Plath's "Notes on Neighbours" offers another kind of parataxis, presenting the unfolding narratives of her relationships with each neighbour alongside each other. But she was fascinated by the continuities and connections within and across the entries of Woolf's diary, reading her "blessed diary" as a model for the kinds of continuities she might allow in her life as well as in her writing. Anxious that she is "becoming too happily stodgily practical" with her baking of apple pies, she feels liberated by Woolf's description of "cleaning out the kitchen" and cooking "haddock & sausage." Her own diary entry about reading Woolf mirrors the movement between domesticity and intellect that she seeks in Woolf's writing, beginning with her anxiety about cooking pies instead of reading Locke, and then going on to find solace not only in Woolf's example but in Woolf's writing and her recollections of reading *Mrs Dalloway* and *To the Lighthouse*. (As she puts it in the next passage, borrowing Woolf's use of the ampersand, she wants for her life "Books & Babies & Beef stews." (269))

The relationship between diarist and reader, as between one diary entry and another, can be understood in terms of connection as well as distance. Reading Woolf's diary, Plath writes, "I feel my life linked to her somehow. I love her . . . " (269). This is the kind of reading celebrated by Jeanne Braham, in her essay "Lens of Empathy." Writing about diaries, memoirs, and personal essays, she discusses personal writing as a grounding of identity in relation to another consciousness and as a form of conversation.[11] Focusing more precisely on the diary as a distinctive genre, Sinor rejects this "lens" for a "diurnal lens" she sees as more true to the diary form. Reading diary writing as conversation, she argues, suggests an "emphasis on content" and "narrative qualities" that she doesn't find in the "more ordinary diaries" with which she is concerned.[12]

Sinor's argument that a conversational quality is too literary a feature to look for in the ordinary diary is surprising, however, since the conversational and the literary are more often seen as in opposition to each other. Roman Jakobson proposes that poetics is the study of what *distinguishes* "verbal art" from "other kinds of verbal behaviour" (such as, presumably, talking).[13] Even Tom Paulin's celebratory review of Elizabeth Bishop's *Selected Letters*, in which he so invitingly calls for a poetics of the familiar letter as a contribution towards a poetics of prose, nevertheless questions whether letters should be seen as possessing "literarity," arguing that they "construct themselves on an anti-aesthetic, a refusal of the literary" in favour of the "dialogic energy" belonging to the moment of writing and the moment of reading.[14] Genette suggests that "Of all the raw materials that humanity can use to artistic ends among others, language is perhaps the least specific, the least narrowly *reserved* for such a purpose." Sinor's objection to a "lens of empathy" or a "literary lens" in reading the diary is that it leaves out the ordinary diary, the diarist "not shaping a narrative."[15] Of all the literary genres, perhaps it could be said the diary is one of the least specific, least narrowly reserved for a literary purpose. Yet if the object of poetics, as Roman Jakobson claims, "is not literature but literariness," a poetic of the diary must be concerned with the literary potential of the diary form, even if this potential is not always met in the ordinary diary. Even poetry, arguably the most literary of literary forms, is more often than not written for purposes other than the purely literary. Poetry has an important place in cards for loved friends or relatives, in memorial verses in the newspaper, at weddings and other special occasions. A study of these poems in terms of their literariness would miss the point of them just as much as a study of Annie Ray's diary in terms of its literariness would miss its point.

Although the diary is not addressed to a reader in the same way a personal letter is, it can as we have seen have a great deal of dialogic energy, and the prose typically shares the same kind of "spontaneous and improvisatory" quality Paulin attributes to the letter. The dash that is typical of the diary entry—and of the personal letter—expresses this improvisatory, dashed-off quality of diary writing, though so too can an idiosyncratic use of any other punctuation mark. Plath for instance often uses the colon where another writer might use the dash, expressing perhaps a forward-looking urgency typical of her attitude, even when she is insisting on slowing down, observing:

> I catch up: each night, now, I must capture one taste, one touch, one vision from the ruck of the day's garbage. How all this life would vanish, evaporate, if I didn't clutch at it, cling to it, while I still remember some twinge or glory. Books & lessons surround me: hours of work. Who

> am I? . . . I shall ruminate like a cow: only that life end not before I am born: the windows jerk & sound in their frames. (328)

The sentence fragment likewise suggests a spontaneous, informal approach to writing, even when it is used, as Cheever uses it, to expressive effect, to heighten and slow down the attention to the detail it describes. Both the dash and the sentence fragment, as well as the questions and exclamations that evoke audience, are features more typical of conversational than literary effect, though, as Sinor points out, conversation is not without aesthetic or narrative demands. Yet their use in diary prose, though it may borrow a conversational quality, is altered through this literary context. Orton's use of the sentence fragment plays on diary conventions more directly than it plays on the patterns of conversational speech. Plath's use of the colon allows an unusual combination of note-like exhortation, rumination, and attentiveness to her surroundings to be expressed in vivid prose. Mansfield's use of the dash and of ellipses borrows from the Romantic tradition, while conveying too a modernist "fastidiousness" for form.

While such features as the dash, the sentence fragment, questions, and exclamations are typical of diary prose in general, each diarist makes their own idiosyncratic use of them. While Woolf's writing reveals that she knows, as Hermione Lee writes, "all the problems that arise from treating books like people and people like books," she nevertheless confidently conveys the character of a writer she knows only through his works. Of William Hazlitt, for instance, she writes after reading his essays, "we cannot read him for long without coming in contact with a very singular character—ill-conditioned yet high-minded; mean yet noble; intensely egotistical yet inspired by the most genuine passion for the rights and liberties of mankind."[16] She recognises character not only through the themes and content of a writer's work, but through the style of writing. She enjoys Sidney's "The Countess of Pembroke's Arcadia" for the "liveliest delight" he reveals in "the syllabling of words," and the personal excitement that can be detected in "the little tremor that stirs and agitates a sentence" that would otherwise remain coldly symmetrical.[17] She is aware of how much more than personality any literature represents, interested in what makes literature "Elizabethan" or "Greek," and in the demands and possibilities of genre and tradition, but then these same constraints and possibilities attend, as she recognises, the construction of self also.

Writing in the diary might be, as Cheever acknowledges, "a kind of retirement from the excellence of life," but it is also a search for the "truth or beauty" that gives life its excellence and a day its shapely form. Such a search may involve the will as much as perception; it may depend on habit as much as on will; it is shaped by the diary form in which it takes place and shapes, in turn, the particular form an individual diary takes. The diary form can result in truth (and beauty) emerging in quite startling ways. Antonia White records a "most odd nightmare" she dreamed the night before the 16th of January, 1962: "I was with Moll at some convent function and I began to vomit and vomit, bringing up the most extraordinary things, old silver spoons, pieces of wire and metal etc."[18] Her search for truth through analysis suggests an interpretation: "It was an odd 'displacement' for on Sunday I had been telling Moll I wanted to scold E. A. C. a little about the dining room episode and was afraid I'd lose my temper and say too much" (64). It is a typically insightful interpretation, but the place of this entry in the sequence that leads up to it suggests further significance too. Since the beginning of the year, she has been describing in her diary rearrangements she has been making to the furnishings of her flat. This has been a recurring preoccupation since she moved into a new flat in July of the previous year, but is particularly striking in the entries leading up to the silverware dream. The entry just before the dream entry, for the 15th of January, suggests that this obsession with interior decoration might be understood as a form of displacement:

> I really should be ashamed of myself. I did only one page yesterday. A fortnight of my precious working months gone already. And all this morning fidget, fidget, fidget about my workroom shifting chairs and ornaments, rushing to P[eter] J[ones] to change the chintz . . . A room is just like a sentence—a change of one object, even an ashtray, can mean revising the whole thing to get the balance and colour right. (64)

She was working at the time of this entry on what would have been the fifth book in the series that began with *Frost in May*, the fourth book of what became the Clara sequence after she changed the name of her heroine. She had begun working on this book four years earlier, but work on this "meaningless mess" as she described it was interrupted by a libel suit filed against the third novel in the series, *The Sugar House*. For several years after the libel suit, she put this draft of "Clara IV" aside to write translations. It is not surprising that she should feel anxious about returning to the Clara sequence after these years, to write the novel which would give a fictionalised account of her relationships with the fathers of her two daughters. She may well have been worried about what she would let spill out. As a writer of fiction, her work is to control the revelation of meaning through arrangement and rearrangement right down to the level of the sentence. The diary is a messier genre, but the dream imagery of silverware nicely suggests the value that might be found in the diary's messy form.

Notes

NOTE TO THE INTRODUCTION

1. Sylvia Plath, *Letters Home*, ed. Aurelia Plath (London, 1978), 31.
2. Tim Kendall, "Showing off to an Audience of One," *Times Literary Supplement* (5 May 2000).
3. Harriet Blodgett, *Capacious Hold-All: An Anthology of Englishwomen's Diary Writings* (Charlottesville, 1991).
4. Sarah Gristwood, *Recording Angels: The Secret World of Women's Diaries* (London, 1988), xi.
5. Robert Fothergill, *Private Chronicles: A Study of English Diaries* (London, New York, and Toronto, 1974), 2.
6. James Olney, preface to *Metaphors of Self* (Princeton, 1972), viii, xi.
7. Domna Stanton, ed., *The Female Autograph: Theory and Practice of Autobiography from the Tenth to the Twentieth Century* (Chicago and London, 1987), vii.
8. Bella Brodzki and Celeste Schenck, eds., *Life/Lines: Theorizing Women's Autobiography* (Ithaca, 1988), 12.
9. Personal Narratives Group, ed., *Interpreting Women's Lives: Feminist Theory and Personal Narratives* (Bloomington, 1989).
10. Liz Stanley, *The Auto/biographical I: The Theory and Practice of Feminist Auto/biography* (Manchester, 1992).
11. Marlene Kadar, *Essays on Life Writing: From Genre to Critical Practice* (Toronto, Buffalo, and London, 1992).
12. Suzanne Bunkers and Cynthia Huff, *Inscribing the Daily: Critical Essays on Women's Diaries* (Amherst, 1996).
13. Tracy Brain, "Dangerous Confessions: The Problem of Reading Sylvia Plath Biographically," in *Modern Confessional Writing: New Essays*, ed. Jo Gill (London and New York, 2006), 11–32.
14. Sylvia Plath, *The Unabridged Journals of Sylvia Plath*, ed. Karen V. Kukil (New York, 2000). Also published as *The Journals of Sylvia Plath 1950–1962* (London, 2000). All subsequent references are made to the English edition.
15. Katherine Mansfield, *The Katherine Mansfield Notebooks*, ed. Margaret Scott (Wellington, 1997); Katherine Mansfield, *Journal of Katherine Mansfield*, ed. John Middleton Murry (London, 1954).
16. Elizabeth Podnieks, *Daily Modernism: The Literary Diaries of Virginia Woolf, Antonia White, Elizabeth Smart, and Anaïs Nin* (Montreal & Kingston, 2000).
17. Alan Bennett, *Prick Up Your Ears: Screenplay* (London, 1987).

18. Virginia Woolf, *A Writer's Diary*, ed. Leonard Woolf (London, 1953), viii.
19. Virginia Woolf, *The Diary of Virginia Woolf*, ed. Anne Olivier Bell, assisted by Andrew McNeillie (Harmondsworth, 1978–1984; first published 1977–1984).
20. Sylvia Plath, "Notes on Neighbours," published as "Appendix 15" in *The Journals of Sylvia Plath 1950–1962*, ed. Karen Kukil, 630–674.
21. Le Anne Schreiber, *The New York Times* (21 April 1982).
22. Peter Davison, "Sylvia Plath: Consumed by the Anxieties of Ambition," *The Washington Post* (18 April 1982).
23. Anita Helle, *The Unraveling Archive: Essays on Sylvia Plath* (Ann Arbor, 2007).
24. Michael Sheldon, "The Demon that Killed Sylvia Plath," *The Daily Telegraph* (13 March 2000), 19, cited in Brain, "Dangerous Confessions," 11. I look in more detail at the myth of Plath's narcissism and the conflation of her life and work in an article "Sylvia Plath's 'Exaggerated American Grin': Anti-American Sentiment and the Reception of Plath's Poetry," *Journal of Transatlantic Studies*, 2007, 117–32.
25. Tom Paulin, "Writing to the Moment," in *Writing to the Moment: Selected Critical Essays, 1980–1986* (London, 1996), 215–39, 220.
26. Variability in the effects of prose features is a subject which has been analysed in detail by Hugh Craig, in "Authorial Attribution and Computational Stylistics: If You Can Tell Authors Apart, Have You Learnt Anything About Them?" *Literary and Linguistic Computing,* 14 (1999), 103–13. He observes that while statistical analyses of prose features to determine authorship need to be based on quantifiable measures (such as the number of times an author uses the form "while" as opposed to "whilst"), the *effects* of such differences, while being harder to measure, must also vary according to author. Yet the effects, or interpretative significance, of the measurable stylistic differences between authors have received little consideration, even though, as Craig argues, "there is an odd asymmetry in the notion that frequencies of linguistic features can classify a style and yet cannot play a part in describing it" (104). His own analysis of the distinctive features of Thomas Middleton's style, such as the frequent use of the words "now," "that" in its demonstrative sense, and "there," demonstrates how such quantifiable differences can be applied to an interpretative description of Middleton's style, a "style strongly dependent on context," in which "characters [. . .] point instead of tell" (111). Of course many stylistic approaches to writers have included at least a degree of computational analysis; Josephine Miles, for instance, uses a quantifying stylistics to distinguish stylistic traits both of individual writers and of literary periods; while most of the *Essays in Stylistic Analysis* collected in Howard Babb's 1972 anthology include some "computation" of stylistic frequencies, if not necessarily by computer. But what is particularly pertinent to this study is how alert Craig is to variant, even contradictory, effects of these quantifiably characteristic features in Middleton's writing, with the use of "now," for example, by one character to express "complacent anticipation" and by another character to suggest "the changeability of things and especially of affections" (110)
27. Steven Kagle's study of *American Diary Literature 1620–1799* (Boston, 1979), for instance, argues that the diary should not be read as a literary test since the subject matter, being limited to the real, is "unimaginative"; the private nature of the diary, the absence of an addressee, leads to indeterminacy, gaps in the narrative, or an absence of background information, which the diarist has not needed to include for his or her own reading; and

the periodic production leads to a lack of perspective, consistency, and unity. Most studies of the diary from the early twentieth century, including Arthur Ponsonby's *English Diaries* (1923), P.A. Spalding's *Self Harvest: A Study of Diaries and the Diarist* (1949), and Robert Fothergill's *Private Chronicles* (1974), are sympathetic towards these unliterary qualities of the diary, reading them as evidence of the integrity of the "self" portrayed, or, at the very least, the integrity of the portrayal.

28. Laurie McNeill, "Teaching an Old Genre New Tricks: The Diary on the Internet," *Biography*, 26:1 (2003), 24–47.
29. Madeleine Sorapure, "Screening Moments, Scrolling Lives: Diary Writing on the Web," *Biography*, 26:1 (2003), 1–23.
30. See Douglas Hewitt's *English Fiction of the Early Modern Period 1890–1940,* particularly the Introduction (London and New York: Longman, 1988); John Gross, *The Rise and Fall of the Man of Letters* (London and Edinburgh: Morrison and Gibb, 1969); "Modernity and Print 1: Britain 1890–1970" by Jonathan Rose, in *A Companion to the History of the Book*, edited by Simon Eliot and Jonathan Rose (Malden, Oxford, and Carlton: Blackwell, 2007).
31. *The Orton Diaries,* edited and with an introduction by John Lahr (London, 1989), from the Introduction, 13.
32. Sylvia Plath, *The Journals of Sylvia Plath*, ed. Hughes and McCullough (New York, 1982), 306.
33. John Cheever, *The Journals*, ed. Gottlieb (London, 1993), 351.
34. Antonia White, *Diaries 1926–1957*, ed. Chitty (London, 1991), 66.
35. *Diaries 1926–1957*, 108.
36. Angela Smith, *Katherine Mansfield and Virginia Woolf: A Public of Two* (Oxford and New York: 1999).
37. Mansfield, *Notebooks*, 2:125.
38. *Notebooks*, 2:168.
39. Ben Cheever, "Introduction," Cheever, *The Journals*, x–xi.
40. Jennifer Sinor, *The Extraordinary Work of Ordinary Writing: The Diary of Annie Ray* (Iowa, 2002), 12.
41. Steven Kagle and Lorenza Gramegna, "Rewriting Her Life: Fictionalization and the Use of Fictional Models in Early American Women's Diaries," in *Inscribing the Daily* (Amherst, 1996).
42. Woolf's terms for these "genres" come from her diaries, 4:129, 3:139; 4:159, 3:34.
43. Hughes, introduction to Plath, *Journals* (1982), xiv.
44. Hermione Lee, *Virginia Woolf* (London, 1996), 402.

NOTES TO CHAPTER 1

1. Antonia White, *Diaries 1926–1957*, ed. Susan Chitty (London, 1991).
2. Cited in Felicity A. Nussbaum, "Towards Conceptualising Diary," in *Studies in Autobiography,* ed. James Olney (New York and Oxford, 1988), 128–37; 128.
3. Elizabeth Podnieks, *Daily Modernism: The Literary Diaries of Virginia Woolf, Antonia White, Elizabeth Smart and Anaïs Nin* (Montreal and Ithaca, 2000).
4. Margo Culley, ed., *A Day at a Time* (New York, 1985).
5. Antonia White, *Frost in May* (London, 1978).
6. Antonia White, *Strangers* (London, 1981).

7. *Diaries*, introduction, 8.
8. Jenny Diski, "Perfect Light," *The London Review of Books* (July 1992), 11.
9. Hermione Lee, introduction to White, *Strangers*, v.
10. White, *Frost in May*, 79.
11. *Diaries*, 87.
12. White, *Frost in May*, 46.
13. White, "The Saint," in *Strangers*, 67–68.
14. Susan Chitty, introduction, *Diaries*, 9.
15. *Diaries*, 260.
16. Katherine Mansfield curiously uses the same metaphor of writing as digestion, to criticise writing that she regards as too processed: in a letter to Dorothy Brett she criticises contemporary writing as "little predigested books written by authors who have nothing to say," quoted in Sarah Sandley, "The Middle of the Note: Katherine Mansfield's 'Glimpses'," in *Katherine Mansfield in from the Margin*, ed. Roger Robinson (Baton Rouge and London, 1994), 72.
17. Elizabeth Podnieks is one scholar who gratefully acknowledges Chitty's generosity in providing access to the diary manuscripts she refers to in *Daily Modernism.*
18. Chitty, introduction, *Diaries*, 10.

NOTES TO CHAPTER 2

1. Blake Bailey, "Oh, What a Chaos It Seems," in *Slate* (3 April 2009). The story the shapely day quote comes from is "The Country Husband."
2. Edgar Allen Beem, "Cheever's Keeper," a profile of Blake Bailey, *The Boston Globe* (5 June 2005).
3. *The Journals of John Cheever,* ed. Gottlieb (London, 1993), 141, 92, 98.
4. Cheever, *Journals*, 5.
5. Ted Solotaroff, "The Cheever Chronicles," *The Nation* (18 November 1991), 616–620, this quote 616.
6. Blake Bailey, *Cheever: A Life* (New York, 2009), 59.
7. Cited in Bailey, *Cheever: A Life*, 59.
8. Cited in Bailey, *Cheever: A Life,* 146.
9. Ted Solotaroff, "The Cheever Chronicles," 616.
10. Bailey, "Oh, What a Chaos It Seems," *Slate* (3 April 2009).
11. L.S. Klepp, "The Journals of John Cheever," *Entertainment Weekly* (11 October 1991).
12. Herbert Mitgant, "Books of the Times; Reading the Notebooks of a Sad, Anguished Man," *The New York Times* (2 October 1991).
13. Philip Roth, "Editorial review" cited by all the leading on-line book sites such as Amazon.com and Powell's Books.
14. Ben Cheever, in an e-mail correspondence held with me, June, 2009.
15. Robert Gottlieb generously spoke to me about editing the Cheever journals in June 2009.
16. See for instance Jennifer Sinor's account of reading her great-great-aunt's "ordinary diary" as a matter of learning not to "read past the repetitions, the daily, the chores, and the tedium . . . the very qualities that mark the diary as a distinct kind of writing" *The Extraordinary Work of Ordinary Writing: Annie Ray's Diary* (Iowa, 2002), 15.
17. Blake Bailey commented in an e-mail to me (June 2009) that although this is essentially how Gottlieb worked, it would be misleading to suggest that he

never intervened in a passage. More often in the later entries, Gottlieb would occasionally "trim some superfluous after-thought from an entry," or even "bits of filigree in the body of an entry as well . . . if it detracted from the integrity of the entry." Bailey adds that he himself "generally agreed with these decisions."

18. Rebecca Hogan, "Engendered Autobiographies: The Diary as a Feminine Form," in *Prose Studies*, 14:2 (1991), 95–107.
19. Naomi Schor, *Reading in Detail: Aesthetics and the Feminine* (New York and London, 1987).
20. *The Chambers Concise English Dictionary* (Glasgow, 1992), 354.
21. *The Oxford English Dictionary* (Oxford, 1989), 542.
22. Cheever, "The Sutton Place Story," in *The Stories of John Cheever* (New York, 1978). All other references made to Cheever's short stories are taken from this edition.
23. Cheever, *Journals*, 106.
24. Emerson, 'The Over-Soul' in *The Collected Works of Ralph Waldo Emerson*, ed. Joseph Slater (Cambridge and London, 1979), II, 157–176, 160.
25. Andrew Ashfield and Peter de Boola, ed., *The Sublime: A Reader in British Eighteenth Century Aesthetic Theory* (Cambridge, 1996), 213, 100.
26. Schor, *Reading in Detail* (1987).
27. Cited in Schor, 25–26. Any further extracts from Hegel's *Aesthetics: Lectures on Fine Arts* are also taken from Schor.
28. For examples see 4–5, 13, 32, 39.
29. Susan Cheever, *Home Before Dark* (London, 1985), 218.
30. See also 92, 116, 181, 269, 275, 383.

NOTES TO CHAPTER 3

1. Joe Orton, *The Orton Diaries*, ed. John Lahr (London, 1989).
2. Maurice Charney, *Joe Orton* (London and Basingstoke, 1984), 124.
3. Christopher Innes, *Modern British Drama: The Twentieth Century* (Cambridge, 2002), 296.
4. Orton's attention to working class speech is described in John Lahr, *Prick Up Your Ears: The Biography of Joe Orton* (London, 1978). Innes cites Orton's staging directions to the Royal Court, regarding the 1967 production of *The Ruffian on the Stair*, which demand that "the extravagance of the dialogue" is contrasted with an "absolute realism" in the acting, Innes, *Modern British Drama* (Cambridge, 2002), 297.
5. Lahr, *Prick Up Your Ears* (London, 1978), 125–26.
6. Lahr, *Diary of a Somebody* (London, 1989).
7. Alan Bennett, *Prick Up Your Ears: Screenplay* (London, 1987), 14.
8. Orton, *Diaries*, 38.
9. Orton, *Complete Plays* (London, 1980), 117.
10. Mark Finch, "Business as Usual: Substitution and Sex in *Prick Up Your Ears* and Other Recent Gay-Themed Movies" in *Coming on Strong*, ed. Simon Shepherd and Mick Wallis (London, 1989), 86–87.
11. Bennett, *Prick Up Your Ears: Screenplay*, 74.
12. Finch, "Business as Usual," 81, 78.
13. Bennett, *Prick Up Your Ears: Screenplay*, 1, 2.
14. Orton, *Diaries*, 266.
15. Bennett, *Prick Up Your Ears*: *Screenplay*, 15.
16. Simon Shepherd, *Because We're Queers: The Life and Crimes of Joe Orton and Kenneth Halliwell* (London, 1989).

17. Bennett, *Prick Up Your Ears: Screenplay*, 13.
18. Orton, *Diaries*, 106.

NOTES TO CHAPTER 4

1. Katherine Mansfield, *Journal of Katherine Mansfield*, ed. John Middleton Murry (London, 1927).
2. Katherine Mansfield, *The Katherine Mansfield Notebooks*, ed. Margaret Scott (Canterbury and Wellington, 1997), 2:136. Subsequent page references are to this edition unless otherwise noted.
3. Ian Gordon, "The Editing of Katherine Mansfield's Journal and Scrapbook," *Landfall*, 13 (1959), 64.
4. C.K. Stead, introduction to Katherine Mansfield, *The Letters and Journals of Katherine Mansfield: A Selection* (London, 1977), 14.
5. Virginia Woolf, *The Diary of Virginia Woolf*, ed. Anne Olivier Bell and Andrew McNeillie (Harmondsworth, 1978–1984), 3:26.
6. Antonia White, *Diaries 1926–1957*, ed. Susan Chitty (London, 1991), 135.
7. Sylvia Plath, *The Journals of Sylvia Plath*, ed. Ted Hughes and Frances McCullough (New York, 1982), 18.
8. The title of Derek Jarman's journal, *Modern Nature,* alludes to this concern, referring both to the "modern nature" of his surrounding landscape and of the garden he cultivates, in view of the nuclear power station of Dungeness, and to his own "modern nature" as HIV positive, gay activist, film maker. Derek Jarman, *Modern Nature* (London, Sydney, Auckland, and Johannesburg, 1991).
9. Mansfield, *Journal* (Murry), 86–87.
10. Susan Sontag, *Illness as Metaphor* (New York, 1978).
11. Alice James, *Her Brothers, Her Journal*, ed. Anne Robeson Burr (London, 1934); W.N.P Barbellion, *The Journal of a Disappointed Man; & A Last Diary* (London, 1984).
12. They impinge on her, in fact, the way attacks of illness impinge on a healthy person. And for a wonderfully immediate account of an attack of illness impinging on a healthy person, it is hard to improve on Siegfried Sassoon's entry in his 1924 diary, interesting too as an example of the power of an interruption generally to give a sense of the moment of writing:
    It is now 4 a.m. and I've just had some tea and bolted three sponge cakes. I now take my pen and wonder inkily what I've got to *show* for my nocturnities of tea and toil since October 1. *Then* I said "No hunting; no sociability; five months of seclusion—if I can achieve it—and we'll see what happens." No more was demanded of the lustrum of dark months than that I should add 350 lines of *Recreations* stuff.
    As regards the *Recreations* part of the programme (sponge cakes are causing abdominal pains—a three-cornered fight, I suppose) I have added 132 lines to the previous 628, but only 69 lines are *new*.
13. Katherine Mansfield, *The Collected Letters of Katherine Mansfield*, ed. Vincent O'Sullivan and Margaret Scott (Oxford: Oxford University Press, 1993), Volume 3: 5, 24.
14. Mansfield, *Journal* (Murry), 101.
15. Although I am referring to the effects of the rhymes in the manuscripts I consulted in the Turnbull Library, I have used Margaret Scott's transcription here (*Notebooks*, 2:266).
16. Mansfield, *Journal* (Murray), 11.
17. Scott, introduction to Mansfield, *Notebooks*, xiii.
18. Gordon, "Editing Katherine Mansfield's Journal.", 69

19. Mansfield, introduction to *Notebooks*, xxiii.
20. Murry, introduction to Mansfield, *Journal*, xv.
21. Mansfield, *Journal* (Murry), 22.
22. Gordon, "Editing Katherine Mansfield's Journal."

NOTES TO CHAPTER 5

1. VirginiaWoolf, *The Diary of Virginia Woolf*, ed. Bell and McNeillie (Harmondsworth, 1978–1984), 3:67.
2. Elizabeth Podnieks, "Virginia Woolf's Diary: 'The Proper Stuff of Fiction,'" in *Daily Modernism: The Literary Diaries of Virginia Woolf, Antonia White, Elizabeth Smart, and Anaïs Nin* (Montreal & Kingston, 2000), 97–164.
3. Leonard Woolf, introduction to Woolf, *Writer's Diary* (London, 1953), viii.
4. Woolf, *Diary* (Bell and McNeillie), 3:212, 3:198.
5. Extracts of these reviews are printed on the cover of the 1954 edition of *A Writer's Diary* (London: Hogarth Press), from which I am quoting them.
6. Thomas Mallon, *A Book of One's Own: People and Their Diaries* (London, 1985), 29–34.
7. Woolf, *A Writer's Diary*, 3:233.
8. Louis Simpson, "American Poetry," *Selected Poems,* cited by Tom Paulin, "Introduction" to William Hazlitt, *The Plain Speaker: The Key Essays* (Oxford and Malden, 1998), xiii–xiv.
9. Paulin, introduction to Hazlitt, *The Plain Speaker*, xiii.
10. Ted Hughes, introduction to Plath, *Journals* (Hughes and McCullough), xiv.

NOTES TO CHAPTER 6

1. Jacqueline Rose, *The Haunting of Sylvia Plath* (London, 1991), 1.
2. Janet Malcolm, *The Silent Woman: Sylvia Plath and Ted Hughes* (London and Basingstoke, 1994).
3. Philip Matthews, "Among the Elements," *New Zealand Listener* (17 January 2004); see also John Brownlow's introduction to *Sylvia: The Shooting Script* (New York, 2003).
4. Brownlow, *Sylvia: The Shooting Script*, and "Who's Afraid of Sylvia Plath?" *Guardian* (Friday 22 August 2003); see also my article on the Plath myth and its origins, which includes a discussion of the film *Sylvia*, "Sylvia Plath's 'Exaggerated American Grin': Anti-American Sentiment and the Reception of Plath's Poetry," *Journal of Transatlantic Studies,* 5:2 (2007), 117–32. For a film review that takes some of these issues into account, see my review article "Sylvia and the Headscarf," *Landfall*, 207 (2004), 190–95.
5. Sylvia Plath, *The Journals of Sylvia Plath, 1950–1962*, ed. Karen V. Kukil (London, 2000).
6. See for instance Ted Hughes, "Sylvia Plath and Her Journals," in *Winter Pollen: Occasional Prose* (London, 1994); Hughes, "Sylvia Plath," in *Winter Pollen: Occasional Prose.*
7. Plath, *The Journals of Sylvia Plath,* ed. Ted Hughes and Frances McCullough (New York, 1982), 226.
8. Kukil is careful, too, to transcribe the less frequent crossed, wavy lines that end some entries and the circles that Plath draws around the numbers heading the entries from entry number 55 onwards.

9. Tim Kendall, "Showing Off to an Audience of One," *Times Literary Supplement* (5 May 2000), 12.
10. Rebecca Hogan, "Engendering Autobiographies: The Diary as a Feminine Form," in *Autobiography and Questions of Gender*, ed. Shirley Neuman (London, 1991).
11. Judy Nolte Lensinck, "Expanding the Boundaries of Criticism: The Diary as Female Autobiography," *Women's Studies*, 14 (1987), 39–53. Other writers on women's diaries who make connections between the gender of the writer and their use of the diary form include Suzanne Bunkers and Cynthia Huff, editors of the collection *Inscribing the Daily* previously referred to in my introduction, and contributors to that collection Lynn Bloom, Steven Kagle and Lorenza Gramegna, Geneva Cobb-Moore, and Trudelle H. Thomas; anthologists of the diary Sarah Gristwood, Harriet Blodgett, and Katie Holmes; and Judy Simons, author of *Diaries and Journals of Literary Women from Fanny Burney to Virginia Woolf*. Arguments that account for the historical association of women with the diary genre seem to me more valid, and more interesting, than arguments about the feminine "nature" of the diary form. Cinthia Gannet's study of the journal as a pedagogical tool, *Gender and the Journal: Diaries and Academic Discourse* (Albany, 1992), usefully examines the association with women and girls with the diary in terms of its contemporary effects in the classroom. Her analysis suggests that the association is more to do with genre than form—taking genre to mean not just the formal qualities of a group of texts, but rather texts grouped together according to an intersection of form, content, and historical association. Gannett discusses the efforts of teachers and school authorities to disassociate the academic journal from the diary—devalued as a personal and as a feminine genre—by an intriguing mixture of approaches, with as much attention to terminology as to content and form. While the academic journal shares with the diary a structure of "selection and accumulation," it is not intended to share the gendering of the diary as female. However, Gannett reports that female students are markedly more comfortable with the journal form than are male students, precisely because of the close links between the journal and the diary form.
12. Sylvia Plath, *The Journals of Sylvia Plath, 1950–1962*, ed. Karen V. Kukil (London, 2000), 672.
13. Plath, *Collected Poems* (London, 1991), 222.
14. Plath, *The Journals 1950–1962* (Kukil), 543–46.
15. Malcolm, *The Silent Woman*, 31–42.
16. Plath, *Letters Home*, 27.
17. Ibid., 3.
18. Ted Hughes, 'Notes on the Chronological Order of Sylvia Plath's Poems,' [1966], in Newman, Charles (ed), *The Art of Sylvia Plath*, Indiana: Indiana University Press, 1971. 48.

NOTES TO CHAPTER 7

1. E-mail correspondence, June 2009.
2. Anne Olivier Bell, preface to Virginia Woolf, *The Diary of Virginia Woolf*, ed. Bell and McNeillie (Harmondsworth, 1978–1984), x.
3. Virginia Woolf, "Women and Fiction," *Forum* (March 1929), 179–83.
4. Leslie Stephen, *Men, Books and Mountains* (London, 1956).
5. Woolf, *Diary* (Bell and McNeillie), 2:105.

6. Antonia White, *Diaries 1926–1957*, ed. Susan Chitty (London, 1991), 43.
7. Woolf, *Diary* (Bell and McNeillie), 1:239.
8. Emily Dickinson, *The Complete Poems* (London, 1987), 238.
9. Cristanne Miller, *Emily Dickinson: A Poet's Grammar* (Cambridge, Massachusetts, 1987).
10. Woolf, *Diary* (Bell and McNeillie), 4:102, 2:56.
11. Miller, *Emily Dickinson: A Poet's Grammar*, 10.
12. Susan Chitty quotes Julien Green writing in his journals about "telling myself about myself" in her introduction to *The Diaries of Antonia White* (London, 1992), 8.
13. Brett, Simon, ed., *The Faber Book of Diaries* (London, 1987), 468–69.
14. Katherine Mansfield, *Journal of Katherine Mansfield*, ed. John Middleton Murry (London, 1927).
15. Woolf, *Women and Fiction*.
16. H. Porter Abbott, "Old Virginia and the Night Writer: The Origins of Woolf's Narrative Meander," in *Inscribing the Daily: Critical Essays on Women's Diaries*, ed. Bunkers and Huff (Amherst, 1996), 236.
17. Woolf, "Romance and the Heart," in *The Essays of Virginia Woolf*, ed. Andrew McNeillie (London, 1988), 3:367.

NOTES TO CHAPTER 8

1. Ronald Koertge, *Diary Cows* (Los Angeles, 1982). Koertge has experimented in several works with combinations of poetry and the diary genre. His YA novel *The Brimstone Journals* (Madison, 2004) is a collage of journal entries from fifteen different teenage students; *Shakespeare Bats Cleanup* (Madison, 2006) is a fictional teenager's journal in poetry form. Another really excellent example of a literary text making parodic use of the sentence fragment as a convention of the diary is Jackie French's children's picture book, *Diary of a Wombat* (Sydney: Harper Collins, 2002). The pictures do a lot to make up for the limitations of a strict diary style (sample text: "Morning: Slept. Afternoon: Slept. Evening: Ate grass. Scratched. Night: Ate grass), though the move from eating grass, to carrots, to oats provides some narrative excitement.
2. Joe Orton, *The Orton Diaries*, ed. John Lahr (London, 1989), 87, 136.
3. John Cheever, *The Journals* (London, 1993), 4.
4. Anaïs Nin, *Incest* from *A Journal of Love: The Unexpurgated Diary of Anaïs Nin* (London, 1993), 49.
5. Elizabeth Smart, *On the Side of Angels* (London, 1994), 34.
6. Alice Van Wart, introduction to Smart, *On the Side of Angels*, 9.
7. Smart, *On the Side of Angels*, 14.
8. VirginiaWoolf, *The Diary of Virginia Woolf*, ed. Bell and McNeillie (Harmondsworth, 1978–1984), 5:199.
9. Hermione Lee, *Virginia Woolf* (London, 1996), 341–61.
10. Quoted in Lee, *Virginia Woolf*, 690.
11. Sylvia Plath, *The Journals of Sylvia Plath, 1950–1962*, ed. Kukil (London, 2000), 519.
12. This same couplet appears in another sonnet, "April Aubade," written "in the three or four years preceding 1956" and published in the "Juvenilia" section at the end of the *Collected Poems* (312).
13. Van Wart, introduction to Smart, *On the Side of Angels*, 11.
14. Woolf, *Diary* (Bell and McNeillie), 2:105.

NOTES TO CHAPTER 9

1. Arthur Ponsonby, *English Diaries* (London, 1923), 35.
2. Elizabeth Hampsten, *"Read This Only to Yourself": The Private Writings of Midwestern Women, 1880–1920* (Bloomington, 1982); Penelope Franklin, *Private Pages: Diaries of American Women 1830s-1970s* (New York, 1986).
3. Judy Simons, *Diaries and Journals of Literary Women from Fanny Burney to Virginia Woolf,* (Basingstoke and London, 1990), 3.
4. Katie Holmes, *Spaces in Her Day: Australian Women's Diaries in the 1920 and 1930s* (St Leonards, New South Wales, 1995), ix–x.
5. Domna Stanton, preface to *The Female Autograph* (Chicago, 1987), vii.
6. Lawrence Rosenwald, *Emerson and the Art of the Diary* (New York and Oxford, 1988), 95.
7. William Jones, quoted by Robert Fothergill, *Private Chronicles* (London, 1974), 95.
8. Fothergill, *Private Chronicles*, 95.
9. Mansfield, *Journal* (Murry), 45.
10. Antonia White, *Diaries 1926–1957,* ed. Susan Chitty (London, 1991), 59.
11. John Cheever, *The Journals*, ed. Robert Gottlieb (London, 1993), 42.
12. Sylvia Plath, *The Journals of Sylvia Plath 1950–1962,* ed. Karen Kukil (London, 2000), 545.
13. Cheever, *The Journals*, 29–30.
14. Woolf could be said to have an iconicity within and beyond autobiography studies that is in a sense similar to the iconicity of Shakespeare within literary studies as a whole, and beyond, as a cultural icon. Brenda R. Silver's study of "Virginia Woolf" as a cultural icon, *Icon: Virginia Woolf* (Chicago: University of Chicago Press, 1999), reprints a *New York Review of Books* advertisement depicting David Levine's caricatures of Shakespeare and Woolf, which invites readers to select an image for their t-shirts (56). Paradoxically, the greater the writer, the more over-rated he or she is likely to be; however, Silver's study makes it clear that Woolf's more complicated and disputed status as iconic writer is determined as much by cultural politics as by the poetics of Woolf's own writings.
15. Virginia Woolf, *The Diary of Virginia Woolf,* ed. Bell and McNeillie (Harmondsworth, 1978–1984), 3:141.
16. Lawrence Rosenwald, *Emerson and the Art of the Diary* (New York and Oxford, 1988), 95.
17. Woolf, *Diary* (Bell and McNeillie), 3:311.
18. And two entries later, the reader, at least of the original manuscripts, can literally "Behold, the rather familiar experiment—a new pen, a new ink." (3:325).

NOTES TO THE CONCLUSION

1. Robert Fothergill, *Private Chronicles* (London, 1974), 3, 192.
2. Felicity Nussbaum, "Toward Conceptualising Diary," in *Studies in Autobiography,* ed. James Olney (New York and Oxford, 1988), 132.
3. Jill Price, *The Woman Who Can't Forget* (New York, 2008).
4. Hermione Lee, "Virginia Woolf's Nose," in *Body Parts: Essays on Life-Writing* (London, 2005), 28.

5. Rebecca Hogan, "Engendered Autobiographies: The Diary as a Feminine Form," in *Autobiography and Questions of Gender,* ed. Shirley Neuman (London, 1991), 103.
6. Podnieks, *Daily Modernism*, 91.
7. Rachel Blau DuPlessis, "For the Etruscans: Sexual Difference and Artistic Production—The Debate over a Female Aesthetic," in *The Future of Difference,* ed. Hester Eisenstein and Alice Jardine (Boston, 1980), 136.
8. Sinor, *The Extraordinary Work of Ordinary Writing,* 157.
9. Woolf, *Diary* (Bell and McNeillie), 1:266.
10. Hogan, "Engendered Autobiographies," 101.
11. Jeanne Braham, "A Lens of Empathy," in *Inscribing the Daily*, ed. Suzanne L. Bunkers and Cynthia A. Huff (Amherst, 1996), 56–71.
12. Sinor, 53–55.
13. Roman Jakobson, *Language in Literature,* ed. Krystyna Pomorska and Stephen Rudy (Cambridge, Massachusetts and London, 1987), 63.
14. Tom Paulin, "Writing to the Moment," 216.
15. Sinor, 17–19.
16. Virginia Woolf, "William Hazlitt" in *The Essays of Virginia Woolf,* Volume 5, ed. Stuart N. Clarke (London, 2005), 495.
17. Woolf, *Essays,* Volume 5, 369.
18. Antonia White, *Diaries 1958–1979*, 64.

Bibliography

PRIMARY TEXTS

Unpublished

Mansfield, Katherine, unpublished papers, held at the Turnbull Library, Wellington, New Zealand.

Plath, Sylvia, unpublished papers, held in the Mortimer Rare Book Room at Smith College, Northampton, Massachusetts.

Published

Cheever, John, *The Journals*, ed. Robert Gottlieb, London: Vintage, 1993; first published by Jonathan Cape, 1991.

Mansfield, Katherine, *Journal of Katherine Mansfield*, ed. John Middleton Murry, London: Constable, 1927.

———, *The Katherine Mansfield Notebooks*, ed. Margaret Scott, Canterbury and Wellington: Lincoln University Press and Daphne Brasell Associates, 1997.

———, *The Letters and Journals of Katherine Mansfield: A Selection*, ed. C.K. Stead, London: Allen Lane, 1977.

Orton, Joe, *The Orton Diaries*, ed. John Lahr, London: Minerva, 1989; first published by Methuen, 1989.

Plath, Sylvia, *The Journals of Sylvia Plath*, ed. Ted Hughes and Frances McCullough, New York: Dial Press, 1982.

———, *The Journals of Sylvia Plath 1950–1962*, ed. Karen V. Kukil, London: Faber and Faber, 2000 (also published as *The Unabridged Journals of Sylvia Plath 1950–1962,* New York: Anchor Books, 2000).

White, Antonia, *Diaries 1926–1957*, ed. Susan Chitty, London: Constable, 1991.

———, *Diaries 1958–1979*, ed. Susan Chitty, London: Constable, 1992.

Woolf, Virginia, *The Diary of Virginia Woolf*, ed. Anne Olivier Bell, assisted by Andrew McNeillie, 5 vols, Harmondsworth, Middlesex: Penguin, 1978–1984; first published by Hogarth Press, 1977–1984.

———, *A Writer's Diary*, ed. Leonard Woolf, London: Hogarth Press, 1953, repr. 1954.

SECONDARY TEXTS

Ashfield, Andrew and Peter de Bolla, ed., *The Sublime: A Reader in British Eighteenth-Century Aesthetic Theory*, Cambridge: Cambridge University Press, 1996.

Babb, Howard, ed., *Essays in Stylistic Analysis*, New York: Harcourt Brace Jovanovich, 1972.

Bailey, Blake, *Cheever: A Life*, New York: Alfred A. Knopf, 2009.
———, "Oh, What a Chaos It Seems," *Slate*, 3 April 2009.
Barbellion, W.N.P., *The Journal of a Disappointed Man; & A Last Diary*, London: Hogarth Press, 1984; first published as *The Journal of a Disappointed Man*, London: Chatto and Windus 1919, and *A Last Diary*, London: Chatto and Windus, 1920.
Battersby, Christine, *Gender and Genius: Towards a Feminist Aesthetics*, London: Women's Press, 1994.
Beem, Edgar Allen, "Cheever's Keeper," *The Boston Globe*, 5 June 2005.
Bennett, Alan, *Prick Up Your Ears: Screenplay*, London: Faber and Faber, 1987.
Blodgett, Harriet, *Capacious Hold-All: An Anthology of Englishwomen's Diary Writings*, Charlottesville and London: University Press of Virginia, 1991.
Brett, Simon, ed., *The Faber Book of Diaries*, London and Boston: Faber and Faber, 1987.
Brodzki, Bella and Celeste Schenck, eds., *Life/Lines: Theorizing Women's Autobiography*, Ithaca and London: Cornell University Press, 1988.
Brownlow, John, *Sylvia: The Shooting Script* (New York: Mewmarket Press, 2003).
———, "Who's Afraid of Sylvia Plath?" (*Guardian*, Friday 22 August, 2003).
Bundtzen, Lynda K. *The Other Ariel* (Massachusetts: University of Massachusetts Press, 2001).
Bunkers, Suzanne and Cynthia Huff, *Inscribing the Daily: Critical Essays on Women's Diaries*, Amherst: University of Massachusetts Press, 1996.
Charney, Maurice, *Joe Orton*, London and Basingstoke: Macmillan, 1984.
Cheever, John, *The Stories of John Cheever*, New York: Alfred A. Knopf, 1978.
Cheever, Susan, *Home Before Dark*, London: Weidenfeld and Nicolson, 1985.
Cixous, Hélène, "Sorties: Out and Out: Attacks/Ways Out/Forays," in *The Newly Born Woman*, Hélène Cixous and Catherine Clément, Minneapolis: University of Minnesota Press, 1986.
Craig, Hugh, "Authorial Attribution and Computational Stylistics: If You Can Tell Authors Apart, Have You Learnt Anything About Them?" *Literary and Linguistic Computing*, 14 (1999), 103–13.
Culley, Margo, ed., *A Day at a Time*, New York: Feminist Press at CUNY, 1985.
Davison, Peter, "Sylvia Plath: Consumed by the Anxieties of Ambition," *The Washington Post*, 18 April 1982.
Demoriane, Hermine, *Life Star*, London: Ross, 1969.
———, *The Tightrope Walker*, London: Secker and Warburg, 1989.
Dickinson, Emily, *The Complete Poems*, London and Boston: Faber and Faber, 1975.
Diski, Jenny, "Perfect Light," *The London Review of Books*, 9 July 1992, 11.
DuPlessis, Rachel Blau, "For the Etruscans: Sexual Difference and Artistic Production—The Debate over a Female Aesthetic," *The Future of Difference*, ed. Hester Eisentein and Alice Jardine (Boston, 1980).
Eisenstein, Hester and Alice Jardine, *The Future of Difference*, Boston: Barnard College Women's Centre, 1980.
Eliot, Simon and Jonathan Rose, *A Companion to the History of the Book*, Malden, Oxford, and Victoria: Blackwell, 2007.
Emerson, Ralph Waldo, *The Collected Works of Ralph Waldo Emerson*, ed. Joseph Slater, Cambridge and London: Harvard University Press, 1979.
Finch, Mark, "Business as Usual: Substitution and Sex in *Prick Up Your Ears* and Other Recent Gay-Themed Movies," in *Coming on Strong*, ed. Simon Shepherd and Mick Wallis, London: Unwin Hyman, 1989.
Fothergill, Robert, *Private Chronicles*, London: Oxford University Press, 1974.

Frank, Thaisa and Dorothy Wall, *Finding Your Writer's Voice: A Guide to Creative Fiction*, New York: St Martin's Press, 1994.

Franklin, Penelope, *Private Pages: Diaries of American Women 1830s-1970s*, New York: Ballantine, 1986.

Gannett, Cinthia, *Gender and the Journal: Diaries and Academic Discourse*, Albany: State University of New York Press, 1992.

Gill, Jo, ed., *Modern Confessional Writing: New Essays*, London and New York: Routledge, 2006.

Gordon, Ian, "The Editing of Katherine Mansfield's Journal and Scrapbook," *Landfall*, 13 (1959), 62–69.

Gristwood, Sarah, *Recording Angels: The Secret World of Women's Diaries*, London: Harrap, 1988.

Gross, John, *The Rise and Fall of the Man of Letters*, London and Edinburgh: Morrison and Gibb, 1969.

Gusdorf, Georges, "Conditions and Limits of Autobiography," in *Autobiography: Essays Theoretical and Critical*, ed. James Olney, Princeton: Princeton University Press, 1980.

Hampsten, Elizabeth, *"Read This Only to Yourself": The Private Writings of Midwestern Women, 1880-1920*, Bloomington: Indiana University Press, 1982.

Hassam, Andrew, "Style and Convention in the Diary: An Investigation with Reference to the Reader," Ph.D. Thesis, University of Wales, 1983.

Hazlitt, William, *The Plain Speaker: The Key Essays*, Oxford and Malden: Blackwell, 1999.

Helle, Anita, *The Unraveling Archive: Essays on Sylvia Plath*, Ann Arbor: University of Michigan Press, 2007.

Hewitt, Douglas, *English Fiction of the Early Modern Period 1890–1940*, London and New York: Longman, 1988.

Hogan, Rebecca, "Engendered Autobiographies: The Diary as a Feminine Form," in *Autobiography and Questions of Gender*, ed. Shirley Neuman, London: Frank Cass, 1991.

Holmes, Katie, *Spaces in Her Day: Australian Women's Diaries in the 1920s and 1930s*, St Leonards, New South Wales: Allen and Unwin, 1995.

Hughes, Ted, *Birthday Letters*, London: Faber and Faber, 1999.

———, *Winter Pollen: Occasional Prose*, London: Faber and Faber, 1994.

———, 'Notes on the Chronological Order of Sylvia Plath's Poems.' [1966], in *The Art of Sylvia Plath*, ed. Charles Newman, Indiana: Indiana University Press, 1971.

Innes, Christopher, *Modern British Drama: The Twentieth Century*, Cambridge: Cambridge University Press, 2002.

Jackson, Anna, "The *Notebooks*, *Journal*, and Papers of Katherine Mansfield: Is Any of This Her Diary?" *Journal of New Zealand Literature*, 18/19 (2000/1), 83–99.

———, "Sylvia and the Headscarf," *Landfall*, 207 (2004), 190–95.

———, "Sylvia Plath's 'Exaggerated American Grin': Anti-American Sentiment and the Reception of Plath's Poetry," *Journal of Transatlantic Studies*, 5:2 (2007), 117–32.

Jakobson, Roman, *Language in Literature*, ed. Krystyna Pomorska and Stephen Rudy, Cambridge, Massachusetts and London: Harvard University Press, 1987

James, Alice, *Her Brothers, Her Journal*, ed. Anne Robeson Burr, London: Macmillan, 1934.

Jarman, Derek, *Modern Nature*, London, Sydney, Auckland, and Johannesburg: Century, 1991.

Jay, Paul, *Being in the Text: Self-Representation from Wordsworth to Roland Barthes*, Ithaca and London: Cornell University Press, 1984.

Jelinek, Estelle C., *The Tradition of Women's Autobiography from Antiquity to Present*, Boston: Twayne, 1986.
Kadar, Marlene, *Essays on Life Writing: From Genre to Critical Practice*, Toronto, Buffalo, and London: Toronto University Press, 1992.
Kagle, Steven, *American Diary Literature 1620–1799*, Boston: Twayne, 1979.
Kendall, Tim, "Showing Off to an Audience of One," *Times Literary Supplement*, 5 May 2000, 12.
Klepp, L.S., "The Journals of John Cheever." *Entertainment Weekly* (11 October 1991).
Koertge, Ronald, *Diary Cows* (Los Angeles: Little Caesar Press, 1982).
———, *The Brimstone Journals* (Madison, Wisconsin: Turtleback Press, 2004).
———, *Shakespeare Bats Cleanup* (Madison, Wisconisn: Turtleback Press, 2006).
Lahr, John, *Diary of a Somebody*, London: Methuen, 1989.
———, *Prick Up Your Ears: The Biography of Joe Orton*, London: Lane, 1978.
Lee, Hermione, *Body Parts: Essays on Life-Writing*, London: Chatto and Windus, 2005.
———, *Virginia Woolf*, London: Chatto and Windus, 1996.
Lejeune, Philippe, "The Autobiographical Contract," in *French Literary Theory Today: A Reader*, ed. Tzevtan Todorov, Cambridge: Cambridge University Press, 1982.
Lensinck, Judy Nolte, "Expanding the Boundaries of Criticism: The Diary as Female Autobiography," *Women's Studies*, 14 (1987), 39–53.
Malcolm, Janet, *The Silent Woman: Sylvia Plath and Ted Hughes*, London and Basingstoke: Picador, 1994.
Mallon, Thomas, *A Book of One's Own: People and Their Diaries*, London: Picador, 1985.
Mansfield, Katherine, *The Collected Letters of Katherine Mansfield*, ed. Vincent O'Sullivan and Margaret Scott (Oxford: Oxford University Press, 1993), Volume 3: 5, 24.
Mason, Mary, *Journeys in Autobiographical Writings by Women*, Boston: G.K. Hall, 1979.
Matthews, Philip, "Among the Elements," (*New Zealand Listener*, 17 January, 2004).
Matthews, William, *American Diaries in Manuscript*, Athens: University of Georgia Press, 1974.
———, *British Autobiographies: An Annotated Bibliography of British Autobiographies Published or Written Before 1951*, Berkeley, Los Angeles, and London: University of California Press, 1955.
———, *British Diaries: An Annotated Bibliography of British Diaries*, Berkeley: University of California Press, 1950.
———, *Canadian Diaries and Autobiographies*, Berkeley: University of California Press, 1950.
McNeill, Laurie, "Teaching an Old Genre New Tricks: The Diary on the Internet," *Biography*, 26:1 (2003), 24–47.
Miles, Josephine, *Continuity of Poetic Language: Studies in English Poetry from 1640's to 1940's*, Berkeley and Los Angeles: University of California Press, 1951.
———, *Poetry and Change: Donne, Milton, Wordsworth, and the Equilibrium of the Present*, Berkeley and Los Angeles: University of California Press, 1974.
Miller, Cristanne, *Emily Dickinson: A Poet's Grammar*, Cambridge, Massachusetts: Harvard University Press, 1987.
Mitgant, Herbert, "Books of the Times; Reading the Notebooks of a Sad, Anguished Man," *The New York Times*, 2 October 1991.

Moffatt, Mary Jane, ed., *Revelations: Diaries of Women*, New York: Random House, 1974.

Nin, Anaïs, *Incest* from *A Journal of Love: The Unexpurgated Diary of Anaïs Nin, 1932-1934*, London: Peter Owen, 1993.

Nussbaum, Felicity A., "Towards Conceptualising Diary," in *Studies in Autobiography*, ed. James Olney, New York and Oxford: Oxford University Press, 1988, 128–37.

Olney, James, ed., *Autobiography: Essays Theoretical and Critical*, Princeton: Princeton University Press, 1980.

———, *Metaphors of Self: The Meaning of Autobiography*, Princeton: Princeton University Press, 1972.

———, ed., *Studies in Autobiography*, New York and Oxford: Oxford University Press, 1988.

Orton, Joe, *Complete Plays*, London: Methuen, 1980.

Pascal, Roy, *Design and Truth in Autobiography*, London: Routledge and Paul, 1960.

Paulin, Tom, "Introduction" to William Hazlitt, *The Plain Speaker: The Key Essays*, Oxford and Malden: Blackwell, 1998.

———, *Writing to the Moment: Selected Critical Essays, 1980-1996*, London: Faber and Faber, 1996; contains his essay "Writing to the Moment," 215–39.

Perloff, Marjorie, "The Two Ariels: The (Re) Making of the Sylvia Plath Canon," *American Poetry Review* 13 (November-December 1984).

Personal Narratives Group, ed., *Interpreting Women's Lives: Feminist Theory and Personal Narratives*, Bloomington: Indiana University Press, 1989.

Plath, Sylvia, *The Bell Jar*, London: Faber and Faber, 1966.

———, *Collected Poems*, London: Faber and Faber, 1991.

———, *Letters Home*, ed. Aurelia Schober Plath, London and Boston: Faber and Faber, 1978 (first published by Faber and Faber, 1976).

Podnieks, Elizabeth, *Daily Modernism: The Literary Diaries of Virginia Woolf, Antonia White, Elizabeth Smart, and Anaïs Nin*, Montreal and Kingston: McGill-Queen's University Press, 2000.

Ponsonby, Arthur, *English Diaries*, London: Methuen, 1923.

Price, Jill, *The Woman Who Can't Forget*, New York: Simon and Schuster, 2008.

Rose, Jacqueline, *The Haunting of Sylvia Plath*, London: Virago, 1991.

Rosenwald, Lawrence, *Emerson and the Art of the Diary*, New York and Oxford: Oxford University Press, 1988.

Salomon, Charlotte, *A Diary in Pictures*, London: Collins, 1963.

———, *Life? Or Theatre?* London: Royal Academy of Arts, 1998.

Sandley, Sarah, "The Middle of the Note: Katherine Mansfield's 'Glimpses'," in *Katherine Mansfield in from the Margin*, ed. Roger Robinson, Baton Rouge and London: Louisiana State University Press, 1994.

Sassoon, Siefried, *Diaries 1923—1925*, ed. Rupert Hart-Davis, London: Faber and Faber, 1985.

Schor, Naomi, *Reading in Detail: Aesthetics and the Feminine*, New York and London: Methuen, 1987.

Schreiber, Le Anne, "Books of the Times," *The New York Times*, 21 April 1982.

Shepherd, Simon, *Because We're Queers: The Life and Crimes of Joe Orton and Kenneth Halliwell*, London: GMP, 1989.

Shumaker, Wayne, *English Autobiography: Its Emergence, Materials and Forms*, Berkeley and Los Angeles: University of California Press, 1954.

Silver, Brenda R., *Icon: Virginia Woolf*, Chicago: Chicago University Press, 1999.

Simons, Judy, *Diaries and Journals of Literary Women from Fanny Burney to Virginia Woolf*, Basingstoke and London: Macmillan, 1990.

Sinor, Jennifer, *The Extraordinary Work of Ordinary Writing: Annie Ray's Diary*, Iowa City: University of Iowa Press, 2002.

Smart, Elizabeth, *By Grand Central Station I Sat Down and Wept*, Ottawa: Deneau, 1982.

———, *On the Side of the Angels*, ed. Alice Van Wart, London: Flamingo, 1994 (first published by HarperCollins 1994).

Smith, Angela, *Katherine Mansfield and Virginia Woolf: A Public of Two*, Oxford: Clarendon Press and New York: Oxford University Press, 1999.

Smith, Sidonie, *A Poetics of Women's Autobiography*, Bloomington and Indianapolis: Indiana University Press, 1987.

Solotaroff, Ted, "The Cheever Chronicles," *The Nation*, 18 November 1991.

Sontag, Susan, *Illness as Metaphor*, New York: Farrar, Straus and Giroux, 1978.

Sorapure, Madeleine, "Screening Moments, Scrolling Lives: Diary Writing on the Web," *Bibliography*, 26:1 (2003), 1–23.

Spalding, P.A., *Self Harvest: A Study of Diaries and the Diarist*, London: Independent Press, 1949.

Spender, Stephen, *China Diary*, London: Thames and Hudson, 1982.

Spengemann, William C., *The Forms of Autobiography: Episodes in the History of a Literary Genre*, New Haven and London: Yale University Press, 1980.

Stanley, Liz, *The Auto/biographical I: The Theory and Practice of Feminist Auto/biography*, Manchester: Manchester University Press, 1992.

Stanton, Domna, ed., *The Female Autograph*, Chicago and London: Chicago University Press, 1987 (first published 1984 as Volumes 12–13 of *The New York Literary Forum*, Jeanine Parisier Plottel).

Stephen, Leslie, *Men, Books and Mountains*, London: Hogarth Press, 1956.

Stevenson, Anne, *Bitter Fame: A Life of Sylvia Plath*, London: Penguin, 1998 (first published 1989).

White, Antonia, *Frost in May*, London: Virago, 1978 (first published 1933).

———, *Strangers*, London: Virago, 1981 (first published Harvill Press 1954).

Woolf, Virginia, *The Essays of Virginia Woolf*, ed. Andrew McNeillie, London: Hogarth Press, 1988.

———, "Women and Fiction," *Forum* (March 1929), 179–83.

———, *The Essays of Virginia Woolf*, Volume 5, ed. Stuart N. Clarke, London: Hogarth Press, 2009.

Index

For Product Safety Concerns and Information please contact our EU representative GPSR@taylorandfrancis.com
Taylor & Francis Verlag GmbH, Kaufingerstraße 24, 80331 München, Germany

www.ingramcontent.com/pod-product-compliance
Lightning Source LLC
Chambersburg PA
CBHW071411100726
47908CB00004B/1140

* 9 7 8 1 1 3 8 8 8 3 6 1 1 *